Can These Bones Live? is a book much needed for the so-called "small" church and its leadership! This is a book that is both spiritual (rooted in the scripture and the Holy Spirit) and down to earth (with real-life experiences)! It is a book that calls me to a more faithful ministry!

Dr. Paul D. Schoonmaker
Pastor Emeritus
Calvary Baptist Church
Providence, Rhode Island

Joshua McClure is recognized as a man who hungers and thirsts after God's own heart. His book *Can These Bones Live?* is timely. I am sure; this book will liberate the body of Christ from the conclusion that the mega church is the emblem of success. I personally endorse and recommend that every preacher, who desires nothing less than to live out the vision of God, should read and add this book to their personal collection as a present and future resource.

Rev. Dr. Kelly Littlejohn, Jr, Pastor
New Beginnings Christian Church
Windsor, Connecticut

Pastor McClure's understanding of where vision originates is very crucial to any of us being able to do the will of God. The real life experiences that are illustrated seem to jump right off of the pages and become such that the reader can almost feel like he/she is right there in the midst of what is happening

Once the understanding of God's vision for the church comes, then surely these bones can live.

Rev. Dr. Vincent L. Thompson, Jr., Pastor
Community Baptist Church
Newport, Rhode Island

can these bones live?

THE MIRACULOUS STORY OF WHAT CAN HAPPEN TO A CHURCH THAT FOLLOWS GOD'S VISION

Joshua A. McClure

Tate Publishing & *Enterprises*

"Can These Bones Live" by Joshua A. McClure

Copyright © 2006 by Joshua A. McClure. All rights reserved.

Published in the United States of America
by Tate Publishing, LLC
127 East Trade Center Terrace
Mustang, OK 73064
(888) 361-9473

Book design copyright © 2006 by Tate Publishing, LLC. All rights reserved.
No part of this publication may be reproduced, stored in a retrieval system or transmitted in any way by any means, electronic, mechanical, photocopy, recording or otherwise without the prior permission of the author except as provided by USA copyright law.

Unless otherwise noted, Scripture quotations are taken from the *Holy Bible, New Living Translation*, Copyright © 1996. Used by permission of Tyndale House Publishers, Inc. All rights reserved.

Scripture quotations marked "NIV" are taken from the *Holy Bible, New International Version* ®, Copyright © 1973, 1978, 1984 by International Bible Society. Used by permission of Zondervan Publishing House. All rights reserved.
Scripture quotations marked "KJV" are taken from the *Holy Bible, King James Version*, Cambridge, 1769.

This book is designed to provide accurate and authoritative information with regard to the subject matter covered. This information is given with the understanding that neither the author nor Tate Publishing, LLC is engaged in rendering legal, professional advice. Since the details of your situation are fact dependent, you should additionally seek the services of a competent professional.

ISBN: 1-5988647-2-6

06.07.27

This Book is dedicated to two most wonderful people

Rev. Albert Theodore McClure
Dorothy Josephine McClure

Thank you for introducing me to your God.
Thank you for teaching me how to live.
Thank you for being love.

A grateful son.

and to

Doris, Debbie, and Esther.

The flickering flame of life was snuffed out all too soon.

A loving brother

Acknowledgements

A debt of gratitude to some very special people who wouldn't allow me to quit: for helping, tolerating, resuscitating, and for indulging me during the writing of this book.

Tom O'Connell and Youlander Bethel—two very gifted writers who teamed up and provided the initial impetus for the writing of this book. They supported me and encouraged me to go forward when it seemed so far away.

Dion Haynes—for prevailing upon me to find my voice in writing. You were a great coach and kept me from wandering 40 years in the wilderness.

Arline Fitzhugh, my sister—who provided invaluable information, when my memory began to dim. I sensed the rekindling of our love for each other.

Bruce McDonald—who provided important insights, and a fresh set of eyes when mine began to weaken.

Ellyn Santiago and Dave Panciera for their editing skills in helping to transfer a raw manuscript into a finished product.

And to all of you who have helped and encouraged me in any way I am grateful. You may be too numerous to mention on the pages of this book, however, my heart has a record of each one of you.

And to my church family:
The members of Pleasant Street Baptist Church—my life is so much richer after knowing all of you.

And to my family:
My wife Ida—who has put up with my many life changes and is still around wondering what I am going to do next.

Allison, Leslie, Dorothy and Wesley—three beautiful daughters and a wonderful son, all who have taken my heart hostage.

And to the readers—most of you I'm meeting for the first time. As you read this book you are giving me your most precious commodity, your time. I pray that I prove worthy of your trust.

Contents

Foreword — 11
Preface — 13
Introduction: How It All Began — 15

Divine Initiative
1. A Living Organism — 25
2. Beginnings ... Early Church Life — 37
3. Family Life — 47

God's Calling
4. Divine Call — 57
5. The Mystery Revealed — 63
6. To Be Discerned — 69
7. Opportunities At Hand — 81
8. A Greater Glory — 89

God's Voice
9. Life In Earnest — 101
10. Out of the Shadows — 115
11. Moving Day — 119
12. Its Not Supposed to Hurt — 129
13. When You've Lost the Star — 135

Vision Manifest
14. A Meeting of the Heart — 147
15. Miracle in Our Midst — 157
16. Visions in the Heart — 169
17. Seven Bassinets — 179
18. Life at Pleasant Street — 183

Promised Fulfillment
19. Without a Vision 195
20. Difference Makers 203
21. Christ Our Life 215
22. Vision Unveiled 223

Epilogue   **231**
Index   **235**
Bibliography   **247**

Foreword

On the following pages a story of faith is told. Like Joshua of the Old Testament, God has given to this "Joshua" a vision and a promise. The Old Testament vision given to Joshua was one of expansion for the people of Israel. The promise to him was that God would be there for him as God had been there for Moses and that no matter what the situation the Lord would not fail or forsake him.

Here we have the opportunity to walk with Pastor McClure as he unfolds the challenges he encountered while attempting to remain faithful to the vision that God gave him. In the end, we hear this pastor's testimony of how God has kept His promise.

What is revealed here is a congregation modeling the New Testament paradigm of what Jesus mandated the church to be. In this telling we hear the long ago directives of Christ, who implored the disciple community not to be enslaved to tradition, put into contemporary praxis. This pastor challenges the status quo and offers a vibrant alternative to despair.

Here is told the story of how God honors faith. This witness is a source of encouragement for all those who are trying to do ministry, often in the context of hopelessness. It is here that some pastors struggling with despair and overcome by expectations too grand to achieve, may find a fresh witness to the power of faith. The experiences of this pastor and people shared here are existential evidence that the biblical canon is not closed. God continues to reveal God's self and engage God's self in the affairs of the human predicament.

This book is one pastor's contribution to the conversation of how the sovereign Lord works in the lives of people to realize God's will and bring forth redemptive transformation. It is a conversation worth sharing for it testifies to a reality worth knowing. Moreover, we have here, an epistle of hope for the church today. We taste here sweet water in the desert, a note of triumph for despairing and failing congregations throughout our nation.

I am certain that those who read this witness of faith will find, as I have, new inspiration in the knowledge that God is still working in the lives of the faithful. God's voice yet speaks new life into dead situations.

>W. Franklyn Richardson
>Senior Pastor
>Grace Baptist Church
>Mt. Vernon, New York

Preface

The church is a living organism birthed by the Holy Spirit to manifest God's Kingdom in the world; it is His reign and rule in the hearts of lost people.

The omnipotent, omniscient, omnipresent God calls unspiritual people, born in sin, out of the world, to receive a new birth into His Kingdom. Among the called are certain men and women who are destined to lead people from the darkness of sin to experience God's mercy and grace.

Each person ordained to lead must first receive God's vision and direction for the church. Pastors and church leaders without divine vision are like captains of ships without sails. They are merely drifting along, like pilots of boats without rudders. Lacking direction, they are like the Israelites wandering in the wilderness for forty years slowly expiring. Without divine direction from God, the church is destined to stagnate and decline, heading undeniably toward a spiritual graveyard.

Churches today are still challenged by God's query to the prophet Ezekiel concerning His people's demise, *"Son of man, can these bones live?"* The prophet's answer was clear and indisputable,

"O Sovereign Lord, you alone know." [Ezekiel 37:3, NIV] The question remains: Can present-day stagnant, expiring church bodies live again? God alone knows!

Joshua A. McClure

INTRODUCTION

How it All Began

Two compelling forces came together to forge my decision to write this book. One was the result of what I saw happening in the church today. This led me to capitulate to the many people prodding me to record the unveiling of God's vision for Pleasant Street Baptist Church; too many to be deemed coincidental. The other was internal and had to do with my own spiritual journey.

Though the theme of this book did not originate in our times it is irrefutably appropriate to them. It is called forth by a condition which has existed in the Church for many years and is steadily growing worse. I refer to the loss of vitality and fervor, and the fact that the Church has lost direction in meeting the needs of people: lost, hungry, hurting, and powerless people in particular. The contemporary church should be basking in this time of opportunity, since God has given His church authority to declare to the world that there is a sovereign, living God who is a source of grace and truth. The message is that *"the power of God at work"* changes hearts and lives. But, the church has bought into the value system of society and consequently both are feeling the same loss of power and direction. Preoccupation with these secular values of materialism, status and bigness has profaned the church's message.

Contained within the October 2003 issue of the Journal of the Southern Baptist Convention *SBC LIFE* are the churches statistics which span denominational lines. At the time, the journal noted that eighty percent of North American churches were stagnant or in decline. And upwards of 3,500 to 4,000 U. S. churches close each year. Today the numbers have even grown worse. The message once only hinted at is now bared and much too somber to be ignored.

In light of these alarming and depressing conditions in the church today, the most relevant question before church leaders is, Can these dead and dying churches mired in a spiritual graveyard live again? Can stagnant, decaying, church bodies be revived? As church leaders, the sense of frustration and helplessness leads to a heavy reliance on how-to manuals, well scripted programs, or tools heavy with human effort in an attempt to stimulate spiritual and numerical growth. It is certain that the church cannot be cured by church growth tools because the church is not a "thing". It is people, and people have distinctive qualities, spiritually formed lives that they bring into any setting. This is what must be transformed—lives. Otherwise, all of our efforts are in vain.

Dr. Ed Stetzer, author of *Finding New Life For Struggling Churches* says, "Dead and dying churches should concern us all ... most of us know the statistics but few of us care enough to engage these churches ... Churches need to change to reach their communities, and denominations need to help them do that ... we must engage dying churches not out of guilt, but because of their potential—to be used of God again in a powerful way ... Many pastors are reading this right now and saying, "That's us." What can we do?"

The answer for today is not unlike that which Ezekiel declared to God in reply to His query concerning His exiled people, scattered and dead in Babylon: Can these bones live?

The prophet determined it was in God's hands if the nation was to live again. His answer was clear and specific "*O Sovereign Lord, you alone know the answer to that.*" God has been the life and hope of the church since its birth at Pentecost, but somehow its flame, fire and vitality have been reduced almost to intellectual ash. And yet God's answer for the church, His formula for growing vital, alive, churches has remained intact since the early church. The Bible, the only comprehensive instruction manual, attests that church growth is not measured by how many people occupy the pews on a given Sunday morning, nor how large the real estate, neither is it calculated on the quantity of programs and "how-to-grow" materials. Church growth commences with the gospel truth of Jesus Christ's death, burial, and resurrection leading to the deep conviction of the heart crying out, "*Brothers, what should we do?*" [Acts 2:37b]

Hence, the vision of the church is manifest as *"each day the Lord added to their group those who were being saved."* [47b] The evidence of growing churches today is characterized by the same attributes as that of this group of early believers. Preaching of the cross results in a deep respect and awe of God; Spirit empowered leadership; needs-oriented ministry; exalting worship; and reverent communal relationships. The message is clear; without a vision of God's heart for the church, real growth is not possible. Preoccupation with anything other than maintaining healthy spiritual values can only compromise and pervert God's message to the world. Thus, disappointment ensues in both the church and the world. However, faith confidently declares that God's vision is the prerequisite to transforming dead or dying churches into vital, living organisms that reclaim broken lives, change hearts, heal hurts, and bring glory to Him.

As I saw what was happening around me, I also became aware of something happening inside me. This surfaced several years ago when I was experiencing one of those periods of spiritual dryness we all encounter. Deep within my spirit I knew I had yet many unanswered questions. In spite of my leadership in the church, in spite of all the good I had done in the ministry, I knew in my heart I had to do something. I wanted to know Jesus in a more personal way. I wanted to have real peace inside. I no longer wanted to do things just because I felt they were right. I desired to know the Lord's will for me and to have the courage to follow His divine direction.

I soon found myself on my knees, deep in prayer, in awe of God's absolute holiness. It was a life-changing experience and I gained a completely new understanding of the holy God I believe in and worship. From that moment on, things began to change in my life. Christ had become more real to me. My desire no longer was just to be a good church member, but now I was focused on becoming more like Jesus. The Scriptures I had read many times before now took on greater meaning. When I read the Bible, words would virtually leap off its pages. My hunger for the word of God increased so that I could not get enough, and passion for Jesus was now my joy. In the midst, I discovered a passage of Scripture that to this very day has become the hallmark of my daily life. It is my testimony and my experience:

"I have been crucified with Christ. I myself no longer live, but Christ lives in me. So I live my life in this earthly body by trusting in the Son of God, who loved me and gave himself for me." [Galatians 2:20]

After that, my relationship with God is hard to describe except to say that I wanted more of God and more from God. I sensed there was more to come, yet not knowing where or how it would come, until that Sunday in December 1976 when God's heart became visible on the wall of my living room. In retrospect, I believe God had been preparing me since birth for this hallowed image now fixed on the horizon. Much of what had previously happened in my life was about to be wonderfully established into God's plan.

Dr. Myles Monroe, in his latest book, *The Principles and Power of Vision* asserts, "Vision is the source and hope of life. The greatest gift ever given to mankind is not the gift of sight, but the gift of *vision*. Sight is a function of the eyes; vision is a function of the heart. Eyes that look are common, but eyes that see are rare."

Vision, then, is not by chance, it is by divine appointment. It is ordained of God; hence vision makes the unseen visible and the unknown possible.

When the vision appeared to me, I was firmly established in business on the threshold of achieving my life's goals, and making plans to live out the American dream in peace and comfort. Little did I realize that God had chosen me to be the conveyor of His heart to a people in need: people who were isolated, nameless and faceless; homeless people, hopeless people, disenfranchised people; youth in trouble, people in darkness, those suffering from the illness of addiction; those in pain, fearful and alone, lacking strength; those in danger of slipping through the cracks with few caring if they were ever seen again.

In and of itself the vision demanded patient obedience and complete trust in God's ability to rescue the objects of His compassion and love. Though the vision was given to attract people of all ages, races and ethnicities, socioeconomic and educational levels, it became difficult to understand when it was revealed that the host community was overwhelmingly Caucasian and 90% Catholic. But most surprising of all was that God's choice of the man sent to bear His vision to a small, sequestered church in Westerly, Rhode Island, was an "African American pastor!" What is certain is that only God knew the portent of the vision, and He would demand deeper trust and greater intimacy before *"the evidence of things we cannot yet see"* [Hebrews 11:1b] would materialize.

This is a book of faith. It is a vision of ministry. Not vision in general, but vision in particular. The book describes a vision birthed in the heart of God directed towards a people in danger of perishing without it. The writer of Proverbs [29:18, KJV] counsels, *"Where there is no vision the people perish."* Thus, this book is not about grandiose churches or church buildings. It is not about locating well traveled church growth programs, nor is it about following a step by step How –To manual for growing churches. It is about faithfully following a God-ordained vision and believing God will accomplish the task. It is about Abraham, [Genesis 12:1] who was told, *"Leave your country, your relatives, and your father's house, and go to the land that I will show you."* Abraham went as directed. It is about a Saul, [Acts 9:6] who encountered the Lord Jesus on the road to Damascus and was told, *"Now get up and go into the city, and you will be told what you are to do."* Saul [who later became Paul] went as commanded. It is about Joshua, [Joshua 5:14b] who fell on his face before the angel of the Lord in reverence, and cried out, *"I am at your command ... What do you want your servant to do?*It is about this Joshua, who was asked the personal, probing, penetrating, question of Jesus [John 21:15-17] *"Do you love me?"* When the reply came in the affirmative, humanity surrendered to Divinity and this man's heart was taken captive by God's directive to, *"Feed My sheep."* And Joshua has done as directed.

Thus, the substance of this message is that God's vision, lodged in the heart of just one faithful servant, can set aflame a ministry so far reaching and so dynamic that it can heal hurting people, resurrect dead and dying congregations, restore hope, reclaim smaller churches, and turn communities to Him. When vision is manifested people from far and near will appear at the door and buildings to support this new ministry will arise. Vans to transport people to and fro will arrive. Gifts to enable ministries will be granted. Children will flock to the church. Pastors and churches will once again see vision, and no longer will people lament "We can't." Now there will emanate a resounding echo: God will, as vision manifests before their very eyes

This book is about the miracles wrought by vision. It is about seeing through eyes of faith. It is akin to the Prophet Elisha's prayer for his servant boy, "*O Lord, open his eyes and let him see!*" [2 Kings 6:17] Elisha wanted the lad to see that God is doing far more for his people than we can ever realize through sight alone. If people faithfully follow God's heart wherever it may lead, their eyes will be opened to see miracles. Then God's desire will be realized: to bring the radiance of His Son Jesus Christ into the midst of a community of people walking in darkness.

The apostle Paul reproves those who are motivated for personal gain, who "*brag about having a spectacular ministry rather than having a sincere heart before God.*" [2 Corinthians 5:12] The question is not whether we can bring large numbers of people into the church, but rather, are we growing large numbers of disciples for Jesus Christ? Success in church programs and measured church goals may somehow contribute to changed behaviors. But God alone is able to change lives, reform behaviors and reclaim the hearts of people to Him. When the focus of the church is on getting people to hear God's voice, miracles will happen. One will discover for certain that the faithfulness of the God who ordains vision can and will write His vision on the hearts of the lost and hopeless, leading to the greatest discovery of all: once vision is received in the heart, that vision is inescapable and eternal.

This story of transformation of individual people, churches, and communities is for the church at large today. It is not exclusive to the traditional "White" church. It is not exclusive to the neighborhood "Black" church, nor is it exclusive to any named church or denomination. This is a story for the whole church of Jesus Christ, the church in the world, consisting of all people called by God into His Kingdom.

It is my hope and prayer that pastors, teachers, lay leaders, seminarians, and any disciple of Jesus Christ from any church no matter what size, or any young person listening for God's call will read and surrender to the most urgent message of this book.

Thus, as mentioned, my personal observations of the stagnation of the church coupled with God's prodding have compelled me to write this book. The revelations and the discoveries recounted herein were actuated by the working of the Holy Spirit. But my decision to begin writing came largely because of the many entreaties to make the vision known. I believe they could not all have been of human origin. I believe it is God's desire to make known His heart to a generation fruitlessly searching for Him.

Renewal can be experienced within the pages of this book, and we can become truly inspired participants in a divine drama. By means of a dynamic vision lodged in God's faithful Word, we can move beyond a routine religion of dullness, disappointment, and distraction into godliness, power, and miracle in this present age—a challenge worthy of our greatest energies. Thus, this is a book of beginnings sans endings.

> "For everything comes from him; everything exists by his power and is intended for his glory. To him be glory evermore. Amen."
> [Romans 11:36]

Divine Initiative...

"The Lord gave me a message. He said, I knew you before I formed you in your mother's womb. Before you were born I set you apart and appointed you as my spokesman to the world.

O Sovereign Lord, I said, I can't speak for you! I'm too young! Don't say that, the Lord replied, for you must go wherever I send you and say whatever I tell you. And don't be afraid of the people, for I will be with you and take care of you. I, the Lord, have spoken!"

Jeremiah 1:4-8

CHAPTER ONE

A Living Organism

"Where there is no vision the people perish,"
Proverbs 29:18, KJV

As is the case in many stories, there are two beginnings to this one. The first occurred in a storefront church in Harlem of the 1930's. The Pentecostal Holiness Church of Prayer and Deliverance at 125th Street and Lexington Avenue in New York City was headed by Bishop Rosa A. Horn. My lasting memory of the Pentecostal Holiness Church of Prayer and Deliverance was a sight not easily forgotten. Wooden canes and crutches hung from a wire above our heads as we reached the top of the stairs and entered the sanctuary of the storefront church. They were left there as a visible and touching testament that God heals physical infirmities, just as he delivers from sin. This was my initial introduction to the God who performs miracles in our midst. I was but a boy.

Community and Celebration

The second beginning was on a Sunday morning shortly after 9:00A. M. A small light grey van completing its journey from Norwich, Connecticut, stops in front of a single story elongated white building on Pleasant Street, in the North End section of Westerly, Rhode Island.

The building carries few identifying marks except an enclosed steeple on the far left end and a sign on the front edge of the lawn humbly displaying the name "Pleasant Street Baptist Church". Alighting from the van are a mother and four children ranging in age from eight to fifteen. Two of them are her biological children; the other two are the remnants of a broken family in need of love and parental care.

A short while later a fifteen-passenger Dodge Maxivan proudly displaying its logo "Youth Alive Ministries" stops at the church. Its noisy occupants quickly scurry out of the van, making their way up the few steps into the church, across the fellowship hall and down the stairs to the lower level where their classrooms and teachers await. Most of the youngsters are children from the New London, Connecticut area, ranging in age from three to ten. Soon grandparents drive up from Uncasville, Connecticut in their family vehicle, bringing six of their grandchildren, a nephew and niece. For the next hour, the scene is repeated several times, with other parents, or grandparents, arriving at the church with their children or grandchildren in tow, some from as far away as South Attleboro, Massachusetts, one hour's driving distant.

Cars now line most of the street in front of the church as the last transport vehicle to arrive pulls up and discharges its passengers. A red, fifteen passenger van, having completed the forty one miles from Providence to the church now backs into the driveway alongside the church, parking near the ramp leading to the side door. Its passengers are mostly adults, and among them is a fourteen-year-old boy with his grandmother and great grandmother.

Inside the small church there is much activity. Church school has just concluded and people are preparing for worship. In today's service, the children's choir of forty voices is scheduled to sing along with the adult "Sanctuary Choir" numbering about fifteen people. The excitement is electric and continues to build for both youths and adults as the choirs stand poised, ready to enter the sanctuary. It is a sight to behold, this group of eager little children lined up in the fellowship hall adjoining the sanctuary. Their faces are beaming as they shift back and forth, trying to whisper despite the edict of silence ordained by the choir director. They anxiously await the signal to begin singing and making their entrance into the church filled with worshippers of all ages. When the call is finally given the children begin their march down the center aisle of the church. Their sky blue robes, with contrasting purple scarves adorned with a white dove, are swaying to and fro keeping time with the rhythm and beat of the music. They are led by a tiny two-year-old girl, followed by several three-year-olds leading a contingent of boys and girls up to ten years of age. They are singing the song from which their name is derived. "A Little bit of love goes a long long way, oh, oh, a little bit of love." What a joy to witness this gathering of children with hands raised to the heavens, singing with such deep emotion. Their next selection is "O the blood of Jesus". The most hardened hearts melt before these tiny witnesses of the grace of God.

The adult choir, marching behind the children, gets caught up in the current of emotion along with everyone in the pews. There is singing and clapping and outbursts of joyous praise emanating from thanksgiving for God's faithfulness. One can sense the expectation and hope of the people that God is about to do something wonderful in their lives. Many here were, at one time, among the isolated, nameless and faceless. Many of these people at one time knew the feeling of disenfranchisement and being alone in darkness because of substance abuse. Some came to the church in deep pain and harboring guilt, but the Holy Spirit healed their hurts and restored hope to their lives. Others came seeking help, and God supplied the help along with the necessary resources to care for them. Buildings to embrace ministries, vans to transport people, gifts to support needs, people whose hearts were broken for the lost: thus the ministry at Pleasant Street is manifest in each person.

In January of 2003, I was invited to speak at a Dr. Martin Luther King Jr. Fellowship Breakfast held annually at the Narragansett Electric Company, in Providence. After breakfast, music was to be provided by the South Providence Neighborhood Ministries with schoolchildren from Providence's Sackett Street Elementary School. When breakfast was concluded, around twenty young girls began filing into the room. They took their places in preparation for their songs. When they began to sing, I was moved by the lovely harmony and the feeling of unity displayed among them, but after a few moments I was awestruck by what I realized while searching their wonderfully expressive faces. No matter how I tried, I could not tell what nationality any of them were. I leaned over to the Catholic nun in charge of the Neighborhood Ministries and remarked, "This is what the face of our society is coming to look like; soon there will be no dominant race or color." She nodded agreement.

Today at Pleasant Street Baptist Church people occupying the pews are colorless. There are Native Americans, African Americans, Caucasians and Latinos. I daresay this is what the church of Jesus Christ is called to be. This was the vision afforded to me of God's heart for Pleasant Street. This is confirmation of the vision of the founding fathers that the church would be a place for every man, woman, or child created in the image of God.

As a people, we have reached outside of the church to the religious community in Westerly. Our motto continues to be "Presenting a Living Christ to a Dying World." Because our vision of ministry encompasses all people, we have spent much time in developing a mission statement which describes who we are and what we are about.

"Our mission is to invite all peoples to faith in God through Jesus Christ as Lord, to equip them to grow in His likeness through Bible study, prayer, and intentional witness, to prepare them as a body for ministry, and to send them out into the world to serve and disciple others in love by the power of the Holy Spirit."

To every member at Pleasant Street, these are more than words—they are life. They define who and whose we are as a church. The evidence is in the faces of those before us. What we see each week assures a growing vital church that makes glad the heart of God.

Pleasant Street Baptist Church is alive today. It has people who are alive. It has a vision which is alive because of its credible witness, *"Jesus Christ is the same yesterday, today, and forever."* [Hebrews 13:8] The church is vibrant, pulsating, and energetic. Its people are growing. It has vans to transport people to church and activities for both children and adults. The church has added a ramp and bathroom for disabled people. Its ministry complex encompasses five houses. One building houses a Family Life Center with a conference room, meeting room, computer room, library and kitchen. Another building is planned as a retreat center, and another space will soon house a pre-school. At present there is a parsonage for ministers, another building that hosts the church office, and there are plans to build a large addition for the Living Waters Christian Academy, kindergarten through grade eight. The ministry has extended into the high school and middle school here in Westerly. Our outreach ministry extends to children of all ages in and outside the community.

The spirit of hope resonating in the church today is in sharp contrast to former times when things weren't always pleasant at the Pleasant Street Baptist Church. Previously, the church attracted few people, mostly by its own design. Not long ago, members of the host community merely passed by the little white building on top of the hill on Pleasant Street and gave it little or no thought at all. Yet those who did think to comment on the church described it as "the little Black church on the hill." A reference to the complexion of its parishioners rather than the physical description of the building. Today this growing ministry embraces people of various ages, races, ethnicities, social classes and backgrounds. This same church is no longer struggling to survive. Once thought to be a prime candidate for the spiritual graveyard, it has now been resurrected and renewed. The excitement of people who come to worship at Pleasant Street Baptist Church today is unparalleled. Many members once cited distance as being an obstacle; today, two-thirds of the active members of the church today live in communities outside of Westerly. Many of those are often heard to remark, "There is something going on here. I just can't put my finger on it, but it is something very special. I may not know what it is, but it changes lives. I know because it changed mine."

How did this come about? What happened to change this church? How can a church today find new life, growth, and vitality? Turning back the Pleasant Street curtain to the time God first announced His vision, and looking at what God has accomplished, the only credible explanation for what has happened is God. There is no other way it can be explained. Whenever the seed of a church is birthed in the heart of a people, God already has a vision of His church in eternity. What He needs to fulfill His vision is to find the Isaiah, or the Paul, or any person who will deny self and surrender all to His divine vision. Confirmation of this surrendered heart is manifested in the words, *"Lord, I'll go! Send me."* [Isaiah 6:8b]

Church History

Isabelle Smith Dortch, the clerk from 1927 to 1971, compiled a history of the church which disclosed that the modest white clad building now proudly perched on Pleasant Street was first incorporated as the Advent Christian Colored Church in March of 1874. Henry Champlin, Gideon Ammons and Josiah Watson were its first members. Mrs. Dortch states that these few courageous men had a vision of a church that would be a place for every man, woman, and child created in the image of God. No longer would they be segregated to the balconies and dark corners of the larger established white churches. No longer would anyone be disenfranchised because of their race, color, ethnicity, or social status. No one should be made to feel unworthy in a church birthed by the death and resurrection of Jesus Christ. These founding fathers believed strongly in the premise that all men are created equal. Little did they know that 130 years later their vision would be the vehicle God would use to transform the Westerly community and beyond.

The early church initially attracted Native Americans. The original model of the church followed that of the Indian Meetinghouse in Charlestown, Rhode Island. In building the church, the settees [pews] faced the church entrance because its founders believed it to benefit the congregation to see people entering, thereby avoiding, disturbing or annoying the ministers by turning around. Initially, baptisms were held on Easter Sundays, and often took place outside in streams. Even now it causes shivers to think that it was sometimes necessary to break the thin ice at the shoreline to enter the water. However, no records exist of any fatalities or illness caused by this frigid exposure.

In May of 1934, the church was renamed the Pleasant Street Baptist Church by a vote of 6 to 3. But the struggles of this small group of dedicated people continued, even as they were focusing on their goal: "To serve God, and minister to the needs of others." Not much had changed until the church celebrated its 90th anniversary on April 18, 1964. Five days later, on Thursday, April 23, tragedy struck as most of the church building and its contents were destroyed by a devastating fire. Those were difficult days for the members of Pleasant Street. They were days of uncertainty, and there was a great sense of loss, which conjured up many questions about what to do next. But through great faith, and God's leading, hope returned. In September, 1964, the members voted to restore the church and add a new fellowship hall wing to the original building. It was a courageous decision on the part of the congregants; however, the new building construction would contribute indirectly to their own demise.

Signs of a Dying Church

The church owned a property immediately to the east containing five apartments. This house, which gave them income and afforded them the opportunity to reach out to the needs of the community, was sold for $10,000 to finance the new fellowship hall, thereby signaling their intent to retreat inwardly and serve the members who were part of the flock. They became an island to themselves shunning future growth because the land behind the church dropped off sharply to a depth of at least 40 feet. The house just to the west of the church was perched precariously on the same hill, making expansion impossible. The fellowship hall would be constructed not for church growth or outreach, but for the comfort of the few. From then on, forward progress began to wane as the ministry began to focus internally on families of the church in detriment to their stated goal to minister to the needs of others. The congregants failed to reach out to the community around them and, unknowingly, they associated themselves with the growing number of U. S. churches in decline. The common signs among this group of churches even today are manifest:

- Worship services are uninspiring. The singing lacks joy, reverence and spirit.
- The sermons are not centered on the Scriptures. "Christ and him crucified" is rarely heard.
- Few visitors attend and there are fewer baptisms.
- There is a lack of new and young families, and an absence of children.
- There is little excitement for outreach, mission or evangelism to save the lost.
- Church work is perceived as what takes place inside the church building only.
- A prevailing sense of complacency prevails among members.
- Leaders and members function out of a sense of duty, rather than out of joy and vision.
- Witnessing and outreach efforts are done mainly by the pastors.
- Real decision-making is done in a small group of older, better-known members.

Ask yourself, do any of these symptoms describe my church?

The members of Pleasant Street occupying the little white building on a side street in the North End of Westerly for the past 130 years had lost the vision for the church. They had evolved into a union formed of members of several old-line families. Many were reaching an age which was dangerously past maturity, without the awareness of the need for new churchgoers. Children had left and moved away. The church, no longer vibrant, was barely surviving in a sea of other places of worship. The church members rested contentedly in the way things were. They felt no compulsion to admit new people, and, especially, new ideas for growth. Notions of activities which didn't include present service attendance only were to be abandoned on the front steps. What the members did not sense was that their church had become moribund, on the way to extinction. This closed society of Baptists had become so pleased with their own interests and narrow needs that they excluded almost all potential members from their company. They had morphed into "a church", which is to say that they had identified themselves with the real estate they owned, and avoided their stated reason for being. They should have been a group of believers who comprised a living ministry. Instead, the people inside had ceased to reach out to others to proclaim the good news of God's love for all of mankind. A vacuum had been allowed to open in their souls. A yawning chasm had replaced the fervor and vitality of the earlier days of their founders' fellowship. Even more damning was the congregation's failure to have a plan to fend or stave off the impending doom. No leaders had come forward with sufficient verve and know-how to direct the flock. There was no vision.

King Solomon's ominous warning, "*Where there is no vision the people perish,*" fell on deaf ears. Pleasant Street Church as a living organism was on the brink of spiritual and temporal extermination. Attendance at services had declined. No new members were sought out. The collective will, a guttering candle, was all but snuffed. The words of the writer of first Samuel were like a sonic boom, "*Now in those days messages from the Lord were very rare, and visions were quite uncommon.*" [3:1b]

On December 26, 1976, God made His presence known to me in a vision where He revealed His heart, and called me to leave my comfortable home and business in Providence to become His hands and heart for hurting people. Little did I know that I would eventually end up in Pleasant Street Baptist Church to carry on the work of reviving His church. For years, God had been making preparation to bring His vision to this small Westerly congregation, but first I had to be convinced of the task and receive assurance He had already prepared the way to accomplish His will. My previous church and business experience had uniquely qualified me for the work ahead. However, God's initial task would be to change my attitude and my desire to be my own man. I saw myself as one who might implement what God had revealed to me. However, He had much more convincing to do before I would agree to go. It was even more difficult when I learned that Pleasant Street Baptist Church might be my destination. I was more determined than ever not to go there. The church was very small, consisting of around 35 members comprised of two or three families. The families were tucked away in a far corner of the southernmost part of Rhode Island, and appeared to have little interest in changing or reaching out to the community. There was scant organization, few real leaders, a lack of boards and committees, and financially the congregation could not sustain a full-time pastor's salary and it appeared it would rather remain that way. I wanted a healthy church, a financially sound church. I sought out more visible recognition than the church could provide. My desire was for a larger church with more activity and more opportunity for ministry, and yet what was haunting and compelling was the vision of God's will for my life.

Something Alarming

Today's church is reportedly stagnating. By recent admissions of major denominations, nearly eighty percent of churches either reached a plateau or are numbered among dying congregations. Pleasant Street Baptist Church was sharing the same sense of frustration and helplessness as church leaders today who are at a loss for what to do about it.

Ed Stetzer, Ph. D., author of *Planting New Churches in a Postmodern Age*, and director of the Nehemiah Project of the North American Mission Board of Southern Baptist Churches explains: "Over time, most churches plateau and most eventually decline. Typically they start strong or experience periods of growth, but then they stagnate. Patterns and traditions that once seemed special eventually lose their meaning. Churches that were once outwardly-focused eventually become worried about the wrong things. … Each year fewer churches baptize large numbers and more churches baptize no one. These trends are alarming, yet few churches are addressing their own decline.

In the 1980s, Ross Perot spoke about the national budget deficit as "the crazy aunt living in the basement that nobody wants to talk about." We have our own crazy aunt—tens of thousands of dead or dying churches. She is crazy but we do love her and want to treat her with dignity. But, ultimately we think she is hopeless and best ignored."

Many churches and church leaders recognize their plight. Tom Harper, publisher of *Equipping Leaders to Grow Healthier Churches*, writes, "Hundreds of churches close their doors every year, never to reopen again. After years of service to their communities and expansion of the Kingdom they are forced to shut down. ... Across the world and right in your hometown churches are struggling to stay open, struggling against declining attendance—struggling for survival."

Another headline avers: Churches at a crossroad: Five denominations in decline. *The Journal News* of the Episcopal Diocese in New York suggests the game plan for church growth is "a shared ministry" between denominations. "We didn't get the growth we expected or the interaction with the community that we expected. Our expectations, I'm afraid, were not realistic," said a parishioner of one of the churches involved.

A leading church growth scholar, Thom S. Ranier, dean of the Billy Graham School of Missions, Evangelism and Church Growth at Southern Baptist Theological Seminary, will soon publish the results of a major new study which asserts the Southern Baptist Convention is evangelistically "on the path of slow but discernable deterioration." Rainer concludes, "Evangelism and church growth does benefit from innovative programs. Research is helpful to grasp possible future paths of evangelistic strategy. But ultimately, evangelism is a matter of the heart between the believer and a sovereign God. It is truly a spiritual matter."

Lyle Shaller, a widely known church consultant, writing in the *New England Baptist Monthly* stated, "Church members today expect their involvement in a local congregation to transform their lives, not just enrich their lives." Further, Schaller says, "Discipleship and ministry, not baptism or active church membership, are the marks of a true Christian."

More recently a book by George Barna titled, *REVOLUTION: Finding Vibrant Faith Beyond the Walls of the Sanctuary* appears to be most disturbing of all. Barna, author of over thirty-five books and founder of the marketing-research firm Barna Group points to research data that documents the failure of churches to do their job of developing mature disciples. He writes, "Whether you become a Revolutionary immersed in, minimally involved in, or completely disassociated from a local church is irrelevant to me [and, within boundaries, to God]." Armed with the results of his study George Barna suggests we abandon the local church for "mini-movements" such as home schooling, house churches, Bible studies at work and Chris Tomlin worship concerts.

Apart from these many voices of church declivity is the fact that God has not abandoned His church.

He still speaks through visions, but the church must be open to see and hear. Vision is the way back to the flame, zeal, and power of the early church. God's plan is to restore His church to its rightful place. He called the church into being and He knows what the church requires to revive itself. Our churches and community need to link together leaders hearing and heeding this call from the Holy Spirit for renewal.

CHAPTER TWO

BEGINNINGS...
EARLY CHURCH LIFE

> "You know how full of love and kindness our Lord Jesus Christ was. Though he was very rich, yet for your sakes he became poor, so that by his poverty he could make you rich."
> 2 Corinthians 8:9

One of my favorite authors, Calvin Miller, in his book *Into the Depths of God* ruminates on the fact that children are forever drawing pictures during his sermons. At first it haunted him because he felt they were drawing out of boredom, and maybe if he preached better the drawings would diminish. At the conclusion of the worship service they often gave him their pictures at the back door of the church. Miller said, "One such child drew a picture of me in the pulpit with Jesus hovering over me in midair. Was it good enough for the Louvre? Not the point! She achieved a worldview of Christ as she wanted him to be and I needed him to be."

It brings to mind the many pictures I have received from my granddaughter Cinphany when she came home from pre-school. Each day the pictures were different as her active mind depicted her grampoppie in various ways, daily changing faces, sizes, colors and caricatures. In reflection, I wonder if God in fact does not at times see us that way. Drawing a picture of us on His divine canvass at birth and then following closely our progress during our perilous journey along the way. Each incident in our lives, the joy, the pain, the sorrow, all help the Artist to blend the colors and character together until one day the subject and the Artist merge and we become sharers of the divine image.

F. B. Meyer, a prominent Baptist preacher and author, writes: "What startling differences there are among men. We are sometimes tempted to attribute their special powers and success to their circumstances, times, parents, and teachers. But there is a deeper and more satisfactory explanation. Adopting the words of the forerunner, men have nothing that they have not received from heaven, by the direct appointment and decree of God.

This is a golden sentence, indeed!—'A man can receive nothing except it be given him from heaven.' Do you have great success in your life work? Do crowds gather around your steps and throng your auditorium? Do not attribute them to yourself. They are all the gifts of God's grace. You have nothing that you have not received. Be thankful but never vain, because He who gave may take. Great talents given imply great responsibility in the day of reckoning."

Meyer makes me keenly aware that what I am today, what I have achieved in life, the granting of a vision of God's heart is a direct result of divine grace, even though some credit may be attributed to the strengths embedded in my genetic composition. My paternal great-grandfather, Jerry Honor, was a full-blooded Mohawk Indian. He married Hannah Lowry, a full-blooded Cherokee Indian. Hannah was from King's Mountain, North Carolina. Their fourth oldest child, Della, my father's mother, married William McClure on December 28, 1899, in Chester, South Carolina.

Here is where I believe much of my independent character trait was birthed. Jerry Honor was a slave given the Abel family name by his white owner. He drove a surrey—a-four-wheel, light pleasure carriage— for the Abel family before the Civil War. My great-grandfather Jerry fought in the Civil War and earned an honorable discharge. [To this day it mystifies me how he came to receive a pension from both the North and the South. The South, however, caught up to him after three years and severed his windfall.] After his discharge, Jerry Honor continued to drive the surrey for the Abel family who suggested his name be changed to Arnold. Jerry was now a free man and was determined he would no longer allow anyone to dictate to him, especially his family name. He changed his last name to Honor, and settled in Chester, South Carolina, where he became a successful landowner. Evidence of the respect tendered to him is found in Chester today, on Honor Street which bears his name and still hosts some of the original family homes.

Charles Benjamin Stedman, my maternal grandfather, was born in New Haven, Connecticut, in 1880. He married Josephine Queen Esther Dunn, a full-blooded Blackfoot Indian, who was born in 1883 in Lawrenceville, Virginia. It is worthy of note that the officiating clergy at their wedding in 1902, in New Haven, was the Reverend Adam Clayton Powell, who then presided at the Dixwell Avenue Congregational Church, and later became pastor of the well known Abyssinian Baptist Church in New York. His son, Rev. Adam Clayton Powell Jr., who succeeded his father at the church, was the first African American to become a powerful figure in the United States Congress.

Just after the turn of the twentieth century, my parents were born in distant parts of the United States. My father, Albert Theodore McClure, came into the world on February 7, 1902, in Lowryville, Chester County, South Carolina. Like many young men of his day he saw little opportunity for respect and felt powerless to achieve his potential at home, so he traveled north, settling in New Haven in his late teens. There he first met a lovely young woman, Dorothy Josephine E. Stedman, who had been born on August 28, 1903 in New Haven. They were married in New Haven in 1922. My dad was a tall, thin man: dark, very handsome, distinguished in suit and tie. He had left school in the eighth grade and forfeited his potential for higher paying jobs, so he spent most of his life working multiple jobs as a laborer to compensate for his lack of education. My dad was a strong man who was gentle, compassionate and caring, but most of all he had an incredible capacity to love. The life lesson that I learned from my father is that a man can possess all of these seemingly less-than-masculine characteristics and still be respected as a man.

My mother, on the other hand, was just the opposite. In stature she was a full ten inches shorter than my dad, coming up to the top of his shoulders. She was fair skinned, medium build, with hair extending almost to her shoulders. She was an attractive woman with soft features. My mother was a woman with bearing. In her presence you became aware of an IQ above the norm. She had high ideals, was goal-oriented and self-assured with a determination to accomplish her aims. Her parents and family often questioned her good judgment in marrying my dad, but who knows the workings of love? The earliest picture I have of them together was standing in front of their church in New York, with their hands resting on a Bible.

The following year witnessed the arrival of the first of my brothers and sisters. Five girls and five boys were born to my parents over the next twenty or so years. Early in their marriage they found a place in Brooklyn where my oldest sister, Doris Helen, was born. Doris was followed by Deborah Mae [Debbie], and Arline Dorothy, and later in New Haven, Beverly Ruth, and finally my youngest sister Esther Frances was born. My oldest brother, Wesley, died in infancy. Then came my brother Edward Daniel [Eddie] was born in 1928, followed by myself, Joshua Alvin. I was the second boy and middle child, born on October 12, 1931, at 536 Herkimer Street, Brooklyn. Several years later my brother Warren Joseph came into the world in New Haven, and finally in 1945, Joel Arnold greeted the world in that same city.

The wide age differential that separated us influenced the order in which my own children were born, for my children are hardly one and a half years apart. Because of the difference in ages of my brothers and sisters, our experiences varied growing up. As the middle child I was not always able to relate to what was going on in their lives.

My father, now responsible for a large family, worked practically around the clock to feed, clothe, and house us. This left my mother to assume the role of disciplinarian, educator, and main caregiver. She became the family's center. Although neither my mother nor father was high school graduates, my mother knew intuitively that education was a *must* for her children. Thus, before sports participation, before social activities, schoolwork was the preeminent focus for all of us. My mother strictly enforced her education program by means of a strenuously applied code of disciplined behavior, manners, and dress. She said, "You're not like all the other kids, you're McClures." Her code was reinforced by the precepts of the church we attended which was, as far as I was concerned, very rigid. My mother was pro-education almost to the point of obsession. She sacrificed everything in her life so that each one of her children would graduate from high school and receive a college degree, an achievement she somehow managed almost single handedly. Only today have I come to realize what an enormous feat she accomplished. Only one of her children did not attain a formal college education—and that only by chance. I would say that was quite an accomplishment for a mother of ten who took in laundry to supplement her husband's income.

The Brooklyn Church

Memories of our first home on 536 Herkimer St. in Brooklyn are sparse, but I do recall some of the details after we moved to 976 Gates Ave. My parents relocated to be nearer to the church in which they first gave their lives to Jesus Christ. They had become members of the Pentecostal Holiness Church of Prayer and Deliverance, 125th Street and Lexington Avenue, New York City. The church was headed by Bishop Rosa A. Horn.

"Mother Horn" as she was affectionately known, was a church leader who started several similar congregations on the East Coast. One of the largest was in Baltimore. She was a woman of average height and medium build, standing about 5 feet 5 inches tall and weighing between 150 and 160 pounds. Her ministry rose to a level that rivaled some of the best known churchmen of her time, such as Father Devine.

Mother Horn was the overseer, an imposing figure sitting on the big soft chair in the center of the rostrum dressed in a floor length white robe with the top of her head covered with a small crocheted scarf pinned at the sides. She looked very regal, and commanded great respect and no one could question who was in charge. Her age and previous activity had caused her to limit her preaching to special services. She surrounded herself with a cadre of ministers, both men and women, approved by her to address the congregation during worship services. Her closest companion and church leader was Sister Gladys Branhagen, who did most of the talking and preaching in her stead.

The church was dominated by women, but Mother Horn had a substructure of men, called elders, who were also leaders of the congregation. Among them were: elders Harry, Green, Lightfoot, Mauchaud, Boxdale and McClure, my father, who was among Mother Horn's favorites.

Bishop Horn lived in a mansion in New Rochelle, New York, and also owned a large estate in Long Branch, New Jersey. The church owned several limousines which were Mother Horn's means of transportation. By contrast, most of the members of the church, including my father, had southern roots. Most had large families and worked very hard but lived in poverty because they gave nearly all of their money to the church.

The block in which the church was located on Lexington Avenue was typical of most streets in the area. Rows upon rows of mom-and-pop businesses lined the street, with a door in between the stores leading to the second floor where other less visible businesses were located. This is where the church was housed.

The sanctuary was a large square space which encompassed the area of five or six of the businesses below. People would walk up a long flight of stairs to get to the sanctuary level where worship took place. Behind the sanctuary was the living quarters, separated from the sanctuary by a large curtain stretched from floor to ceiling. The living area included a kitchen and pantry, a sitting room, and several sleeping rooms with cots. Only the inner circle of people was allowed to go behind the curtain.

Mother Horn treated my father as one of her sons and referred to my parents as "Allen" and "Dot". This meant we were among the privileged few. In between services, we ate meals in the back of the building behind the long curtain, and we took naps right there in the church.

As I previously mentioned, the sight of many canes and crutches hanging on a wire near the entrance to the Sanctuary left a lasting impression on me. This visible proof of God's prowess leads me to this day to believe strongly in intercessory prayer and divine healing as essential to our faith.

The church held three worship services each Sunday. The morning and evening worship services lasted four to five hours, while the afternoon service was shorter. The most notable time of worship was a convocation of sister churches for a Service of Consecration. This special worship was held twice a year, and the churches under Mother Horn would gather with the mother church to celebrate. It was one of the few times Mother Horn actually led the worship. The women, all dressed in white with their little crocheted hats on their heads, proudly marched down both sides of the center aisle of the church, with a certain bounce in their step, almost a strut, swaying to the beat of the music. I can see them now and hear them singing with celebratory ardor, their voices rising far above the chords of the piano. "It's a highway to heaven; none can walk up there, but the pure in heart. It's a highway to heaven, walking up the King's highway," they sang.

It was a sight to behold, a church filled with women, singing and praising the Lord, coming to give more of themselves to the Lord, expecting a rich blessing in return. The men in attendance were nattily dressed in black suits with thin gray ties, the three buttons on their suits fully secure. Their attire contrasted with the garments worn by the women. In the front of the altar the Service of Consecration would include prayers of forgiveness, personal dedication to the Lord, commitment to holiness and cleanliness and sanctification, setting aside of self to God. The Consecration Service culminated with each person being anointed with oil on the forehead. Many years later my sister Debbie remarked, "Every time I hear that song, Highway to Heaven, I think of Mother Horn. I can see the saints all dressed in white marching down the aisles of the church."

It brings to mind that great vision of the apostle John exiled to the isle of Patmos.

> "After this I saw a vast crowd, too great to count, from every nation and tribe and people and language, standing in front of the throne and before the Lamb. They were clothed in white and held palm branches in their hands. And they were shouting with a mighty shout, 'Salvation comes from our God on the throne and from the Lamb." [Revelation 7:9, 10]

Mother Horn's church also hosted a radio program on Sunday nights, a live broadcast of the evening service. It often lasted beyond midnight, but boasted a large following and attracted many people off the street. I can remember many times at night riding home in the car listening to Bishop Rosa A. Horn's Church of Deliverance on the radio.

My father at this time had become a very strong, popular church elder and leader. He was often called on to preach. He was a strong influence in the church and in our lives during these formative years, the church became almost an extension of our family. We were expected to commit Sundays entirely to worship, and the church doctrine dictated we, its members, become models of decorum for the community at-large by means of virtuous comportment and fastidious attire. On

Sundays, men like my father appeared on the street in neatly pressed suits, starched and ironed shirts, an appropriate necktie, shined shoes, and carefully selected and maintained hats. Proper clothing for the ladies was body concealing dresses, or long skirts with long-sleeved blouses buttoned to the throat, hats suitable for church, sensible shoes, and hair formed into a bun at the top of the head. As kids we emulated the sartorial splendor of our parents and always sat in the front row. Sitting there all dressed up and on our best behavior, we were learning discipline and total respect for the House of the Lord. Church life heavily influenced everyday life.

My older brother Ed tells the story of when he and my father were traveling to church on the subway. In an attempt to save his father some money, Ed slipped under the turnstile. He says, "I felt this strong hand grab me by the collar and pull me back." My father reprimanded him, "Don't you ever do that again. That is wrong. It's the same as stealing."

Ed confessed to me, "That's why I can't steal today." The effect of the church still lingers for good or ill in our family. My older sister Doris had doubts about the church. She was filled with anger and bore a negative image of the church almost to the day she died. As a child growing up in the church, she reported to my mother and father that she had experienced inappropriate touching by one of the leaders of the church. When this was reported to Mother Horn, she convinced my parents not to pursue the accusations to the detriment of the church. Doris felt hurt, angry, betrayed and disillusioned by the experience and remained at odds with the church for its hypocritical stance in dealing with a human life. Looking back, "the influence of" our early days in the Brooklyn church have proved to be inescapable for each of us to this very day.

In concord with the church, the Brooklyn years awakened in me a sense of family. For the most part, our lives were an amplification of the church. For instance, Debbie, my older sister, was given preferential treatment. Debbie would be off to Coney Island and some other entertaining locales with my Aunt Helen, my father's youngest sister, all the while Arline, my younger sister by two years and myself would be stuck with several chores to perform. We often had to scale and clean fish that would be sold in the restaurant owned by Aunt Helen. I can still recall Debbie, arrayed in her pretty dresses with pigtail coiffed hair, recklessly spinning herself round and round and round on the eating-place's stools, until the centrifugal force of her efforts seemed to catapult her out the door to a fabulous afternoon of fun. Arline and I, left behind, were furious as we were forced to settle for a date with some cold fish.

All was not lost, however. Justice and compassion prevailed sometimes. Aunt Gertie, a close family friend and restaurant worker, who observed our distress, set about to make things right for us. She would seize upon the pie man's periodic refill stops at the eatery to bring us one of his freshest treats, usually a huge apple pie. Aunt Gertie's after work treat for us came to include a good hot, soapy, soaking bath and an overnight sojourn at her home. Those evenings' activities were capped by sinfully delicious slices of hot apple pie straight from the oven. While Debbie managed to keep her experiences separate, Arline and I had our own exclusive secret from her.

Brooklyn's P. S. 129 was where I began my public school career. My mother found work there in the cafeteria. She further augmented our family's income by taking in ironing and cleaning other people's houses. When Arline, in particular, learned of the verbal abuse her mother received from her clients, she became infuriated, and yet, mama was determined to do the best she could for her family no matter what.

CHAPTER THREE

FAMILY LIFE

"Teach your children to choose the right path, and
when they are older, they will remain upon it."
Proverbs 22:6

The McClure family left New York and moved to New Haven, Connecticut, when I was seven years old. Deeply devoted to their church, my dad and mom would drive the Merritt Parkway weekly back to New York from New Haven to attend services. Evening prayers for the health and security of their children were the norm for my parents. A scene I will never forget is the picture of my mother and father kneeling beside their bed in the flickering yellow-white glow of an oil lamp, reciting each child's name aloud for the Lord's special notice. I can hear them now: "Lord will you please bless my son, Joshua. Make him wise and strong, and lead him to one day come to know you."

My father's new job at the Cooper Tire Company necessitated the move to New Haven. He also earned extra money by driving a tractor-trailer to and from Edgewater, New Jersey, for the Ford Motor Company. Sometimes he would take us along with him. Some of our happiest times were riding along with Daddy in the cab of that giant truck. We looked forward to being with him because he was absent from home so much of the time.

It was here in New Haven that life began to unfold for me. Here I truly began to develop as an individual. In New Haven, the experience that would ultimately shape my life began. Our family moved to 114 Dixwell Ave. into a building nicknamed "Oatmeal Flat", which derived its name from the cereal its residents consumed vast portions of. Not an elegant edifice, the three-story apartment house contained twelve units, four apartments per floor with a furniture store anchoring the ground floor. On each floor families had their own bathroom accessed from a common hall outside the individual apartments. Inside, all of us slept in one bedroom: the girls on one side, the boys on the other. The middle space between the children's areas contained the pee pot so necessary during the night. Each of us, in turn, was assigned the daily task of disposing of its contents. A lasting memory of Oatmeal Flat is standing on the back porch with its loose, unsafe railings. There was a pile of trash in the backyard, and I remember standing three stories up throwing rocks down at rats as big as cats.

I didn't realize it at the time, but those New Haven years were the 1930's, the Depression era, brought on by the crash of the stock market in 1929. President Franklin Delano Roosevelt would eventually present social programs to help the poor. But for a while, the poor were on their own. We were poor and we practiced economics on a grand scale. Bargains were assiduously hunted at the First National, Mohegan, and A& P food stores. Armed with newspaper ads clipped out by my mother, my sister Arline and I walked many miles between those food stores buying only those items offered at sale prices. Wind, rain, and snow often buffeted us on our journey as we pulled our wagon along the hungry streets. When available, Wonder Bread bakery's day-old bread, cupcakes and rolls were a welcome supplement to poor families' diets. I created a new delicacy—a cup cake sandwich. I did this by slicing sweet cup cakes and inserting them as the filling between two bread slices. It prolonged the taste and extended the range of the cupcake treat.

There were rationing queues for cheese, butter, sugar, dry beans and bread during those lean years. I remember standing in the "bread line" to get our portion; I hardly noticed that I had something in common with everyone else who stood with me. The black shoes we wore stigmatized each one of us who stood in line. Everyone wore them because that is what was issued by the city to impoverished individuals. We were on city support, but I still did not realize it. I suppose I was not very observant of my surroundings. Or there may have been another reason. My mother was so gifted and so skilled in making things go a long way that we never really felt the lack of anything.

We made the most of the resources we could get hold of. Mothers in those days would make delicious stews from beef bones and chicken feet. Old clothes were kept serviceable by frequent careful mending. My brother Eddie's knickers were tailored to fit me after he outgrew them. When I received the knickers it was just as if my parents had bought me new clothes. The same thing happened with suits or coats. We took especially good care of our clothing because we expected the garments to be handed down to our younger brothers and sisters when we outgrew them.

Life in Connecticut with my mother was a learning experience. One might say it was here the McClure family life was altered. My mother would tell us over and over again, "People who live in a ghetto are not there because they want to be." She realized that the neighborhood offered her children temptations which they might not be able to resist; therefore, she arranged to supervise our activities closely. We went to school and returned directly home to read and study. No loitering on the streets was allowed. Most of us had an intense dislike for Saturdays, because Saturday was cleaning day. We stayed home and did the chores around the house. I tried to forget, but Arline reminded me mama outlawed mops from the repertoire of cleaning utensils we could employ to do the work. We scrupulously scrubbed the floors on our hands and knees until the color disappeared from the linoleum and in its place the black backing underneath popped up. Our furniture was polished, dusted and burnished until it shimmered. The porcelain and chrome fittings of the household plumbing fixtures, though a little rusty and peeling, were made to gleam. Beds were changed. Rooms aired. Stairways swept and scrubbed. Windows admitted God's nourishing sunshine and soul refreshing light through spotless panes. We wondered if mama was only being a meticulous housewife, or was there a not so subtle message for us in all this gritty manual labor. After the tasks were satisfactorily completed, she always had a reward. She treated us to a plate of broken, half price, day-old-yet-tasty cookies from the bakery. Then it was time for some entertainment—checkers. We were allowed to play the game on the newly scrubbed black and white pattern linoleum floor. Who could be blamed if kings were made by "mistake" on a surface scrubbed almost to a homogenous color? Of course, Sunday meant the long jaunt back to a day of church exercises in New York City.

Perpetually penurious, "Dot"—her sister Frances and close church friends called her—was compelled to devise schemes and strategies to meet her objectives for her kids' betterment. Books, she understood, were at the core of the education she planned for her sons and daughters. But how to obtain them, new and free, was the problem. One day she noticed encyclopedia salesmen plying their trade in the area. She found out that the salesmen would offer, as an inducement for buying beautifully leather-bound twenty-four volume encyclopedia sets, a series of science books, biographies, histories, etc. Dot reasoned that the local libraries bought new sets of these volumes of knowledge at regular intervals. Her children could use the newest encyclopedias there for free. But she wanted books in her home for her children to read and enjoy. So she ordered the big sets of books accompanied by those free books. She would return the encyclopedias but keep the free books for us to read.

Sibling Relationships

In New Haven, my sister Debbie, too, underwent a transformation. She became my protector when Eddie wasn't there, which was all too often. In those years, I was a stout little fellow whose diffidence was a magnet to bullies. We walked several miles to school everyday to reach Dwight Grammar School. Buses were unheard of for us. Those miles could be an endurance test, a cold gauntlet past which I had to speed to reach the minimal security of the schoolhouse. Not a bold youth, I would offer only verbal defiance to my tormentors, but that was as far as I would dare go, especially if I had no protection. Not only that, I was bound by my mother's stricture not to fight. I would leave for school meticulously attired; a fight in those clothes could produce a rip or a tear and would have brought me severe consequences when I arrived back at home.

Being weight conscious, I often felt isolated. I lacked self-confidence, had few close friends, was very shy, kept very much to myself and spoke only when spoken to. A cousin, Lucille (Walker) Sewell, with whom I recently renewed an acquaintance after a forty year break remarked, "I can remember you as not having much to say, and when in the company of adults, you spoke only when spoken to." I must admit I attempted to live very much the way my parents wanted me to. When I violated their rules, which was very infrequently, I could be sure of swift and harsh punishment from either of my parents.

As previously noted, my mother told us we were "McClures". That meant we were expected to set an example for the other neighborhood children. Our family life was centered on the church. My parents were completely committed to living disciplined lives for Christ Jesus. Hence, it followed that each one of us were counted on to emulate their example.

Debbie, Arline, and I were seen by others in the neighborhood as the "Preacher's Kids" always on a pedestal. We acted differently. We were forbidden to do certain things such as attend movies, stay out late, smoke, drink, have groups of friends without bringing family members along, all things which many of our friends and classmates took as natural rights. Some peers even viewed us as anti-social. We were always properly dressed for school, clean and neat. We had to go straight to the school and return home immediately after school was over. At times my Lord Fauntleroy finery drew threats from other kids. That's why I needed Eddie or Debbie for protection.

Unfortunately, my brother Eddie wasn't around much. He had figured out how to get around my parents' rules and restrictions. Though only four years apart, our worlds were vastly different. Eddie was an imposing figure: broad shouldered, wide bodied and a great candidate for a football lineman.

On the other hand, I was shy, not heavy into sports, and inclined to stay near home. Eddie established a shoeshine business at Pierson Gate at Yale University. He met many people and established many contacts, and for the most part, the core of his activity was outside the home. My memories of Eddie as a big brother tend to focus on the times he left me at the mercy of the New Haven bullies. My mother told him to watch out for me, but Eddie's interest was either football or cozying up to one of the sweet young local girls. He paid little attention to me and I became a prime target for the local toughs. On Saturday afternoons when my mother went shopping, she would often come home and find Eddie and me fighting, with me usually on the bottom. That is why I preferred Debbie to be my protector; she took the responsibility for my safety seriously.

Growing up, my younger brother Warren had his own circle of friends. Though I was four years his senior, he looked to Eddie as the older brother and was more inclined to follow his lead. Eddie was worldly wise, and had much to say about life in general. On the other hand, I had little in the way of experiences to offer. Today, Warren and I have become extremely close. I had the privilege of introducing Warren to Jesus Christ.

My older sister Doris grew up to be a very beautiful woman. She had ideal facial features and a natural beauty that rivaled the most glamorous movie stars. She maintained a near perfect figure, dressed meticulously and appeared as if she had stepped out of the pages of *Harper's Bazaar*. Doris had left home in 1941, in defiance of my parents, when I was ten years old. She moved to New York, so my relationship with her was mostly confined to the few times she would pay us a visit. Even with our limited time together, I was probably closer to Doris than anyone in the family. Certainly that was so at the end of her life when she surrendered to the Lord. Her bitterness and anger toward the church had simmered throughout most of her life, to the point no one felt safe even talking about church. A slip would invite a torrent of words and change of personality.

In July of 1979, I received a call from a close friend of Doris to say my sister was in the hospital and had recently undergone surgery for cancer. Doris insisted no one in her family be told of her cancer. However, the friend felt her condition warranted informing the family.

One of the times I visited Doris, I gingerly broached the subject of having peace in her life, and that Christ had died to take away anger and replace it with joy. Doris listened intently but said nothing. I counted it a miracle that I received no angry response and felt none of her rage.

On December 31, 1979, the family had gathered at Arline's home in Sharon, MA. We proposed to bring Doris so she could see all her siblings and her nieces and nephews. The dining room was just adjoining the kitchen and everyone was either around the dining room table or downstairs in the family room. Doris and I sat alone at the kitchen table and during those precious moments she received Jesus Christ as her Lord and Savior. In the following days she rejoiced in her newfound faith.

However, she insisted she was not ready to be baptized, even though she was growing weaker and weaker. Early in April, she must have resigned herself to the fact she would soon die, so she said, "Josh, I'm ready to be baptized." I spoke to Jack San Filippo, pastor of the

Coney Island Gospel Assembly Church, and we arranged a date for her baptism.

On Thursday, April 12, 1980, I baptized my beautiful sister Doris, and twelve days later on Thursday, April 24 she died. I officiated at her funeral from the Coney Island Church on Monday, April 28, and laid her to rest in Pinelawn Memorial Cemetery, Farmingdale, New York. Doris was fifty-six years old when she died.

My younger brother, Joel, and Beverly and Esther, my younger sisters, were so young we could only have a little brother-kid sister relationship. And yet many years later, I became Esther's legal guardian, and once again faced the prospect of burying a sister.

My sister Arline and I enjoyed a wonderful relationship growing up. We had a close bond that remains to this day. We were so close we often felt like twins, we did so many things together. My mother often spoke to us as a pair, whether it was about going to the store, or cleaning the house, or cleaning fish at Aunt Helen's restaurant. The instructions were always: Arline and Josh, or Josh and Arline do this. Our early years were spent close to home trying to adhere to our parent's wishes. When I left Chelsea, Arline was living in the apartment downstairs, still close to home helping to care for her younger sisters and brother.

Rules or not, I did on occasion sever the bonds of parental control, but not without retribution. There was the time when I just couldn't resist pitching rocks at some bottles lined up on a fence behind the apartment house. Someone heard the sound of shattering glass and called the police. I ran into the basement hoping to elude the police and escape involvement in the crime, but that's where the police found me. I confessed straightaway hoping that would help. It didn't. That was when I was twelve or thirteen years old.

It seemed like a great idea and fun at the time, but when I tied a small bottle with string around its neck and swung it around in front of a large dresser mirror, disaster followed. The bottle slipped the string's grip and smashed my reflection. Bad luck came in the form of my father's administration of punishment with his leather strap.

Then there was the time I was told by my mother she was going to the store and I was not to leave the house. She said, "Joshua, don't leave this house, don't you set foot out of this door." I reasoned she meant the front door by which she left. So, I climbed out of a side window. Didn't I get a nail stuck in my foot? I found it's not easy to be a transgressor.

God's Calling …

"Then the Lord told Abram, Leave your country, your relatives and your father's house, and go to the land that I will show you. I will cause you to become the father of a great nation. I will bless you and make you famous, and I will make you a blessing to others. I will bless those who bless you and curse those who curse you. All the families of the earth will be blessed through you."

Genesis 12:1-3

CHAPTER FOUR

DIVINE CALL

"Yes, your servant is listening"
1 Samuel 3:10b

Bill Hybels, senior pastor of the globe-spanning Willow Creek Community Church in South Barrington, Illinois, in his recent book, *Courageous Leadership,* cites the names of several well known leaders who in some way contributed to world change: John Adams, one of America's founding fathers; William Wilberforce, who advocated the abolition of slave trade; Wilbur and Orville Wright, inventors of the airplane; Henry Ford, who produced the first affordable automobile; Billy Graham, a world known evangelist; Dr. Martin Luther King Jr., who advocated a policy of non violent protest, and dreamed of a time of freedom, opportunity and justice for all. ; Dr. Gilbert Bilezikian, professor at Wheaton College, Wheaton, Illinois. More than 30 years ago, Dr. Bilezekian's passionate teaching ignited a vision in the heart of his student, Bill Hybels. Hence, Willow Creek Church was birthed. All these leaders had one thing in common: a compelling vision.

Hybels reiterates, "Vision is at the very core of leadership. Take vision away from a leader and you cut out his or her heart. Vision is the fuel that leaders run on. It's the energy that creates action. It's the fire that ignites the passion of followers. It's the clear call that sustains focused effort year after year, decade after decade, as people offer consistent and sacrificial services to God …. But when a church needs a God-honoring, kingdom-advancing, heart-thumping vision, it turns to its leaders. That's because God put in the leader's arsenal the potent offensive weapon called vision."

From 1973 to 1975, after the Rev. Jack Clark resigned as pastor of Providence's Pond Street Baptist Church, due to illness; I was reluctantly thrust into the role of interim pastor. I served in that position within the church until another pastor was called. It was soon after in December of 1976, after serving as a member of Pond Street for 15 years and successfully running several businesses for more than 17 years, I received a revelation from God. It was a "vision of ministry" so clear and so compelling that it gripped my heart, and I became a man willing to leave all behind to follow Jesus.

The plans had been made and confirmed that our family would spend that Christmas holiday in Philadelphia with my wife's parents. The kids were excited and looking forward to the trip. They enjoyed traveling, and since the day each of our four children was born, they became the reason for us to continually buy bigger cars. A few weeks before the time to leave arrived, a strange thing happened. In the midst of my busyness, I thought I heard a soft voice speak to me and cancel my trip to my in-law's home. My wife continued preparations, but once again several days before Christmas the voice returned with the same words; "You are not going to Philadelphia." This time I took notice because the voice seemed more of a personal plea rather than a demand, and more determined in its effort to get my attention. Not only did I take notice but I responded to the declaration, asking, "How do I tell my wife?" I knew my wife Ida would not even hear of my missing this trip with the family, and at Christmastime? I queried once again, "How do I tell Ida I'm not going?" After a moment of silence that seemed like forever, I heard two simple but assuring words, "Tell her."

For a time I avoided conversation with my wife as I pondered the whole meaning of what I had experienced. I even wondered if all of this was true or whether I was hallucinating. In retrospect, I was reminded of Elijah waiting on the mountain for God to reveal Himself. After a windstorm, earthquake, and the fire God spoke in *"a gentle whisper."* [1 Kings 19:12.] When I finally summoned up the courage to approach Ida, I said to her yet with some trepidation, "Honey, I can't go to Philadelphia with you." I feared this would not be a pleasant moment for us; in fact, I expected a loud outburst of disappointment and anger. To my surprise it never came. Ida looked at me and before she responded, I knew. God had already prepared her heart and she reached out, touched my arm and said, "Okay." The power of this moment would later prove to be instrumental in my struggle to leave Providence for Westerly.

In reflecting on this incident, I realized a peace and calm about what was happening to me. In the last few years, my relationship with the Lord had been deepening, and my times of worship and prayer were becoming more intimate. I had no thought of why God had singled me out; however, I was certain that God wanted time alone with me. Indeed, I soon learned the reason for His call.

Sunday, December 26, 1976, in the late afternoon I was sitting in my living room reflecting on events. The day was much like other Sundays, everything seemed very normal. I felt no unusual anxiety, and yet I was aware that I was alone. Prior to leaving church, several people insisted I have dinner with their family so as not to be alone, but when I declined I was treated with the remark, "I don't know how your wife could leave you alone on the holidays." In my heart, I knew I was home not because my wife insisted, but because of God. Soon thereafter, God came and revealed to me His heart for wounded, broken, lost and hurting people. My whole being trembled when I realized the *vision* now etched upon my heart was a picture of God's heart for people and my appointment to ministry. I knew then God's plan for my life was fixed and following him was inescapable. During Christmas of 1976, at home in my living room, I saw the Lord.

The Vision

I was alone when it happened. In my solitude, I became aware of an image projected as a picture upon my living room wall. It was a startling visitation I later reasoned could only have been God-sent. Muffled voices, garbled, indistinct, seemed to emanate from the picture. Then parts of the spectral portrait became unified as if they were all parts of a mosaic. I rubbed my eyes several times in amazement and incomprehension, not yet sure of what I was seeing. Slowly the vision cleared. Shapes began to form. Then I realized that the activity in the picture was caused by the movement of outstretched hands gesturing in my direction. I perceived them not as a threat, but more as though begging, yearning, beseeching, desiring some response from me. I could not answer at the moment; I was transfixed, as if frozen in time. As my perception became more acute, faces emerged from the bleak, grey-red, dimly lit background. Images with eyes that were sad, hopeful, pleading, tears could be seen falling, mouths were opened wide. The people appeared to whisper plaintive words, seeking food, clothing, a place to live, work, a guide to living, sage advice, the Word of God in their lives; hands, faces, voices became incarnate. I was seeing and sensing needs as never before, yet I was unaware what the vision's portent was for me. In my puzzlement and despair, I began to pray intently for understanding. I wanted to know what I was seeing and why. I waited and listened: nothing; silence. No still small voice, no *gentle whisper*. I began to pray anew, this time with greater concentration and persistence. Again, I waited. I listened more attentively. In my heart I heard God tell me He had important work for me to do and it was imperative that I yield to Him. The assignment meant a complete change of the work I had been successfully engaged in for many years. I would have to leave the business world, abandon my personal goals and the desires I had held since a child. My way of life and my family's would be altered irretrievably. No longer was there doubt in my mind and heart of what I had been blessed to witness. This vision became my destiny on earth. I had been called to serve the Lord with all my heart, soul, mind and strength. At that moment I gave little thought as to how I could run a full-time business, continue to be heavily involved in the community, maintain my loyalty and devotion to Pond Street church and still complete a demanding four-year college program. Relying on my own strength it could not be done, so I made a life decision to rely totally on the Lord. I would serve Him completely. He would provide these answers and make clear His plans in His own time and schedule. He had captured my heart.

Which Way, Lord?

In an effort to sort out what this haunting visitation from God implied for my family, my business and the church, I immediately sought out the Rev. Dr. Eugene Motter, then executive minister of the American Baptist Churches of Rhode Island, for advice. As a result of our discussion, I enrolled in the Denominations Certified Lay Ministry Program, which would allow me time to figure out what all of this signified. Though I needed more time, I did not want to be delayed. Thus I requested that I be allowed to accelerate the program by doubling up my courses. The committee agreed, so I entered the Certified Lay Ministry Program in 1977 and completed it by the summer of 1978. A few months later, in the fall of 1978, I enrolled in Barrington College as a Biblical Studies major.

Shortly after the vision, I excitedly told my pastor about the revelation from God. He rebuffed me and said he was too busy then and would deal with it later. This translated into early May, six months later. Our relationship continued to be strained to the point that one Sunday I preached a sermon entitled, "The Peril of Delay," using the *"Parable of the Ten Bridesmaids"* [Matthew 25:1-13] as my text. The point of my message was Christ's second coming will be swift and sudden. There will be no opportunity for last minute repentance or bargaining. The choice we have already made will determine our eternal destiny; there is danger in delaying our decision for Christ.

I had no idea how deep the rift was between us until the very next Sunday my Pastor preached a rebuttal sermon, "The Danger of Mistaken Zeal." He used as his text, Luke 9:49, 50: The disciples saw a man who was not one of their group casting out demons, and they told him to stop. Jesus reprimanded them, *"Don't stop him! Anyone who is not against you is for you."* The pastor made the point how misinformed we can be because of our zeal for the Lord. From that time our relationship continued downhill. It got so bad, and caused me such pain and stress, that I was determined to leave the church that I had called home for so many years of my adult life. I finally approached my pastor after much avoidance to tell him that leaving the church was the best move for my spiritual well being. He replied, "Josh, did God tell you to leave?" Because I knew the answer, I remained at Pond Street Baptist Church for one more year, experiencing deep pain and anger and avoiding confrontations with this man. However, God would not allow the rift to remain. Some fifteen years later he accepted my invitation to come with some of his parishioners to share in a day of worship at Pleasant Street.

Simultaneous with what was happening at Pond Street, I began to realize God was confirming the call upon my life. I was assured this was indeed the place God wanted me to be. During this time of unremitting pain and constant struggle, I began to understand the nature of the ministry I had committed to follow. My own hurt and anguish would help me be sensitive to the pain and affliction of those God was calling me to care for. Earlier it might have been easy for me to turn back to the things

I knew and was comfortable with, but each time my distress increased it seemed that God would draw me closer to Him. I was determined to continue on in spite of the unknown.

CHAPTER FIVE

The Mystery Revealed

"Your word is a lamp for my feet and a light for my path."
Psalm 119:105

There were three sermons I heard during that last painful year at Pond Street. Each of them left a deep and lasting impression upon my life and ministry. They spoke directly to me, but more important, they helped unlock the mystery of God's divine grasp upon my soul. I can still hear these sermons today, nearly three decades later, and they are just as meaningful, just as profound. They happened during the time the Deacon's Alliance of Providence and Vicinity scheduled worship services at different churches. The host pastor was usually asked to preach and his choir to provide the music. The first of the three sermons was on a Sunday evening at Union Baptist Church in Pawtucket, Rhode Island. The pastor was Rev. Ronald Carter, whom I had not previously met. Rev. Carter entitled his sermon "Wounded for the Mystery." It was the story of Jacob wrestling with God all night at the Jabbok River, and Jacob vowing: "*I will not let you go unless you bless me.*" [Genesis 32:26] I do not know how, to this very day, but somehow through my pain I was ministered to by God; each time Pastor Carter called the name Jacob I heard very clearly my name, "Joshua". I was like Jacob in my struggle at Pond Street. I had encountered much pain pursuing the vision.

What I learned was that I had to be persistent in the work God had called me to. Though it led to real struggle and pain it was God's purpose to form my life to His.

The second sermon was preached by Pastor Kenneth Mars at the

First Church of God in Peacedale. The deacons at First Church were not members of the Alliance. However, Rev. Mars was a deeply respected, spiritually gifted pastor and a dynamic speaker. All in attendance were anxious to hear a word from the Lord through his preaching. Pastor Mars used a text from the Gospel of John. He preached about the threefold question of Jesus to Peter inquiring if Peter really loved Him. When Peter responded in the affirmative, Jesus made it clear that love for Him must be manifested in one's willingness to serve His people. When He said to Peter, "*Feed my sheep*" [John 21:17], I knew in my spirit God was directing these words to me. If the love I professed for Him was real, then it must be demonstrated in my love for others. It was my mandate to take care of those that He would entrust into my care. The words of my mouth must find integrity in my care for all who come to me in need. It was easy to say that I loved God. However, the real test was to come in serving Him in spite of my own pain. I was later severely tested in my willingness to serve the Lord under stress.

The third sermon that I heard during this period of time was not so clear to me as the others. Though I did not readily understand it, at the time the impression it left on me would be as deep and lasting as the other two. The sermon preached by the Rev. Cornelius Williams, pastor of the Olney Street Baptist Church in Providence, was entitled "Back to the Old Landmark". The apostle Paul says,

> "And my message and my preaching were very plain. I did not use wise and persuasive speeches, but the Holy Spirit was powerful among you. I did this so that you might trust the power of God rather than human wisdom." [1 Corinthians 2:4, 5]

I now believe that God was urging me to cling to the simple basic tenets of the gospel. My preaching and teaching today have evolved to the point they can rightly be understood by people from eight to eighty. The whole thrust of my ministry has been simple truth, and I cling to the simple gospel of God in Christ Jesus, as did Paul.

> "I passed on to you what was most important and what had also been passed on to me—that Christ died for our sins, just as the Scriptures said. He was buried, and he was raised from the dead on the third day, as the Scriptures said." [1 Corinthians 15:3, 4]

I believe these two verses contain the entire gospel. The word of God, indeed, is so pure and simple that even a child can understand it. This is the essence and foundation for Christian preaching. I needed to get back to the Old Landmark.

It was during this birthing of ministry that I came to adopt the prophet Ezekiel as my role model. I saw Ezekiel as a man much like me, given a vision of the Lord, a revelation of God's truth; and yet, nothing in Ezekiel's previous experience had prepared him for such a display of God's presence and power. Once Ezekiel experienced the vision God then gave him a basic message to deliver to his people. God gave him the difficult responsibility of presenting his message to ungrateful, hard-hearted and stubborn people. Three times, God told Ezekiel not to be afraid or dismayed, but to speak His words to the people. Further, He says, *"You must give them my messages whether they listen or not."* [Ezekiel 2:7] The lesson for me to learn was that the measure of any success in the ministry would not be how well the people responded, but how well I obeyed God and how faithful was my commitment to His call.

I knew that God's message had to sink deep into my heart and show in my actions before I could effectively help others to understand the truth of the gospel.

The turning point came one night as I sat praying and crying out of my seemingly unbearable pain. I was sitting near the foot of my bed, on the floor. The lights had been turned out and my room looked darker than ever before. A few shadows appeared on the blinds because of the absence of light inside. My eyes were held tightly shut to keep the tears from falling on the floor. I prayed to God with a fervor as never before. I asked Him to ease the pain, calm my anxiety, and relieve the stress that had gripped me. I had never felt such helplessness before. I was determined not to rise up until God gave me a clear word about my future. Somewhere in the midst of my tears in that darkened room God answered. I can only describe what appeared to be a sheet descending down around me and then a feeling of complete peace. I had my answer. The next day I could not wait to inform my pastor that it was time to go. My words were met with total silence, and I departed Pond Street Baptist Church.

A Light to My Path

God's divine intervention was the reason I headed to Westerly. In the late 1970s and early 80s, I was heavily involved in the American Baptist Churches of Rhode Island of which Pond Street Baptist Church was a member. I had served on boards and committees of ABCORI, and in 1980 served as president of the denomination in Rhode Island, encompassing approximately 80 churches. At one of the annual meetings, I met Rev. Harold Lambe, pastor of Pleasant Street Baptist Church in Westerly. Little did I know at the time that one day I would be working under Rev. Harold Lambe at Pleasant Street as the associate pastor. I had no thought or desire to be a pastor until the day I received a telephone call from Harold Lambe asking me to come to Westerly and serve at Pleasant Street. I was not prepared for such an offer, so I gave scant thought to his proposal. I simply wanted to get on with my life and be able to find some peace and stability. I was later to find out it was also God's desire, and Pleasant Street was the place He had prepared for me.

During this time of transition, another door seemed to open which would have derailed my move to Westerly. There appeared to be an opportunity to stay in the Providence area. The Rev. Hugh McGhee, a friend and pastor of St. James Baptist Church in Woonsocket, had contacted me to come north and be his assistant. My heart was inclined towards Woonsocket because Hugh McGhee was a mentor and the church had a congregation of more than 300 members. Rev. McGhee spoke with his deacons and they were very enthusiastic about my coming to the church. I was thrilled to think I would be able to minister to a large congregation. Like many younger ministry students coming out of seminary, I, too, had been afflicted with the large-church syndrome. I was enamored of the size of the church, drawn by increased visibility, more job prospects for ministry, accelerated growth and the opportunity to introduce new programs. Rev. Lambe was insistent. He called several more times, and I finally told him of my plans to go to Woonsocket. Either he did not believe me or he had advance word from God, but he left me with the feeling he was not discouraged.

About a week later, Rev. McGhee called and told me there was a slight glitch in his plans. However, it was not insurmountable. One of his deacons, a friend and colleague, raised the issue that some members might be drawn away from Pastor McGhee towards me. Hugh McGhee was unmoved. His offer stood firm and he proposed to go before the church to ratify it. It was recommended by Pastor McGhee that the church set a date to vote on my becoming his assistant. As the time drew near for the Woonsocket church to vote, I found I still could not dismiss Harold Lambe and Pleasant Street from my mind. Harold continued to keep in touch and I constantly struggled about why I should not consider Westerly. Then one day I received a clear confirmation from God. I heard that familiar voice saying, "Westerly is to be your destination." I learned what Harold Lambe already knew. I immediately called Rev. McGhee and told him to cancel any vote on my candidacy because I no longer had a choice. I was going to Westerly. In obedience to God, I left Providence and Pond Street Baptist Church to travel the 41 miles south to Westerly. In July of 1981, I became the associate Pastor of Pleasant Street Baptist Church under Rev. Harold J. Lambe.

I continually asked myself, how did I arrive at this juncture in my life? Why would God call someone like me to carry out His will here in Westerly? What is it that prompts me to engage in life changing decisions without fear? Why would God promise to give me eyes to see far beyond what others can see? Many questions. Few obvious answers. And yet, I believe more than adequate responses to my queries may be found in the details of my life's journey long before God's call to serve the people of Pleasant Street.

CHAPTER SIX

To Be Discerned

"No eye has seen, no ear has heard, and no mind has imagined
what God has prepared for those who love him."
1 Corinthians 2:9

Looking back on that particular time of my youth, I now realize that I lived my life vicariously through my sister Debbie. She was the rebellious side of my emerging personality that I devoutly wished I could unleash, but was fearful of the predictable consequences. For Debbie, the expression of her will was of tantamount importance. She shrugged off the punishment she was dealt as the cost of having the experience. I admired her enormously because she did what I wanted to do. She was a major influence in my life. I wanted to fit in and be accepted by her because her life seemed to be more exciting than mine.

We were forbidden to go to the movies. However, Debbie didn't allow the punishment to deter her. When she got a beating, she never cried, whereas I started crying at the very thought of the razor strap my father kept in the top drawer of his chifferobe. When we did wrong, he would simply tell us to go and fetch it and bring it back to him so he could use it on us, usually on our bare bottoms. Despite that, Debbie's influence won out over the punishment and I went along with her. One night I went with her to the movies. Lo and behold, I always got caught. While my father was beating me I was crying and yelling, "Daddy, I'll take it like a man," hoping that might distract him. When it was over, Debbie would say to me through my sobs, "Josh, you're so stupid for following me; you will never learn."

I remember vividly, one night, the Dixwell Avenue Community

House basketball team, the Rangers, was scheduled to play a team from Bridgeport. Debbie wanted to go to a movie with her girl friend, Dolores Wilson. They only had to ask me once to see *The Bandit of Sherwood Forest* with Cornell Wilde and Olivia DeHavilland. As luck would have it, when we returned home from our night on the town we never noticed the lights were out at the CUE House. We were greeted at the door by my mother who seemed unusually interested in the outcome of the basketball game. She asked, "How did you enjoy the game?" Feeling quite bold, I answered, "It was very good." Her next question was, "What was the score?" Before I could conjure up an answer she said, "Don't keep lying. The Rangers game was postponed this evening." This time my father was waiting for me and as I tried to hide under the bed; I forgot there was too much of me to hide. My father merely sat on the edge of the bed beating my exposed rear with the strap. All of this to the tune of Debbie's taunts, "You are so … stupid."

In New Haven, we took baths in the kitchen because the bathroom was outside in the hall. The water had to be heated in a galvanized tub. Once the tub was filled with the water, it had to be carried to the bathing spot on the far side of the kitchen. One night as Debbie and I were carrying the tub, her hand slipped and I got burned. My mother came running to see what all the screaming and commotion was about. She found Debbie insisting I had dropped my end—even though she tipped the tub over.

The extent of my naiveté in those early years was exposed when I did not discover that girls were really different from boys until I was about fifteen. We had moved to Chelsea, Massachusetts, and I met a friend named Billy Johnson who was crazy about my sister Debbie. He wanted to date her. Billy didn't know very much, but he taught me what little he knew. This opened a huge gap in my social life.

It was at the CUE House that I met the man who would become my surrogate father. George Thompson, a full-blooded Cherokee Indian, offered me advice on how to make the right choices when presented with dilemmas. He was a moral beacon in my life in the absence of my much overworked father. Mr. Thompson, as I called him, taught me to play basketball and the rudiments of woodworking, a talent that served me well for a substantial part of my life. I looked forward to the time I spent with Mr. Thompson, for I felt he was genuinely interested in my welfare.

During my sojourn at the CUE House, I joined the Boy Scouts. This association with like-minded boys gave me another area for growth as well as an opportunity for constructive projects. Added together, the years in New Haven gave me an enlarged picture of the world I had inherited. If a man is to reach a higher plane of attainment or self-realization, he must squeeze from experience, good or ill, some droplets of self-knowledge. During my self-education, my mother was there to encourage me. Sometimes she would utilize my thoughts in her own decision making process. She would give her ideas a dry run with me. She would say, "Josh, you have a good head on your shoulders. What do you think about this?" I don't know how helpful my thoughts were, but it sure made me feel important.

It was in New Haven that I was unknowingly being prepared for my first job. While at Troup Junior High School, Mr. Daniel Santry, my manual training teacher, first directed my natural ability to work with wood into a marketable skill. In his class, I learned how to build furniture and work with light woodworking machines. I loved it and began to think of a career in woodworking. When I confided my aspiration to Mr. Santry, he said, "You have great talent, but it is not marketable. It needs to be refined." This was great encouragement for my ego, and Mr. Santry's statement was to remain with me for over six decades. My teacher's good help and instruction long outlived him.

Lessons From Home

The New Haven years were extremely important in my development. I learned from my parents two of the most important lessons for my life. From my father, I learned how to love. He was the most loving human being I have ever known. He neither allowed his admitted lack of education or circumstances in life to change his gentle, loving character, nor alter his ability to love.

From my mother I learned perseverance. She taught me never to surrender my goals; second place was not an option.

My dad was a strict disciplinarian, especially in response to my mother's prodding. How many times had I heard the fearful words, "Wait until your father gets home." And I waited and waited. One of his most notable qualities was his integrity in dealing with his family and with other people. He could be trusted. If he gave you his word you could expect him to deliver, even if it was the razor strap in the top chifferobe drawer. I loved my Dad very much and we were very close.

One of my last memories of him is of standing beside him stroking his soft wavy, black hair the night before he died, and hearing him say to me, "Son, someday you will understand." He always had this calm peaceful look on his face, but this night he seemed to be even more at peace than ever before. I might even say he was tranquil. My father was my hero. It was he who taught me how to be a man. He was firm, yet at the same time very gentle and compassionate. He taught me that it was okay to show emotion, and that a man can cry and still be respected as a man. The most important lesson he taught me was that a man is known at home and abroad by his integrity. When my mother died, he became the primary caregiver for my youngest brother Joel and my sister Esther, who became stricken with childhood diabetes, which was diagnosed when she was just seven years old. My dad is still very much in my memory. In many ways I believe, much of my character and my ability to love people has been derived from him.

My mother was the cheerleader, counselor, and spiritual guide to her youngsters. My sister Arline and I have been reminiscing about our life with her and the legacy she left us. Now older and wiser, we are better equipped to understand what she tried to do for us. She stands as the most poised, knowledgeable and gracious woman we were privileged to know. Her refinement had nothing to do with wealth or stature as they are usually defined, but rather her engaging manner of self-worth. We recall, for instance, the times when our spirits drooped for any number of causes, she would make a point of informing us, in the strongest possible tone of voice, "You look just as good as those Astorbilts, and are just as special." At the time we had only a vague idea of who those Astorbilts might be. It was sufficient we had received a better than favorable comparison to the renowned Astors and Vanderbilts. My sister Arline remarks today, "I can't even imagine any of us looking like anyone resembling the Astorbilts, with our homemade, often dated, clothes and city (welfare) shoes – but we were always led to believe we were as special and wealthy, in our own way, as those fictitious Astorbilts."

Sometimes, when other kids called us names because we were

overweight, or for any variety of reasons, we had mama's retort ringing in our ears: "No matter what anyone says about you, it won't make you any better or worse than you really are." That advice was helpful for us to remember since we had been instructed not to respond to name calling. "The key to survival," claims Arline, "was to separate which of those names had anything to do with me as a person." This is not an easy thing to accomplish in the throes of a verbal battle. In reality, I was overweight, poor, and a preacher's kid, so for me the hurt came in the derogatory way the names were called and the words that were used. I do not know who originated the childhood verse: "Sticks-and-stones will break your bones, but names will never hurt you." But I take issue with it. Names *do* hurt, especially when you are a child. As a matter of fact, they hurt even now. Back then, it was children or strangers. Now, it's mostly adults and people who claim to know and profess great love for me. But guess what? My mother's words, spoken so long ago, still hold true for me: "No matter what anyone says or calls you – it won't make you any better or worse than you really are." Thank you, mama, for those words of wisdom; they remain in my memory still.

Life Lessons From The Bible

Childhood holds many memories for all of us, but one thing we treasure today is remembering how quickly, absolutely and firmly my mother could come up with an appropriate response to any occurrence or situation deemed to be traumatic, life shattering or upsetting. Such statements always ended with, "And I didn't just make it up." Debbie, outspoken as she was, would often say, "There she goes again—she made that up." Ultimately, however skeptical we were about mama's statements, we found she didn't make them up. Most were found in the Bible, and she merely interpreted them to our young, reluctant ears. Some of her more memorable sayings are based in Proverbs: "A fool is known by the multitude of his words." [17:27] "You can't get justice from an unjust person." [28:5] "Take care of today, you don't know what tomorrow brings." [27:1] "You can paper the walls with diplomas but that doesn't mean there's anything up in the head." [17:16] "Don't waste time trying to convince someone of something you know is true." [23:9] "Listen before you answer." [18:13]. These are just a few of the daily doses of wisdom my mother dispensed. However, just remembering these few, and allowing them to guide my path in life, has helped to keep me humble, less judgmental of others, more understanding, tolerant and confident in who I am, and more important, keeps me focused on *whose* I am.

My mother also taught me that I could not simply be content to be equal to my white counterparts in anything. I must exceed even my own expectations if I was to be successful in my life. I never considered failure a possibility; the word was not a part of my vocabulary. This was the motivation behind the success of my first job, which was also the first time I encountered racial discrimination and was forced to put mama's teachings into practice. My mother never dwelled on the fact that our color is an obstacle, but rather she taught us we could use our difference as an opportunity. "First impressions are lasting and people will not forget their first meeting with you, because your color makes you different in their eyes" she said.

In New Haven, I graduated from Troup Junior High School in 1945. That fall I began attending Hillhouse High School in New Haven. It had one of the top high school basketball programs in the country. With my several years of experience playing on the Dixwell Community House basketball team behind me, I tried out for the freshman team of Hillhouse, and made it. I wasn't tall or fast or very talented, but because I demonstrated good timing, the ability to follow directions, and an understanding of the game's concepts and fundamentals, the coach selected me.

In December 1946, our family left New Haven. Because my dad had spoken of a possible job in Evanston, Illinois, we thought that city would be our destination. Instead, our Packard Roadster carried us, all huddled under blankets, to Chelsea, a city to the northeast of Boston. Since the car had no heat, we arrived on what appeared to be the coldest night of the year. The night is vivid in my memory because of Arline's remark to me: "Josh, we needn't worry about having cockroaches here in Chelsea, because when I opened the kitchen cabinets all the roaches were frozen to death."

Living conditions for the family in Chelsea were not a great improvement over the apartment house complex in New Haven. When we saw the house we were to live in, we were sorely disappointed, but it was the best our parents could afford. I believe my mother and father felt a double disappointment when they heard our disdainful appraisal of their purchase. Little did we know then that my mother had been saving pennies, nickels, and dimes in a big flour jar. She must have been happy when she toted the funds down to the bank for a down payment on the house. The house was ours, so they made the best of it. It wasn't long before we set to work tidying and fixing up the new home. The basement floor was all dirt, so we had to mix cement to pour a proper and level concrete floor before we could store our things in there.

Just like in New Haven, we went to school in Chelsea with sandwiches filled with split hot dogs and fried potatoes. My sister Arline sometimes threw her lunches in the trash. She didn't want anyone to see what it contained, or put on more weight consuming such starchy fare. My greatest disappointment was in not being allowed to try out for the Chelsea High School basketball team. I was a mid-year transfer student. I did, however, find some solace in playing pickup basketball games at a court in Scollay Square in Boston. In retrospect, these were not the happiest years of my life. I was shy. Written under my picture in the 1949 Chelsea High School yearbook were the words, "Cheerful as a bird, always seen never heard."

Turning Point

During the time we resided in Chelsea, my father worked at Pallin's Storage Garage. The owner's name was Ralph Pallin. My dad's job there was to line up and park delivery trucks so they would be ready to be loaded and sent off to their appointed destinations without any delay. It was a job that required my father to be up early in the morning and to be out in the inclement New England weather regardless of the season, the temperature or precipitation. He was such a conscientious employee that he memorized the departure sequence of each vehicle from the loading dock. So responsible was he in this position that he would often arrive well before the 5 A.M. starting hour to ensure the timely exodus of the truck fleet.

My father's employment by Ralph Pallin corresponded with my fourteenth year, a critical turning point in my life. To this day, I retain my vow taken that year to be dependent on no human being for my livelihood. My father's job termination by the Pallins caused me to rethink my entire approach to life.

What occurred to cause such determination and bitterness is still with me. My father wanted to buy a new automobile, a Chrysler. He was a hard worker. He saved his money when he could. He wanted to get the best deal possible for his money. After shopping around at several area Chrysler dealerships, he found the car he wanted in Everett, Massachusetts. He told Ralph about the deal he had struck. Remembering that Ralph's brother Hyman Pallin owned a Chrysler-Plymouth dealership, my dad asked Ralph to talk to his brother about a better price. Hymie not only would not try to beat the deal my father had but he wanted even more money for the same vehicle, so my father purchased the motorcar from the Everett dealership. When Ralph found out about the sale, he fired my dad on the spot. My father had saved about five hundred dollars through his negotiating skills. Ralph Pallin said, "If you can afford to buy this car, you don't need to be working for me." Not only did my dad lose his job, but my sister Arline was removed from her job as a babysitter for Ralph Pallin's children. Never had any event in the family's history had such a profound effect on the psyche of us kids. We were hurt and furious at the injustice and arbitrariness of one man toward another. My diligent, conscientious, work-oriented father had been laid low by the decision of his mean spirited employer. I ruminated on this awful situation for some time. It led to a life-long resolve never to work for anyone and never to allow myself to be put into that vulnerable position as long as I lived. I would start my own business; I would work for no one but me; I would be my own boss.

This jarring event remained fresh in my mind all during my freshman year at Chelsea High School. Life continued, but it was a time when important decisions had to be made. This incident with the Pallins caused me much pain. My dad found another job at Cardi Box Company in Chelsea, but he was never the same man. I watched the hurt and disappointment in my father, and I saw the bend in his shoulders. I was hurt, angry, shaken by *this* betrayal and determined that I would be my own man. I vowed that the only person who could stop me from achieving my goal in life was me. At this point, God was not in my thoughts, or plans, or decision making at all.

Military Service

After graduation from high school, in early 1950, my friend Eddie Fortes and I blithely signed up for a hitch in the U. S. Naval Reserve. Our motivation was simple: the extra cash. A few drills here, a few meetings there, what could be easier? World War II had ended and most people thought they would never see another armed conflict in their lifetimes. We could not have been more wrong. In the ensuing Korean Conflict, we had our Reserve status rescinded. Eddie and I were summoned to Active duty in the U. S. Navy on July 8, 1952, at the height of the war in Korea. The immediate result of the calling up meant a three month stint at the U. S. Navy boot camp at Bainbridge, Maryland.

From Bainbridge I was ordered, in October 1952, to attend the Navy's Damage Control School in Philadelphia. The school was where carpenters and related tradesmen were sent to learn how to fight fires aboard ship. It wasn't what I wanted or expected; however, I was made to know there is a way to complete every task in this life, and I was to learn the Navy's way.

Social Life ... Marriage

It would be inaccurate to say that I was a lively and adventurous young man. However, during my time in Philadelphia at the Damage Control School, I became intrigued by the city's social life. The navy unwittingly supported my curiosity. Because of a Philadelphia bus strike, the navy decided to cancel all leaves and assign sailors to ride the bus routes to keep a lid on trouble spots around the City of Brotherly Love.

Most of us didn't know what we were doing. However, as young sailors we could never have afforded a dating service that allowed us to meet so many young women! Bus patrol was a bachelor's dream job. I learned that most women love men in a uniform, and at 21, I was told I didn't look too shabby in my bellbottom blues. I had a few dates, none really serious, even though I dated some girls more frequently than others.

I had a date one night with a girl I knew. Earlier in the evening we had made arrangements to meet in south Philadelphia at the Elks Club. She gave me the address and we set the time around 8 P.M. She was to be with several of her girlfriends, so I invited a few of my buddies to come along. The evening did not start out very well because I lost the address and had to ask several local people how to find the club. I never connected with my date that night, for the directions I received led me to another club in a different part of the city. At first I was disappointed I could not find my date there. However, at one of the tables we saw six young women sitting together, and we decided this might be an even more appealing place to be. We ordered Cokes [that was the strongest drink I had ever had] and sat at a table adjoining the women; and after a few minutes, we struck up a conversation. I was attracted to one of the young women who told me her name was Queenie. She was what would be termed in those days "a fox". Hardly noticing any of the others, I conversed with Queenie for a while until they all announced it was time for them to go home. Immediately, I offered to drive Queenie to her residence in the city. From that moment on, my recollection becomes progressively fuzzy. The girls seemed to disappear for a short while and when they finally came back, they had some bad news for me. My date had had an unfortunate accident. One of her girl friends, the one named Ida, explained my date accidentally spilled her drink all over her dress. I asked how this could have happened so early in the evening. It seems the chair on which Queenie was sitting had suddenly taken upon itself to inexplicably spill her and her beverage onto the floor. She had to leave and make repairs. I was a man never to pass up present opportunities so I escorted Ida home that evening. Now the former Ida Ruth May is Mrs. Joshua A. McClure.

A mischievous thought still lingers. I find myself musing aloud, "I can not prove it, but my suspicion is that Ida may be the one who pulled the chair out from under her friend … naw, that couldn't be. Or could it?" Ida still insists she had nothing to do with it. Oh well! The rest, as they say is history.

After my discharge from the navy, I returned to live in Chelsea. Three months later, November 6, 1954, Ida Ruth Mays and I were married in Child's Memorial Baptist Church, in Philadelphia. Her pastor, the Rev. Raymond A. Cromwell, performed the ceremony. After a week honeymoon in Goffs Falls, New Hampshire, we moved into our first apartment on 345 Warren Street in the Roxbury section of Boston.

Following my training at the Damage Control School, October 1952 to February 1953, I was assigned to duty at the U. S. Navy Photographic Center, Naval Air Station, Anacostia, D. C. At first the transfer caused me some puzzlement as I had no photographic experience. The Navy's ways are not always clear-cut, but the mystery was cleared up in the person of Chief Petty Officer William Hester, who enthusiastically greeted me, a mere Seaman, upon arrival at the Navy duty station. CPO Hester told me the Navy brass had reviewed my personnel jacket and discovered my civilian cabinetmaking expertise, and they had me assigned to Anacostia because there was a special project that had been laid on the Center. No one at the photographic center possessed the requisite carpentry skill level to complete the project.

The Center had been given the task of taking President Harry S Truman's photo – with a walnut, raised panel wall as a background. The Navy does not tend to have walnut raised panels hanging around, so they had to build one. No one could be found with the ability to fashion such an intricate piece of work, so it became my project. I was thankful to God that I could utilize my skills here in the Navy. I laid out the plan, ordered the materials, and happily set about the task of fashioning this custom wall panel.

I cut the pieces, routed and mitered them, fitted the joints, fastened all of the several parts together, sanded the whole wall and applied several coats of finish. Then it was ready for the Presidential photograph, which later appeared in the Sunday magazine sections of newspapers across the country.

After that I was well known at the center. This experience gave me a sense of achievement and self-confidence and increased my determination to make it on my own.

Looking back, I was glad that I insisted I did not want to be stuck in a classroom like my woodworking teacher, Mr. Santry. My persistence with my mother had already impacted my life. I recall pleading with her to let me attend a trade school. She was stubborn and determined to have her way. Hadn't she planned and dreamed that all of her children would one day be college graduates? The argument see-sawed back and forth. I was as adamant about trade school enrollment as she was stubborn about college matriculation. Sensing my mother would yield to a sincere and logical rationale, I voiced my thoughts to her politely and most firmly: "I do not want to be a manual training teacher all my life," I told her. She finally seemed to relent. I did, however, underestimate her tenacity. She intuitively reasoned that her son was making the right decision, but was seeking the wrong means to achieve that end. Trade school would not really help him to learn woodworking and carpentry skills as quickly and efficiently as he desired.

 I later found out that my mother's seeming acquiescence was a ruse. Without my knowledge, she had been secretly scouring the local newspapers' help wanted sections for cabinetmakers openings. She discovered an ad for such a position at the Furnwood Corporation in Brockton. I figured she really didn't know much about these matters. "You don't just *become* a cabinetmaker, you have to go to a trade school to *learn* the fundamentals," I said. She held her ground, looked me straight in the eye, and said, "Call them. Tell them *you* want to become an apprentice cabinetmaker and you want to *learn* the trade." What else could I do? I would call, but I expected little from the call. The forces of reason and my mother's love trumped all resistance.

CHAPTER SEVEN

OPPORTUNITIES AT HAND

"Unless the Lord builds a house, the work of the builder is useless."
Psalm 127:1

I phoned the company in Brockton. I tried to be firm and self-assured. I knew what I wanted. This approach, the more I thought about it, would be far better than several years at a trade school where my real goal would be postponed. Maybe my mother was right after all. The company agreed to meet with me, and I made an appointment for an interview. Although my parents tried to prepare me for life, I realized I was entering a time when it would be my own experience itself that would shape me and mold a new mental toughness. This would be my awakening to the real world of discrimination. Here I would be singled out by the color of my skin rather than by the content of my character.

My meeting with the plant superintendent, a middle-aged Swedish man, left a life-long impression on me. He was noticeably unfriendly, and at seventeen, I was greatly intimidated by him. This encounter brought to the forefront my mother's teaching, and surely taxed my ability to love people.

I was determined not to miss this opportunity, so with a new found poise, visible self-assurance, and palpable resolve to learn the trade, I must have made a positive impression on the man. When the interview was reaching its conclusion, the superintendent abruptly informed me, "We will take a vote over the weekend whether we want a Negro person in this shop. I will call you and let you know." Late the following week I received a call and I was instructed to report to work on the next Monday.

After an anxious weekend, I arrived at the plant very early Monday morning, quite excited and earnestly determined to show the boss my woodworking skills. Hope and elation were quickly replaced with disappointment and shock when the supervisor shoved a straw broom in my face. He explained dispassionately, "We need someone to keep this place clean." Was this a test or a scare tactic? It was time for me to make another life shaping decision. I could pitch the broom back at the foreman, admit defeat at racism's first unexpected job related appearance, all the while shouting at him, "I didn't come to this factory to be degraded by being made a floor sweeper." Or, my other option was: accept the job and sweep the floor better than anyone had done it before. I preferred the former but accepted the latter. I decided to humble myself. I swept the sawdust from the floors of that shop for a few weeks. Then one day the foreman casually remarked: "You're too good to keep on sweeping floors. I'm going to let you help some of the cabinetmakers here." Was I thrilled! I couldn't wait to tell my mother. My hard work, perseverance, and determination triumphed, and my career was birthed.

I quickly realized that most of the craftsmen at the shop there were immigrants who had learned their trade in Europe, specifically in Italy and Portugal. I also discovered right away the jealous secretive ways of these men, who shielded their talents from my view. They would stand in front of their work at such an angle as to block me from observing what they were doing. This was extremely frustrating for me since their hostile actions ran counter to my purpose for being there.

All was not lost. While the workmen shut me out of their spaces, the foreman took an interest in my plight. Here I was, a kid who was not allowed to learn, who sincerely wanted to learn. All I could think of was my passion for the trade, and my sincerity appealed to his sense of fair play. He then began to allow me more and better opportunities to learn new procedures and hone my raw skills. After some time spent on less challenging projects, I was permitted to work on more intricate, detailed procedures such as matching veneers and inlaying objects into the wood on some very expensive dining and living room furniture. While working at the Furnwood Corporation, I became acquainted with the names of some of the most famous furniture makers—Jens Risom, Chippendale, and Hepplewhite. I worked there for a couple of years and word of my burgeoning woodworking mastery reached the ears of another furniture building company who would afford me the opportunity to enhance my woodworking skills. Now it was now time to move on. So when a position allowing me advancement in the trade was offered, I naturally accepted it. The new factory, Allied Woodcrafters, was located in Charlestown, Massachusetts. By this time I owned my first car, a 1938 Buick, and I was able to drive to work. Brockton had been a decent commute: Charlestown was closer. The man who hired me, Francis Maranhas, a Portuguese immigrant, was the owner.

Mentoring

I now understand that my progress in life was due in part to my penchant for meeting mentors at significant points along the way; however, I believe it has always been the hand of God leading me in the right path. My faith was greatly rewarded at Charlestown in the person of Joseph Marshall, the plant wood-finishing foreman. Joe also knew a lot about carpentry. He, too, was from the old school that did everything by hand. He mixed his own stains from powders and aniline dyes. His talent allowed him to apply exquisite finishes to wood with shellacs and lacquers. He would use colored sticks of shellac, with a heated knife to fill in holes in wood and color light spaces in the wood to blend in with darker ones. Joe, a man of Portuguese descent, had keen eyes. He saw my enthusiasm for the job begin to falter, and he wondered why I appeared to exhibit such an aura of frustration. For me, it was *déjà vu*. It seemed as though the Furnwood shuffle had followed me to Charlestown. The men were giving me the same negative treatment. Joe sensed my anger and distress, and he determined to do something about it.

One afternoon, Joe decided that his personal intervention was required. He called me into his office, sat me down, and detailed his observations of the situation. I agreed that his assessment was entirely correct, and in fact, I was thinking of looking for work elsewhere. Joe was really depressed. He got up from behind his desk. He walked over to where I sat in a pool of gloom. The next words he uttered shook me to the core and caused my insides to leap with joy.

"Listen," he said earnestly. "I like you. I really mean that." He now had my full attention. "As a matter of fact," Joe said, "I am going to teach you everything I know," he paused carefully, "just like my own son."

I will never forget that moment, nor will I ever forget Joe Marshall. My whole perspective reversed itself. I figured I could now endure the trials with the strength and knowledge Joe was willing to offer. With his help, I had really two trades, cabinetmaking and wood finishing. I think it is important to establish this fact because that is exactly what William Bloom & Son, a later employer, needed when they hired me to expand their business to include detailed and intricate wood finishing work in exclusive department stores. There were few in the trade who possessed both skills: knowing the different types of wood, crafting furniture out of that wood, but also having the ability to apply beautiful finishes. Few could reproduce the kind of work Joe taught me. Joe was one of the best; he fulfilled his promise to me, and more.

He even took me to his home in Concord, MA, and introduced me to his wife Mary and his family. He reiterated to them his promise that I would be treated as one of them. They opened their arms to me and later to my family. [Some people may choose to argue about the significance of the Marshall couple's first names, Mary and Joseph. But who knows?]

Removed from the shadow of discontent, I honed my skills and flourished in the light of Joe's attention. I learned everything I could, and Joe was an avid teacher. As fortune would have it, my newfound expertise earned me a promotion, after less than a year at Allied Woodcrafters. Francis Maranhas advanced me to assistant shop foreman under Joe Marshall. In retrospect, I can say Joe Marshall wielded the greatest influence on my career in woodworking. Allied Woodcrafters underwent a company name change to Arlington Furniture Company while I was working there. I worked at that firm until July 1952, as a cabinetmaker.

In retrospect, my employment at Allied Woodcrafters in 1951 was to prove providential as it led me to share the same page as the thirty-third President of the United States, Harry S. Truman.

God Works In Everything

Not all of my experiences in the Washington, D. C. area were of a positive nature. This, in spite of the fact that President Harry S Truman, had by Executive Order #9981 (July 26, 1948) desegregated the Armed Forces.

As an African-American man in a predominately white society, discrimination played a significant role in my life. Initially the anger and pain from the unfair, undeserved injustice to people of color caused me to want to strike out in retribution. However, over time, both my mother's teachings and God's grace prevailed. I determined that if, indeed, all men are created equal, we are all made in the image of God, then I must guard this truth in my heart and live it out in my life. In retrospect, I believe, this was one of the important images that had to be merged upon God's divine canvass before vision could become sight. God's grace and His love for all people becoming one.

While in the Navy, memories of my awakening of discrimination during my first job interview at Furnwood resurfaced again, but this time in a more direct and painful way. I was dressed in my U. S. Navy blue uniform, walking down Pennsylvania Avenue very near the White House. I was accompanied by three of my buddies: one was from Massachusetts, the other from Maine, and the third from Baltimore. The four of us went into a local drugstore to eat. The front of the store contained a lunch counter, so we ordered hamburgers and shakes. The clerk behind the counter was a young African-American male who gave each of us strange looks, and appeared to be quite nervous. I thought nothing of it as I watched him make the shakes and cook the hamburgers. Nearing completion of our order he gestured toward me and remarked to one of my white friends. "He [meaning me] cannot eat here. He will have to eat his food outside."

There I stood in my Navy blues, side by side with other members of our armed forces. Each of us had pledged to defend our country with his life, and now I was singled out and told in essence: You can fight and place your life in jeopardy for your country, but you cannot eat food at this lunch counter. I was angry, hurt and disillusioned, and did an about face and walked defiantly out of the store. My three buddies followed silently behind me; they refused to eat the food or pay for it.

Back at the base my success with the raised panels led to requests that I custom build office furniture. The chief procurement officer, who was a lieutenant in charge of the facility, offered to set me up in business in Silver Springs. The proposition was attractive, lucrative and very promising. With my sponsor providing the financing, the new business would specialize in applying interior trim to new homes. This work required the careful skills of a finish carpenter or cabinetmaker. To make the proposal even more irresistible, the officer gave me permission to take an off-base job in a lumberyard located in the area where the new homes were to be constructed. I was intrigued by the opportunity to have my own business so soon after my active duty expired, so I gave the idea much consideration.

As happy as I thought I would be with the work, I did have some lingering doubts about the racial attitudes of my prospective neighbors should I decide to settle in that area of Maryland. So I called Ida to take a test run with me to survey the area. The locale suited us both in its physical appearance (homes, lawns, clean streets, etc.) and in the busy commercial zone. So after the drive, we decided to have a bite to eat. We stopped for lunch at a drive-in restaurant.

At first, we did not realize every car but ours was getting service. Thinking their lack of attention from the wait staff was merely an oversight on a busy day, we sat there patiently. After almost a half hour of waiting, I noticed the waitresses had been looking at us, but had avoided direct eye contact. We never did get waited on.

That did it for me. My previous experiences with discrimination, coupled with my vow of independence, prompted me not to place myself in a situation where I had to live with outright bigotry because of my skin color. My decision was made.

When I returned to the base I told my supply officer, "Thanks, but no thanks." I was still smarting over the earlier incident in Washington, D. C., and I refused to be treated as a second class citizen. I remembered my mother's words from my childhood. "You look just as good as those Astorbilts, and are just as special." I remained at Anacostia until I was honorably discharged from the United States Navy on August 7, 1954.

Recent reflections on my navy experience lead me to believe that the discrimination and rejection I encountered had greater implications for my life than I could have imagined, and yet other events at the time impacted me equally. The understanding that God can use every experience for our good prompts me to not only view the positive experiences, but also the negative ones for His future glory. The positive experiences appear to be immediately beneficial, whereas the negative ones will be felt for decades to come. Paul writes in [Romans 8:28]

> "And we know that God causes everything to work together for the good of those who love God and are called according to his purpose for them."

CHAPTER EIGHT

A Greater Glory

"So we don't look at the troubles we can see right now; rather, we look forward to what we have not yet seen. For the troubles we see will soon be over, but the joys to come will last forever"
2 Corinthians 4:18

Further reflection on my ultimate call to the pastorate of Pleasant Street Baptist Church leads me to think that much of my preparation for ministry had been carved out of my own personal experiences of pain and loss surrounding the death of loved ones. In death, as well as in life, God is not only able to use our experiences for our eternal good, but more important, he employs them to fulfill His divine purposes.

I am convinced that God works in everything—not just isolated incidents—for our good. This does not mean that all that happens to us is good. Sin and evil overshadow our fallen world, but God is able to turn every circumstance around for our long-range good.

Henri Nouwen, a Catholic priest born and ordained in the Netherlands, has written a classic book titled *The Wounded Healer*. Nouwen suggests in his book what it means to be a minister—a healer—to a rootless generation, to people who suffer loneliness, alienation and pain. He proposes that the wounds of the wounded healer can be a source of healing for others. He stresses that only in one's brokenness before God and humankind can anyone really transform community. His insights have helped me share my own fragility with people to help them relate to God through their brokenness.

Often during personal encounters of suffering and grief, I have felt the throbbing ache of vulnerability. I have lived through the hurt and anguish of standing helpless, watching a loved one suffer intense pain. I have witnessed the heart finally yielding to that last enemy, death, and I have firsthand knowledge that one in the throes of death clings to words of hope until that last breath. What is probably the most important lesson I have learned, which sustains me to this day, is: Death is not forever and we are never alone in it. Through each experience, in learning to seek God's comfort and strength, I have found that in my darkest moments, lurking beneath the layer of pain, the God of all comfort is surely there.

My first experience with death was in 1959 as I stood in Massachusetts Mental Hospital in Boston at the bedside of my father, who had suffered a severe nervous breakdown. His world had been shattered when the hierarchy at Mother Horn's Church changed a long standing belief of baptizing converts "*in the name of the Father and the Son and the Holy Spirit.*" [Matthew 28:18b]They now declared their teaching of many years to be in error and they would adopt the practice of baptizing in the name of *Jesus only*. My father could not accept this doctrinal change, and insisted the Scriptures called for the singular name of the three persons of the Trinity, Father, Son and Spirit, not Jesus alone. He refused to accede to the new teaching and he agonized over their stance. This took such a toll on him that before long his physical and mental state deteriorated to dangerous levels. His physician described his condition as critical. For several days he was incoherent, causing great concern to each of us. I can remember my mother sitting by his bedside wet washcloth in hand, responding to every movement of his body, lightly rubbing his forehead to help control his temperature.

The defining moment came one morning as we stood around the bed. He raised his head ever so slightly, looked at those gathered around the bed and said, "Don't worry about me. I am not the one going to die. God showed me someone else in the family will be dead in six months."

We attributed this to his condition and gave it little credence until a few weeks later when my mother was diagnosed with cervical cancer. My father recovered. However, almost six months from the day he uttered those prophetic words, on December 19, 1958, at the age of 56, my mother slipped into a coma and died at the New England Deaconess Hospital in Boston. On December 21, she was buried in Woodlawn Cemetery in Everett, Massachusetts.

Each of us felt the great loss. A huge hole was left in our lives. She was the glue, the one we went to for answers, the one who dispensed the cod liver oil pills every morning before school. She was the one who ran the house in my father's absence. She was the one who was always there to bind up the wounds and soothe the hurts. Her death would permanently affect each of her children, but none so deeply or as devastating as that of my younger sister Esther.

Esther had been ill as a child, and at the age of seven was discovered to have childhood diabetes. She was an extremely bright girl who always excelled in school from kindergarten all through high school. She had a cherubic face. She was quiet and thoughtful, and spent most of her time at home close to her mother and family. Doctors described her diabetes as quite brittle, meaning it needed careful and constant care. My mother was her primary caregiver. Esther was in her first year at Burdett School of Business in Boston when she first discovered our mother was dying. I could see the change in her personality as she withdrew into herself more and more. She stayed to herself, spending more and more time alone, until that day, December 21, when our mother was laid to rest, not to be seen in this life again. Esther felt lost, abandoned and alone, and all of our efforts to comfort and motivate her were to no avail. She wanted to be with her mother. In the ensuing days and weeks, Esther began to neglect her insulin injections to control her diabetes and her health started to quickly spiral downhill. She missed her mother terribly. With my mother gone, my father now became her primary caregiver, but with all of his efforts he, too, was unsuccessful in motivating her to go on. Esther eventually dropped out of school and after several years ended up in state hospitals in Massachusetts for the mentally disturbed. She had given her life to Christ as a child and all through this period that was the one constant. She maintained her hope that God would one day make things right in her life.

In 1983, Esther's doctors discovered sores on her foot which were potentially life threatening. Because of her lack of care for the diabetes, gangrene was setting in. One or more surgeons recommended amputation of her leg above the ankle. For some time, my sister Arline and I had taken over Esther's care. I had previously been appointed Esther's legal guardian, so the doctors looked to me for permission to go forward with the amputation. I refused to allow it for two reasons: I did not think it was necessary; I wanted the doctors to exhaust every other avenue. The other reason was that I did not think she would survive such an operation. Her will to live was dwindling, and I was sure, facing such trauma that she would give up. After two years of fighting through the court system, the state of Massachusetts prevailed. I was forced to capitulate. Surgeons amputated her leg below the knee. Six months later they returned saying they did not go far enough the first time and they would now have to amputate above the knee. Three months after a second operation, on May 18, 1986, in UMass Medical Center, Worcester, Esther Frances took her last breath. She was 44 years old. On May 21, at Union Baptist Church, Cambridge Mass, I preached Esther's funeral. I likened her somewhat to Job, but I did not allow myself to be so presumptuous to believe that Esther experienced as much misery as Job. However, I did suggest their lives merged. Although we may not be able to understand fully the pain and loss we experience, it can release us to rediscover God. This would lead me to believe that Esther might have declared, "*I had heard about you before, but now I have seen you with my own eyes.*" [Job 42:5] Esther was laid to her final rest alongside our mother and later our father at Woodlawn.

    I believe my learning and preparation approached its zenith when my father died. We were extremely close. I loved my father with all my heart; he was my hero. I never knew a man so trustworthy and so consistent in his faith. He was a man who would discipline you and all the while make you feel sorry you disappointed him.

    My dad was quiet, compassionate, caring and unusually gentle, but always a man. I remember so well in the early 1960's my daughter Leslie was in the Miriam Hospital in Providence for about ten days. My father drove down from Chelsea each night after work, and I can not recall him missing one single day. I have had many memorable moments with him. However, one that especially stands out was during the time of his second nervous breakdown. He was still living in the Chelsea home and by now I was living in Providence. At the time I was a member of Pond Street Baptist Church, but on Sunday evening I would often attend services at Zion Gospel Temple in East Providence. The worship services at Zion were more focused on the gifts and power of the Holy

Spirit, resident in the lives of people. I was feeling a lack of power and identity in Christ in my own church, so I traveled to Zion to worship when I could. I had met the pastor of Zion, Dr. Leonard Heroo, who impressed me as a man truly anointed of God. Pastor Heroo was a powerful preacher who also seemed to possess a God given gift of discernment. He prayed powerfully for healing of people in need and was in demand. In the midst of my father's recovery, I decided that I would take him to the church in East Providence for healing. I had him come down to Providence, and I took off from Sunday worship at Pond Street and attended Zion Gospel Temple. The church held from four to five hundred people and we barely found seats that morning about halfway down from the rear of the church. The worship as usual was awe inspiring. The singing was moving, the prayers were uplifting, and the preaching was dynamic. Following his sermon pastor Heroo began to call out people for prayer. I don't remember how long it was, but Dr. Heroo stood in the pulpit and declared God had shown him a man and then said, "This man is a minister, a man of God. He is from out of town and he is here this morning for prayer of healing." My introduction to physical healing began as I viewed the many canes and crutches hanging above my head many years before at our church in Brooklyn. Now I brought my father before the loving God to be healed.

What gave me great assurance that this moment was from God, was when the pastor left the pulpit, walked down the aisle, and in the midst of hundreds of people came to where we were sitting and pointed my father out. At that moment I was so thankful that God allowed me to be an instrument of my father's healing. Indeed, he walked away that day a changed man.

My father later remarried and lived in Chelsea until the unforgettable Monday morning in October of 1968 when he went home to be with the Lord. It was a notable day. Notable in that all of my father's grandchildren were visiting. I later learned that he asked to see all of his grandchildren on that day. However, I was not aware that they came because of his request or because of divine intervention. When my wife and I arrived at the house in Chelsea, he was sitting in a chair with his robe on. It was not unexpected because my stepmother Clara had explained earlier in the week that the doctor kept him out of work, saying he was suffering from physical exhaustion. After a few more days of rest at home he would be fine, the doctor said. My first clue that something was amiss came when for no apparent reason my father asked his wife to bring him the checkbook. Clara, who had been talking with us, looked over at him surprised. "Allen, why do you want the checkbook," she asked? "I want to pay some bills," he replied. To which Clara asked, "Can't the bills wait until tomorrow? Tomorrow is Monday."

My dad insisted in an unusually firm voice, "No! I want it done right now." My stepmother relented, located the checkbook, and wrote out the checks to be mailed the next day. There was a strange aura in his living room that afternoon. For some reason I felt even closer to my dad than ever before. I still remember the feeling while standing beside his chair running my fingers through his soft black hair. At that moment I just loved him. I wanted him to know how I felt so I told him several times, "Dad, I love you." I did not want to leave him but I knew I would soon have to go home. I somehow knew this was the last time he would be able to hear me say those words. He must have known that I knew, for the last words he spoke to me that night are ever present on my heart. He took my hand and looked at me. "Son, someday you will understand." That night was the last time I saw him alive. Many times since that day I have whispered to him, "Dad, I assure you, I understand."

I was deeply saddened but not surprised when the phone call came early Monday morning that my dad had passed away during the night. On Thursday October 17, 1968, he was laid to rest alongside my mother in the Woodlawn Cemetery.

My recent and most treasured experience of pain and deep loss came on January 10, 1996, when my sister Debbie died of pancreatic cancer at the age of sixty-six. Debbie died as she lived, fearless and courageous. In her death she reasserted her place as one of the greatest inspirations of my life. Debbie had known for several months that her prognosis was not good. She said, "After serving as a nurse for over 45 years, you know that when they take you into the operating room for major surgery and close you up 45 minutes later, there is not much hope." What further endeared me to Debbie was that, though she knew her death was inevitable, she did not miss a beat in living her life to the fullest. When I first heard about Debbie's cancer, I was not only saddened but distressed to the point I could not comprehend how I would be able to go through this again. I thought of my mother and my father. I relived burying my sisters Esther and Doris, and I thought I couldn't do it again.

As I sat ruminating over what to do, God sent a very wise angel to rescue me from my predicament. Minister Margueritta Tucker, a colleague on my ministerial staff, was one of the first people I met upon coming to Pleasant Street. I have always respected Margueritta for her loyalty and her wisdom, but little did I know she would be the one to free me from my deliberations. When she heard about my sister Debbie and watched my struggles with her sickness, she approached me and said in a quiet authoritative voice, "Pastor, why don't you this one time just be a brother to Debbie. Right now that's probably what she needs most." Indeed, Margueritta was right; the many times I saw Debbie after that it was she who was ministering to everyone else.

One of the last and most memorable times of Debbie's life was on Thanksgiving day, 1995, just before she became too weak to travel. When she was brought to my sister Arline's house in Sharon, Massachusetts, to see all of the family, Debbie, as they might say, held court. She sat in the middle of Airline's bed and greeted every member of the family one by one. Each had their time with her, and it was sad but wonderful. Debbie laughed, she joked, she dispensed wisdom, she visited, and she sang. For her and for each member of the family, sisters, brothers, cousins, grandchildren and close friends, it was goodbye until we meet again in heaven. The last thing Debbie said that day was, "If anybody asks you just who I am, tell them I am redeemed!" That was Debbie's song; that is Debbie's song today; that will be Debbie's song in eternity: "Tell them I am redeemed."

A Homegoing Service was held for Debbie on January, 16, 1996, in Northbrook United Methodist Church in Illinois. I offered a prayer and read a scriptural tribute from the Psalms. As I sat there through all of the proceedings I thought, "What an honor just to be Debbie's brother!"

Through these life changing experiences I have learned much about death, but even more, I have discovered that in Christ, death is the pathway to life. I have observed that the Shepherd is always near, so I have adopted for myself the words of the Psalmist, [23:4a] *"Even when I walk through the dark valley of death, I will not be afraid, for you are close to me."*

My personal episodes of that walk have surely been a classroom for ministering to the many people and families who have relied on me to deliver them a word of comfort and guide them through valleys of grief and despair at the last hour. Because of my own experiences with death, I can assure others who arrive at this inescapable moment that they are never alone. God is an ever present companion along the way.

The following letter is from Ray Uzanas, a retired businessman formerly from an exclusive area of Westerly, now residing in Stonington, Connecticut. For the last five years, Ray has been a member of Calvary

Episcopal Church in Stonington, Connecticut. I met Ray several years ago at the YMCA. However, it wasn't until several years later after I learned about the illness of his wife Loretta that our friendship blossomed. Ray later received Jesus as his personal Lord and Savior.

"As Westerly YMCA classmates of several years, Pastor Josh McClure and I shared a mutually enjoyable friendship. We exercised together, played basketball as a two man team (the same team, but often going in different directions), watched sporting events together, occasionally shared conversation over coffee and muffins (always pumpkin raisin). I even purchased a custom designed/built computer from Josh's fledgling computer business. But the essence of our relationship was fostered, strengthened, and secured through the spiritual support and comfort which he provided to my terminally ill wife, Loretta, and by extension to our entire family especially during the final six months of her life on earth.

"Loretta, who had been reluctant to seek spiritual solace from clergy of any faith, found herself truly open to, and comforted by, God's love and caring for her as distilled though her many tableside and bedside conversations with Pastor Josh. During those periods, my primary role was to provide and keep pouring the hot tea with honey and all the other accompaniments requested by Pastor Josh during his visits, some of which became three to four teacup events. And the consequences of his sessions with her were wonderfully transforming.

"Loretta's final moments were spiritually fulfilled and her inner peace at that time was shared by all of us and gave us an enormous sense of well-being and belief in God's love and purpose. The success of Pastor Josh as a messenger of Our Savior, and in conveying the essence of God's role in all our lives, was accentuated through his heartfelt and comforting oratory during Loretta's memorial service where his message resonated among the assembled guests.

"As a personal reflection, our family, and especially my dear Loretta, owes much to Rev. Joshua McClure for his role in showing us God's love and its meaning to us not only during times of grieving, but always."

The apostle Paul assures us that death is not the end; it is merely a pause on life's journey and will be continued when Christ returns to claim His church.

"But let me tell you a wonderful secret God has revealed to us. Not all of us will die, but we will all be transformed. It will happen in a moment, in the blinking of an eye, when the last trumpet is blown. For when the trumpet sounds, the Christians who have died will be raised with transformed bodies. And then we who are living will be transformed so that we will never die. For our perishable earthly bodies must be transformed into heavenly bodies that will never die. When this happens—when our perishable earthly bodies have been transformed into heavenly bodies that will never die—then at last the Scriptures will come true:

Death is swallowed up in victory. O death, where is your victory? O death, where is your sting? For sin is the sting that results in death, and the law gives sin its power. How we thank God, who gives us the victory over sin and death through Jesus Christ our Lord!" [1 Corinthians 15:51-57]

God's Voice...

"Meanwhile, the boy Samuel was serving the Lord by assisting Eli. Now in those days messages from the Lord were very rare, and visions were quite uncommon. One night, Eli, who was almost blind by now, had just gone to bed. The lamp of God had not yet gone out, and Samuel was sleeping in the Tabernacle near the Ark of God. Suddenly, the Lord called out, "Samuel! Samuel! Yes? Samuel replied. What is it? He jumped up and ran to Eli."

Samuel did not yet know the Lord because he had never had a message from the Lord before.

1 Samuel 3:1-5a, 7

CHAPTER NINE

LIFE IN EARNEST

"Commit your work to the Lord, and then your plans will succeed."
Proverbs 16:3

T. E. Lawrence once wrote, "All men dream, but not equally. Those who dream by night in the dusty recesses of their minds awake in the day to find it was vanity. But the dreamers of the day are dangerous men, for they may act their dream with open eyes, to make it possible …"

I believe each one of us has a dream placed in our hearts, though not a dream like winning the lottery, which is really the desire to escape our present circumstances. I am talking about a vision deep down inside that speaks to the very soul. The thing we were born to do that draws from our gifts and talents, appeals to our highest ideals, sparks the feeling of destiny in our life and is inseparably linked to our purpose in life. The dream that links us to the success of our journey between the lines of the time we are born and the time we die.

My dream of being a great cabinetmaker had not yet materialized. Upon returning to work, I was still employed by someone; yet, I had not given up hope that the opportunity would present itself. So my vow made in Chelsea to be my own boss could be fulfilled. Little did I know that it was not far away, for the following year, in the summer 1955, I moved my family once again, this time to Providence.

Joe Marshall again was the key player in my career move to Providence. In his capacity as a wood finishing foreman, Joe had for many years selected and purchased industrial wood finishing products such as lacquers, thinners, shellacs, stains from major manufacturers such as

Lilly Industrial Products and DuPont Chemicals. Sometime before his departure from Arlington Furniture Company in Charlestown, Joe had been approached by a small manufacturer from western Massachusetts, Merrimack Industrial Products. The company's representative had left Joe some samples of his wood finishing products, hoping to steal some business away from the big guys. Joe tested Merrimack's products on various woods and found both product and price to be acceptable so he gave them limited use. This began a business relationship with the company and on occasion afforded the men opportunity to talk shop about the woodworking industry in the New England region. It was during a sales stop at the F. B. Hicks Company that the Merrimack representative passed on information to Joe about a job in Rhode Island. Joe by then was too old for another job change and not inclined to move out of state. He suggested that he knew someone who would be ideal for the position. He offered my name as the man for the job.

Joe told me that a small store fixture company in Providence, William Bloom & Son, was seeking an individual with unique talents and ability. They were offering a management position in the company. The person they were looking for would manage their wood-finishing department. As Ben Bloom, the son of the founder and president of William Bloom & Son, explained, the company needed to grow. It wanted to bid on larger and higher-end department stores the likes of Rich's in Atlanta; Lord & Taylor and Jordan Marsh in Boston; Macy's in New York; and possibly, Nordstrom's in Cleveland. These stores were more demanding in their selections and color matching woods had to be blended, stains had to be customized and interior colors had to be matched under different types of interior lighting. This would allow William Bloom & Son to compete in the "big leagues". In the past they had specialized in building the interior fixtures for small department stores or local finance company offices in New England.

It took a special type of person to satisfy Bloom's requirements. Joe recommended to Bloom that I was the right, and possibly only, man for the position.

With Joe's glowing recommendation, William Bloom & Son contacted me for an interview. My years of training and experience were recognized and rewarded when, after the interview, Bloom offered me the job. This was a major career advancement, a chance to grow professionally along with the company. This was the opportunity to manage an entire finishing department. In addition, the salary they offered me was double my current income. What was there not to like? How could I turn them down? "Principles!" I reasoned. If I accepted this offer I would be compromising my life-long intended goal of being an independent businessman. Should I turn my back on my vow not to rely on any company but my own? Was there a compromise I could live with that the Blooms would accept? Could they even begin to understand my desire for entrepreneurship?

William Bloom, the founding father, had turned the business over to his sons, Ben, Julie, and Abe. Ben, the oldest, was the president of the company. He was the consummate businessman at all times. He appeared stern, straight to the point, no nonsense but fair. Abe on the other hand was Ben's opposite. A former schoolteacher, Abe was energetic, friendly, and always joking. He was the youngest and served as general manager and chief negotiator. He carried out the wishes of his older brothers judiciously. The middle son, Julie, was the company's sales representative. Julie was cordial, approachable, and always on the run. He traveled the country bidding on contracts. Julie didn't spend as much time at the company as Ben or Abe so it was harder to really get to know him.

When I sat with the three brothers to negotiate, I found them to be very amiable, fair and generous. I was impressed by them and their offer, and yet, though tempted, I turned them down. They were startled. Most men, they reasoned, wanted more money, so they offered me more. "No, no, please understand," I said. "It isn't the amount of money. Your offer is very generous to be sure … I have to tell you why I cannot accept it. Long ago while in high school, I made a promise to myself. I pledged that I would start my own business. Because of an incident that happened to my father, I vowed I would control my own destiny. I will not allow anyone else to do it." They stared at me as though I had slipped to the other side of sensibility. They were not prepared for my answer or my stubbornness. "Out of the question," Ben said. "Look," he pointed out, "you will be making more money here than you'll see for a long time." Their assessment was sound and valid but my dream for independence was stronger than their monetary offer. They didn't know how deeply my father was hurt. They weren't there to see the disappointment on his face and the droop of his shoulders when he heard the words, "You're fired."

They could not know the hurt and tears we all suffered. The memory of my father's painful experience in Chelsea would not allow me to do otherwise. I said to them, "I cannot and will not work for you unless I am free to start my own business as well."

Though I was fully aware of how desperately they needed me, I did not feel I was taking advantage of them. What did they have to lose? I was capable and willing to manage two careers at once. They were businessmen. I wanted to become one on my own. The Blooms needed me, and I wanted to help them, so after further thought and realizing how resolute I was, they relented and hired me on my terms, thereby allowing me to one day be my own man.

After a few years, I began pursuing my dream of building my own kitchen cabinet business by working nights and weekends while employed by the Blooms. Ten and one-half years after I was hired, I walked into Ben Bloom's office. "Ben, it's time for me to go. I've reached the point where my business now demands all of my time and effort. I really appreciated working here. Thanks for your support." After agreeing on my final working day at the company, we shook hands and when that day arrived, I left to run my fledgling kitchen business. I maintained amicable relations with the Blooms, and occasionally I returned in a consultant's role to work on special projects.

It is important to know that the ultimate decision to leave William Bloom was not a foregone conclusion. The final decision was made with much thought and anguish on my part. I was not the same person who walked into William Bloom & Sons in 1955. My life and obligations had changed considerably, and the decision to keep my promise to myself now appeared to be predicated on selfish motives. I now had not only a wife, but four young lives in my care, and their futures as well as mine were riding on my dream of independence. No longer could I think solely about assuaging my pain and hurt. And yet my resolve was not lessened by this truth. I talked to many people about my impending decision, and the answer for the most part was the same. "You have a good job, you're on salary, you don't have to work hard, and you have a young family. What more do you want?" I went to a very successful businessman and friend in Providence named Andrew Bell. Andrew was a man I deeply respected; he was my mentor. He listened to my story showing little emotion and at the end agreed with everyone else my plan would be very risky. I spent much time wrestling with my inner self because of the overwhelming advice against leaving Bloom. As I thought more about it, a very simple equation became the deciding factor in my decision for me and my family. Somewhere in my travels I heard the sermon topic, "When you get to where you're going, where will you be?" I asked myself the question and deduced that if Bloom would give me a ten percent increase every year for the next ten years—highly unlikely—I would still not be in the place I wanted to be. The rest was easy. I made my decision. Irrespective of the warnings of my peers, I told Ben Bloom it was time for me to go.

My determination to succeed in business dictated I hone my management skills, so I returned to school, enrolling in several non-degree programs at Johnson and Wales University, in Providence, where I studied small business management. At Roger Williams College, Providence, I studied business administration; at the University of Rhode Island, I took a course in graphic arts design; at Shrello Associates I took a course in cash flow management for non-financial managers, and Bryant College, Smithfield, Rhode Island, taught me the mechanics of how to start a business. The return to school not only helped strengthen my cabinetmaking business, but it afforded me an opportunity to make an impact upon the black community in Providence. Yet education was only a small part of God's plans for my life.

While the Civil Rights movement of the 60's pushed for equal rights and voting rights across the south, I experienced my own share of discrimination. As a black business owner in the northeast, I quickly found that I could suffer disrespect, rejection and often be denied products that my white counterparts could readily acquire.

Failure Is Not An Option

In 1959, I incorporated my business under the name American Custom Kitchens, Inc. I chose the name because the word "American" would place me on the front page of the Providence Yellow Pages directory. I soon found my first home in an old mill building in Olneyville Square, an area in the west of Providence. It proved to be very temporary, as my business was interrupted when the landlord moved me to the third floor of the building to accommodate a company that offered to pay a higher rent. It was not easy lowering cabinets down to the street from the third floor with a makeshift hoist and winch attached to a plywood platform. It forced me to look for a new home for my fledgling company.

Someone told me of an abandoned building on a street located in a neighborhood of low-income projects. Residents there seemed to have nightly reservations on the police blotter. When I saw the place, my heart sank. The building had been vacant for eight years and showed evidence of deterioration. There was one third of a roof left, no doors or windows, rotted beams infested with carpenter ants and a dirt floor.

For any other person, this might have occasioned the abandonment of all hope. However, I had no money, and could not afford to pay high rent. Standing there, I was determined to find a way to make this my business address in spite of the apparent obstacles of the building and the location. I could not allow myself to get discouraged, nor would I surrender my determination to accomplish the task. I had made a vow to be master of my fate, but even more, I saw no other option. How far can a man go without any money? There were no financial supporters and no apparent resources—just dogged determination to succeed. I believed in what I was about.

So I naively asked a local banker from Industrial National Bank to look at the property. Industrial held the present mortgage on my home and I thought they might loan me the necessary money for repairs. The banker took a cursory glance at the property, and after a derogatory remark said, "You're kidding?" He quickly informed me that he had no interest in the building or the neighborhood. "This is impossible. Find another site."

I was more determined than ever not to quit. Every fiber in my being told me I would not fail. I invited another local banker from the Rhode Island Hospital Trust National Bank to take a look. I asked him to grant me a construction mortgage so the building could be renovated in stages. There were no promises made, but the bank suggested that I begin to fix it up and they would return to take a look at my progress. I then went to one of my subcontractors, a roofer, and asked him for help with a promise to pay when the mortgage was granted. Together we added new support beams and in the process dislodged millions of carpenter ants from their comfortable dwelling. When we finished the beams, we put a new roof on the building and in the process I almost got electrocuted because the power had never been turned off to the building. When the roof was completed, I called the banker to take another look at the progress, with scarcely a thought that I would not be successful. I had neither money nor collateral, but I held firm to a dream of owning my business and I allowed no room for failure. The banker returned to look at the property, but this time he was not alone. Bob Baxter, vice president in commercial lending at Rhode Island Hospital Trust National Bank, came with him. I had never met Bob before, but to this day he is still uppermost in my memory. After spending time looking at the building and listening to me describe my dream of being an entrepreneur and owning my own business, Baxter looked me squarely in the eye. "This doesn't make any sense. You don't have any capital or collateral or any of the things that a bank needs to grant a loan. My experience and training tell me this is all wrong. However, after listening to you, I am convinced. I believe you will do what you say. I am going to grant you this loan." American Custom Kitchens soon had a new home at 145 Chad Brown Street in Providence.

The Communion Table

Initially I built and finished all of my cabinets by hand, and among them was an ornamental oak framed communion table with a tapestry of the Lord's Supper adorning the front surface. Little did I know at the time that this piece of furniture would one day prove to be confirmation that God had a plan for my life long before I truly knew Him. Pleasant Street Baptist Church had a long established custom of seeking out ministry students still in seminary during their junior and senior years to pastor its small church.

In September of 1959, the church called a young man named Readus Watkins, a Boston University student, to become its next pastor, and he remained at Pleasant Street until August of 1960. Readus Watkins was married to my sister Debbie, and when my mother died of cancer on December 19, 1959, Readus asked me to build a communion table as a memorial to honor her memory. I built the table and attended its dedication to the Lord one Sunday morning at Pleasant Street, unaware that some 27 years later I would find myself officiating the Lord's Supper to the Pleasant Street congregation from this same table.

On April 23, 1964, 70 percent of the church was destroyed in a disastrous fire. How prophetic that when the smoke had cleared the communion table peered through the darkness like a bright light. It was the one thing that remained intact, unharmed by the heat and thick black smoke. Today it stands as brightly as ever.

First Impressions

During this time, American Custom Kitchens, Inc. was growing in reputation to the point that it was impossible keeping up with the demand. However, I was fully aware that my efforts of hand labor could not produce enough cabinets to sustain a viable business. Reluctantly, I turned to prefabricated factory made cabinets with someone else's name and seal on them. It was not by choice but out ofnecessity that I changed from being a manufacturer of quality cabinets to a representative of products whose workmanship was often in question. The transition was difficult for me because up to now the outstanding quality and workmanship I poured into my cabinets was what sold them. I now had to undergo a major attitude adjustment for I had no experience and little confidence in selling cabinets that were not fashioned by my own hands.

Concurrent with what was happening in my business, I read a trade magazine article about a group of kitchen dealers in the Mid-Atlantic area who had a dream of establishing an association of similar kitchen dealers across the country. I was very curious and eager to meet others in my profession, so I made reservations and attended my first convention of the American Institute of Kitchen Dealers in the fall of 1964. The first meeting was in a hotel in New York City with approximately twenty people in attendance, most of whom were founders of the association. They appeared to be sincerely happy to see me, welcomed me warmly and appeared to be interested in my business in Providence.

My efforts to sell pre-manufactured kitchen cabinets resulted in much disappointment and frustration, and exposed me to further rejection and discrimination. It was not unusual that after making an appointment over the phone and arriving neat, well dressed and on time, a homeowner would be condescending, apologetic, or even unwilling to open the door upon seeing that I was a person of color. I continued this with little success, until meeting a man named Klaus Paradies a few years later while attending the American Institute of Kitchen Dealers convention that was being held at McCormick Place, in Chicago. Klaus was the executive director of the organization and his sales prowess was legendary. It was said that Klaus could sell ice to the Eskimos in the dead of winter.

Early in the morning after the show had closed, several of us were sitting around talking when I felt a gentle touch upon my shoulder. I turned to look square into the face of Klaus Paradies who inquired about my business. I explained my difficulty in trying to peddle someone else's cabinets and the reaction of people concerning my ethnicity. I explained, "I am a man who wants only to sell kitchen cabinets, but people are afraid of me because of my skin color and respond as if I have two heads."

Klaus smiled and his perceptive analysis not only changed my approach to selling cabinets but it also gave direction for my approach to life. Klaus spoke with a heavy European accent and at times was difficult to understand. He reminded me that his unusual speech had also been a hindrance until he learned to use it to his advantage. He said, "People have a fear of other people who are different, no matter what the difference. So instead of waiting for them to initially welcome you into their home, you must use the first few minutes of your appointment to sell yourself and ease their fear that you are not there to commit acts of violence against them or their children, or inflict bodily harm in any way. They need to know you have a wife and kids, and that you want the same things out of life as any other human being. Only then will they hear your offer of a product they will find difficult to live without."

Klaus went on to say, "Turn your difference into an advantage. I assure you, when you speak they will hang on your every word." It was then I remembered the words of my mother many years ago: "First impressions are lasting and people will not forget their first meeting with you because your color makes you different in their eyes." When I took heed of this admonition and put these principles into practice, my business began to grow.

Along with my new found prowess in selling manufactured kitchen cabinets, I next had to wrestle with the problem of getting higher quality cabinets. Many companies, upon finding me a black man, refused to sell me their products. It was a difficult and discouraging time. Many times I chastened representatives from companies who shunned me, telling them, "You will be back." They did come back several years later only to be reminded that I was the same man they had rejected years earlier.

In the next few years, I became very active in the association, and was later elected to serve on the board of directors. The crowning moment came in May of 1973 at The Fontainebleau Hotel in Miami Beach. I was installed as president of the American Institute of Kitchen Dealers, which then numbered approximately 1,300 kitchen firms, retail dealers, distributors and manufacturers from the U. S. and Europe.

That night will be forever enshrined in my memory. Though once a shy young man afraid to stand before a few people, that night I made my entrance dressed in a brown tuxedo with a peach cummerbund onto a stage before hundreds of people. I was prepared to address this large a crowd for the first time in my life because my acceptance speech, in essence, was a testimony of faith in Jesus Christ. I knew in my heart that He was the only reason I was able to stand before them. The stage was set for the future. That night a new man surfaced under the guiding hand of God, and before all of these people I declared that all honor and glory for my success was due to my relationship with Jesus Christ. After the event, many people emerged from the woodwork claiming to be Christians previously afraid to declare their faith. Another visible step in the journey had been made.

I was re-elected in 1974 to serve a second term ending in May of 1975. David Broscious, of Brocious Lumber, Northumberland, Pennsylvania, succeeded me as president of AIKD. Ida and I met David and his wife Joan at a board dinner following one of our meetings at the Concord Resort in Catskill, New York. We instantly bonded and he and Joan remain very close friends of our family to this day. Our children refer to them as Aunt Joan and Uncle Dave. Today they attribute our witness of Christ as a great influence in their decision to surrender their lives to the Lord on January 5, 1975, in Sunbury Bible Church, Sunbury, Pennsylvania.

During my tenure, one of the board meetings fell on a National Day of Prayer. After the meeting began, one of the members thought to remind the group that we should pause and take advantage of the opportunity afforded us to pray. Ray Afflerbach, our executive director was annoyed and promptly asked, "What does that have to do with us?" He was not inclined to give recognition to any religious observance. Ray was the consummate businessman and an extraordinarily gifted administrator. He was no nonsense, direct, and often volatile if things did not go his way. He kept to a schedule and was proud of his efficiency in getting things done, and appeared to have little time for things not easily apprehended by reason.

A few years later, all changed; Ray Afflerbach received Christ Jesus as his Lord and Savior and was baptized in the Assembly of God Church in Washington, New Jersey. Ida and I felt compelled to be there so we drove down from Providence to witness that glorious occasion. Ray and I, as leaders of AIKD, spent much time together. At every occasion, along with the testimony of David and Joan, we witnessed to him about finding peace in his life through Christ. As president of the organization, I prodded him on the need to give God thanks before meals [which was adopted]; in our travels across the country representing the organization I always sought out churches in which to worship. We also spent many nights together talking about the Lord, until late one afternoon I sat with Ray as he prayed to God confessing his sins and asking Jesus to be Lord and Savior in his life. I do not know if it was my constant witness that wore Ray down, or if it was simply God saying, enough is enough. I suspect it may have been a combination of the two that so indelibly touched his heart to surrender it to the Lord. Before his death, Ray's changed life bore great witness to the gospel

> "For I am not ashamed of this Good News about Christ. It is the power of God at work, saving everyone who believes—Jews first and also Gentiles." [Romans 1:16]

Inalienable Rights

My life at AIKD was not without incident. I was often reminded of the difference skin color makes. I recall the time our board was meeting at the Greenbrier Resort, in White Sulphur Springs, West Virginia, and also when we convened at the Fontainebleau Hotel in Miami. At each place, I was refused a room and later offered much lesser accommodations than other members. The issue was finally resolved only when Ray Afflerbach threatened to pull the entire convention out of the hotel if I did not receive the treatment befitting the president of the organization.

Moved by my experiences with discrimination, along with my determination to succeed in business, I was transformed by the Civil Rights Movement into an advocate for change in the business, civic, and educational fields. My focus began shifting to the creation of new opportunities for minorities.

Naomi Brodsky, an English teacher at Lincoln School, a private school for girls in Providence, contacted me concerning the need for diversity and the opportunity to open private schools in the Rhode Island area where minorities were previously excluded. Along with a few parents, we formed Operation Outreach, and our group was successful in getting minority scholarships to Lincoln School, Mary C. Wheeler and Moses Brown in Providence, The Gordon School and Providence County Day School in East Providence, and Rocky Hill School in West Greenwich. A few years later I proposed forming the Progressive Black Businessmen's Association. The group was composed of black business owners, entrepreneurs like myself, who were interested in coming together to use our collective resources to wield economic influence. There were, indeed, problems within the black business community in 1968, and as president of the association it seemed imperative to create a springboard for ailing black businesses. During this time, blacks in the business community lacked economic power. When you need a voice, money talks, so I encouraged black business owners to pool their resources into one bank. These were difficult times for black start-up businesses. For example it was almost impossible to get loans from banks. I proposed that if one member of our association were refused a loan we would tell the bank we would all do business elsewhere. I refused to be cast aside because of my color. Simply put, there was never a time that I felt defeated in trying to make a change for better business opportunities within the black community.

Business Opportunities, Inc. was established in 1968 as a subsidiary of Business Development Corporation, an organization that developed and financed new and promising business endeavors in the Providence area. A board of directors was chosen with an equal number of black and white members. I was chosen as one of the original members of this board.

On August 6, 1979, I was a passenger on the corporate jet owned by Textron Inc., the parent company of Bell Helicopter, as it left the T.

F. Green Airport in Warwick. The jet was heading south, bound for the city that three decades ago refused to serve me at a lunch counter across the street from our nation's capital. Along with several black community leaders, I was flying to Washington, D. C. as a guest of G. William Miller, chairman of the board of directors and chief executive officer of Textron Inc., soon to be sworn in as the 65th Secretary of the Treasury. In July 1977, President Jimmy Carter nominated Miller to be chairman of the Federal Reserve, and on July 19, 1979, he nominated Miller for the U. S. Treasury post. We were invited by Miller to witness the proceedings because of our local efforts to reduce racism in the corporate environment.

It was in 1975 that G. William Miller became interested in some of the inequalities faced by the members of the black community, especially in the field of employment. With the advice and counsel of James N. Williams, then executive director of the Urban League of Rhode Island, Miller decided to promote a program to change the policy of employment within his own company. Bill Miller selected seven black men along with a number of corporate executives to join him and form an integrated board of directors to discuss what actions Textron could take to improve conditions in the city's black community. The integrated group became known as the Rhode Island Urban Project. After a few years the project was so successful it was expanded to other major corporations, and I was asked to become part of the larger organization.

During my tenure on the board, we funded a program called To Increase Minorities in Mathematics and Engineering, called TIME-2. The basic premise of the program was to seek students as early as the sixth grade who might have an interest in engineering or other highly technical professions where mathematics played an important part. Several years later, TIME-2 graduated students from major universities, and today it is a fully operating charter school in Providence.

Ascending Star

The presidency of AIKD and involvement in other business and civic groups in Providence led to my being noticed in the business world. Until the 1970s, no corporations, especially banks and utilities, had ever appointed minorities to their boards of directors. When this fact became an issue, Edward Mulligan, the dynamic president of Narragansett Electric Company, began to search the community for a businessman whom he felt would be a suitable person to be the first black member of the board of directors. After a diligent search, Andrew J. Bell Jr., director of development of the newly built Bannister House Nursing Home, and former owner and operator of the Bell Funeral Service, was chosen. Andrew Bell was an excellent choice, well respected by both the black and white business community. On April 17, 1975, Andrew Bell was formally elected to the board of the Narragansett Electric Company. He was the first black member of the board of directors of any utility in the state of Rhode Island.

Soon after, in February 1976, a vacancy occurred on the board of the parent body of the power company, the New England Electric System. Andrew Bell was interviewed and elected as the first black director on New England Electric System's board of directors. This left a vacancy on the board of Narragansett Electric and Andrew Bell suggested to President Mulligan that I should be named to succeed him. I was then endorsed by President Mulligan and elected to take Andrew Bell's place on the Narragansett board. When Andrew Bell faced mandatory retirement at age 70 from the New England Board, I was interviewed by Guy Nichols, chairman and CEO, and Joan Bok, vice chairman, and was subsequently elected to the board of directors of the New England Electric System. I served for 22 years until NEES merged with a foreign utility in the year 2000 and became National Grid USA.

CHAPTER TEN

OUT OF THE SHADOWS

"The people who walk in darkness will see a great light—a light that
will shine on all who live in the land were death casts its shadow."
Isaiah 9:2

During my early working years in Providence, I was unaware that my determination to achieve my vow to be my own man left me with a deep spiritual void. At this point, I was not involved in the church. I had been away from the church for a long time in fact, I had fallen so far away from God that I hardly thought of Him at all.

I spent many afternoons eating lunches out with some of the men on the job, and I was horrified to find myself using curse words at times without realizing it. I also worked many weekends, which precluded my attending church at all. The turning point came for me one day when a man from Narragansett Electric Company appeared at William Bloom and Sons to adjust the meter. When the man went to remove the glass cover of the meter, it blew up in his face, and he was severely injured.

For the next few moments I stood there looking at the injured man lying on the floor. While waiting for help to come I saw myself and thought, "That could be me lying there. I need to do something about my life." At that moment I decided to get my family and myself back in church.

The spiritual exodus to return began when Wesley, my son and third child, was born. At that point, I felt a need to lead my family to church because of my children, but also because I had drifted away from my roots. I had attended church a few times in the last five years, but I made no serious commitment to the Lord. I didn't want to slip further away from my spiritual upbringing so I determined that immediate change was in order. While at William Bloom & Son, I asked one of my employees, George Martin, who then lived in East Providence, if he knew the churches in the Providence area. George directed the question to his wife Alice, who was a member of Pond Street Baptist Church on the west side of the city. Alice promptly invited me and the family to attend services at her church. One year later, in 1960, I was baptized by Rev. Bernard Holiday and became a member of Pond Street Baptist Church. I worshipped in Pond Street for the next 21 years until I began my journey to Westerly.

Life at Pond Street started out rather innocuously. I was on many boards and committees from 1961 to 1981. My first role in the church in a leadership position was president of the Senior Choir. Remembering myself as president of the Senior Choir causes me to chuckle—I couldn't even hold a note. A few years later in 1963, Pond Street Baptist Church was forced to relocate due to the Central Classical School Redevelopment Project, so the church moved to Chester Avenue in South Providence, where it remains today. My previous business experience led me to play a key role as a member of the Relocation and Redevelopment Committee for the building of the new church.

The people of Pond Street found me to be just as committed a worker for the Lord as I had been in establishing my own business. My responsibilities before coming to the church thrust me into positions of church leadership. At different times I served as church treasurer, chairman of the Deacon and Trustee Boards, and chairman of many committees. It was here I met a man named Clarence "Bubby" McKay. Bubby had been a saxophone player and leader of a small band, which he willingly gave up for the Lord. Now Bubby and his family devoted much of their time to the church.

Bubby and I instantly hit it off and we began to develop a very close relationship. It was a memorable time when Bubby and I were installed as deacons together in 1972 under Rev. Jack Clark. "They had been walking deacons in training for five years before I brought it to Reverend Clark's attention," said Louise McKay, Bubby's wife. Louise recalls that Bubby and I had such a love for people that we tried to visit as many as we could. This was the beginning of the transformation of my heart from pursuit of business goals to caring for people's needs.

Bubby and I visited people in their homes and hospitals in an area from Providence to Narragansett, Jamestown and Newport, in the south, and Woonsocket in the north. A most memorable experience occurred one Sunday as we went to visit one of our members in Providence. Lillian Bailey had been housebound in a wheelchair and could seldom get out to church. When we arrived, we heard a dog barking; we debated who should be the first to enter. Mrs. Bailey's husband, Preston, sat in a chair close by with a huge German shepherd at his side. He eyed our every move and both he and the dog glared at us until we left. It happened every time we went there. Several years later, Preston Bailey asked Jesus Christ into his life and subsequently became a deacon at Pond Street Baptist Church. That was only one of many stories of our ministry at Pond Street. We worked together untiringly to bring hope to other's lives, but sometimes God brings the ministry to our own households.

This was the case with Bubby's son Larry. He was a recent college graduate who didn't want to hear about church and often responded to his parents with the question, "Why do I have to go?" It was Bubby and Louise's nightmare that Larry, brought up in a Christian home, had suddenly rejected the faith. One Sunday, with deep despair, they went to church and left him at home. During the worship service that Sunday morning, just as the doors of the church were opened, Larry came forward to give his life to Christ. "Unknown to us, Josh had been witnessing to Larry and that was only one of many times that he helped our family."

Bubby McKay was a medical marvel because he was on dialysis for 24 years. Bubby continued treatments until his death in 1989. When Bubby died I felt a great void in my life; we had become like brothers, and I mourned the passing of my dear friend and colleague.

In the midst of my heavy involvement with Pond Street church, I made a life changing discovery. I was unable to say with certainty at that time that there existed a real and vital relationship with the Lord Jesus Christ in my life. My testimony begins on a Wednesday evening in August, when members of the small house-church across the street were granted permission to use the Pond Street church for a revival. There were many very small churches in the neighborhood, housed in storefronts. Each of these churches, started by local ministers, numbered approximately 15 to 20 members. The people wanted to be independent of established denominations and felt a special calling from God which could only be realized apart from organized religion. The house church across the street had not yet acquired a building, so they requested the use of our sanctuary.

I attended the revival that night. While entering the foyer I was met by a young woman, a member of the neighboring church who looked at me quite strangely. She asked, "What are you doing here?" I had attended this church for 13 years and no one had ever asked me that question before. Not yet fully recovered from the assault on my haughtiness, I answered, "I came for the revival." She replied, "I thought Baptists didn't usually attend this kind of service." I realized I had been drawn to this place tonight with the prospect of getting to know the Lord Jesus in a deeper and more abiding way.

Revival focuses every bit of energy on God. It begins on ones knees in prayer, pleading and petitioning God for a renewed outpouring of His Spirit. It is characterized by powerful soul, hot preaching and a deeper intimacy and power from the Lord. This I wanted and needed in my life.

The defining moment came some months later, in the fall of 1973, at another revival at the church. This time, the Rev. Frank Scott, a local minister, was conducting a revival for Pond Street. After the sermon the revivalist posed the question, "Do you know for sure where you will spend eternity?" The first time he asked I was content not to deal with the question, all the while knowing I did not have the necessary assurance. The question of the writer [Hebrews 2:3] surfaced in my memory, "*What makes us think that we can escape if we are indifferent to this great salvation that was announced by the Lord Jesus himself?*" I knew I had to do something. I wanted to be sure that I was going to spend eternity with the Lord. I threw all caution to the wind, stood up from my front row seat, and presented my life before the Lord. That night I committed myself a living sacrifice to Jesus Christ and asked Him to forgive me of my sins. As the pianist played the hymn, "I have decided to follow Jesus, no turning back, no turning back." I went forward with tears streaming down my face. My heart was sorrowing, repentant and palpitating at a rapid paceAt that moment I asked Jesus Christ to come live within and be Lord of my life.

CHAPTER ELEVEN

Moving Day

"So Abram departed as the Lord had instructed him."
Genesis 12:4a

After I departed Pond Street Baptist Church, my experience with Christ was still very much in focus. It seemed almost surreal, as if the person I once was no longer existed. The many experiences in my life seemed distant, and my life began to merge into God's divine plan. In particular, my heart was changing toward people. I saw them through different eyes. The anger I once felt because of isolation and rejection due to my color was waning, and I began to see people's needs before I saw their color. God was preparing me for what was ahead.

I cannot help thinking now that God was fashioning me to be His eyes and heart for the ministry in Westerly. Calvin Miller in his book, *The Unchained Soul*, tells the story of how "Scottish patriarchs looking for walking sticks, always passed over the untried wood of the lower slopes. They climbed to the wuthered heights to search for rods made strong by storm and wind.

These iron-strong canes were once young trees that fought the icy Northers. With each storm they bent and twisted and broke a bit inside. But gradually each inner scar became the steely fiber they bought with every storm that endured. Only such woody steel will serve as the rod of God," Miller warns, "But do not let their majesty delude you. These mighty rods were once just spindling trees. Therefore, never bless the rods; rather, bless the gales that broke their sinews, lacing them with stone, until the storms they so despised had changed them into scepters."

God uses our experiences to fashion us into rods that He can use for His glory. He merges us together with Him that we might share in his divine nature. Many times I had been vulnerable, felt beaten up, rejected and broken, but along with each act of bigotry, each derogatory word, each accusation, God was fashioning a stronger, more confident, more durable and wiser man to accomplish the task He had set before me. In the process, I learned that those experiences which do not break us make us stronger and wiser.

To be sure, my arrival in Westerly was a real culture shock. I was in a town which reminded me that once again, because of my color, I was a minority. Westerly held much uncertainty, many questions and no great expectations for me. I was just happy to be out of Providence, to be working in a less stressful environment and to have the opportunity to escape the pain and conflict of my previous ministry at Pond Street. Yet, my earlier experiences of prejudice led me to believe that ministry in Westerly would be testing.

The last 20 years of my adult life in the Christian community had been in Providence, where I was surrounded by several large churches with a membership composed of nearly 98 percent African American people. A negligible number of whites attended these predominately Black churches. So, I could not understand my reason for being in Westerly, and I even queried God if He had not made a mistake—all the while asking myself if I had heard God rightly. I was desperate and in need of getting out of Pond Street Baptist Church, but why here, why Westerly? What could I do here? Pleasant Street Baptist Church had hardly more than 30 members, a few black people, a few whites and the majority Native Americans. The church was surrounded by a vast population of whites with hardly one percent blacks or people of color. Westerly is heavily Catholic, a challenging environment for a Protestant pastor of a small church. It left me confused, to say the least.

It was a far cry from my previous experience of the Christian community in Providence where there were five major Baptist churches. Ebenezer on the South Side, Olney Street and Congdon Street on the East Side, Union Baptist in Pawtucket, north of Providence and St. James far north in Woonsocket. Along with them, there were several

African Methodist Episcopal and AME Zion churches. All were known to have a predominately black membership. Surely, I did not understand it at the time, but what I was certain of was that I was in the place God wanted me to be. I thought often of the words of the writer who noted, *"There is a time for everything, a season . for every activity under heaven."* [Ecclesiastes 3:1]No longer did I question whether I heard God rightly.

I readily confess that I had some problems to overcome regarding race. Since moving to Rhode Island in 1955, we lived in predominately Black communities, and not always by choice. There was a time we pursued buying a house in Warwick, Cowesett, East Greenwich and Pawtuxet only to be told we were not welcome because of our color, and, further, my real estate agent was advised not to bring those "black people" around here again. I could afford the houses, but it made no difference. The residents were advocates of the "NIMBY" principle, *not in my backyard*. They did not want black people living next door.

At the same time, I had deep personal feelings about whites because of my brothers' personal choices in women. It seemed to me that most of their ongoing relationships were with white women, and it bothered me. I asked one of my brothers, why he did not date many black women. His response caught me completely by surprise. He said, "There are no good black women around." When I recovered from the initial shock, I said to him defiantly, "How can that be? Your mother and sisters are black."

I could hardly have believed I would find myself lodged in Westerly, in an all-white community, preparing to follow God's will for my life, committed to proclaiming a living Christ to people of every race, color, and social status. I was cognizant of the Scriptures,

> "There is no longer Jew or Gentile, slave or free, male or female. For you are all Christians—you are one in Christ Jesus." [Galatians 3:28].

Years later, I revealed to my children my earlier experiences and subsequent feelings about race and prejudice. They found it incredible that after knowing me to be so loving, compassionate and colorblind, I could have ever held such feelings in my heart. My ex-son-in-law, Minister Mallory Davis, often takes delight in reminding me that God sent me to Westerly because of His divine sense of humor. "God never took you seriously anyway," he saidHe is probably right. I could not imagine holding a grudge against anyone created in God's image.

The move to Westerly was not made without worrying and agonizing over how to make my family understand that this was not just a means to express my independence. It was not about asserting my authority as head of the family, nor was it one of the sudden irrational or unconventional moves I had been noted for; on the contrary, despite my vow to be an independent man, I was feeling less control and authority over my life for the first time since young adulthood. I was sure about the decision I had made for the future. I had given it much thought and spent much time in prayer before I came to the conclusion I had little or no choice but to surrender to the will of God, leave my home in Providence for Westerly and follow God. I was certain it was I the prophet Isaiah had in mind when he said *"and you will hear a voice say, 'This is the way; turn around and walk here."* [Isaiah 30:21]

In my prior conversation with Pastor Lambe, I confessed that I was at a loss in knowing how to address my family, in particular my wife, concerning leaving Providence for Westerly. Once again, I would be making a sudden change that she was unprepared for. Harold Lambe was a man short of physical stature, but a giant of spiritual wisdom. He asked, "Josh, since you first received the vision from God has He not taken care of everything else up to this moment?" "Yes," I said quietly. "Can you not trust Him now to take care of your wife?"

I then planned to talk to my family the following Sunday after church and tell them of my plans to go to Westerly, to serve at Pleasant Street Baptist Church as Associate Pastor under Rev. Harold Lambe. I was fairly certain of what my wife would say. Ida and I were attending Pond Street along with our daughters Leslie and Dorothy. My son Wesley was playing piano for a youth choir at Olney Street Baptist Church in Providence, while my oldest daughter Allison, now a student at Douglas College, Rutgers University, in New Brunswick, New Jersey, had joined Tabernacle Baptist Church in that same city. That Sunday was a bit cloudy, but it appeared the sun would peek through the clouds at any moment. I was praying it would, because the warmth of its rays might have helped my nervousness and apprehension. Here it was again: another bolt from the blue for my family to digest. How to tell them I did not know, but I had to answer God, and I felt compelled to go to

Westerly. I loved my family and they were all so important to me. I wondered if I could get them to see how this decision had come about. In the next moments as I shared my heart with them, each of the children processed my impending move in different ways. But without my knowing it, my move to Westerly was to have a profound impact on their lives, deeper and greater than I could ever imagine.

Where Is Westerly?

My youngest daughter Dorothy, usually the most outspoken, was now the most subdued. She recalls, "After the talk I remember seeing some things packed up and I realized it could happen, but hoping it wouldn't. I remember a feeling of loss. I felt like you were leaving me. I no longer had a haven to run back to. It was only after I saw you and Mom in Westerly that the reality of it set in, and I just had to accept it." Dorothy had spent 15 years in the financial services field most recently as a trust operations specialist in the trust department of the Washington Trust Bank here in Westerly. A few months ago she sold her home in East Providence and moved to Westerly to be near her parents.

Leslie, my second born child, has been living in Westerly about eight years. She is now a special education assistant at the Tower Street Elementary School in Westerly. She teaches the second and third grade children one-on-one. She also serves as director of youth ministry at Pleasant Street Baptist Church. Of all our children, Leslie was the one who was most emotionally vulnerable. She never wanted to be very far from home, so she attended college at the University of Rhode Island and Community College of Rhode Island. Leslie has since shared her struggles about that Sunday sitting around the table. "My first thought was, what the heck is he talking about? Where is Westerly? Is he leaving us? What about the job? Panic quickly crept in. I think I blocked out most of the conversation after that. All I kept thinking was that my father was leaving. My rock. Who is going to take care of me? I was the one who kept coming back home and now I would not have a home. LeavingProvidence meant loss of security, stability, and support. After I willed my brain to continue to listen, I realized that there was passion in his voice and his eyes told what his heart felt. God told him that He had other plans for his future. My mother just sat quietly, glancing up at him now and then with very little expression. Then she would look at each of us trying to grasp our reaction. I guess I was the hardest because I was not leaving my home. Hey, I even left college and moved back home and when I was at college I went home every weekend; then I transferred to a junior college so that I could be home. Now where was my home going to be? I was being selfish, but I didn't care because Westerly was in another *country* and it was too far away to get the instant reassurance that I needed. Then I heard something about church and you don't have to come – you can make your own decision. How dare you just decide to leave and expect everything to be okay, I said. It's something I have to do, my father said. Don't expect me to leave my home, my friends and my life then. I returned with my arms folded like a defense mechanism … after that he continued to talk about selling the business, the house, etc. My emotions jumped from shock to anger to defiance. I took the decision very personally and actually felt like my parents were running away from me. I was determined not to be supportive or agreeable. I wouldn't like Westerly and I wouldn't help. All this happened in about 15 minutes until I actually felt something go through me that made me look—really look at my dad. His eyes, his voice, his expression were so different, so surreal, so sincere. While his face showed compassion and concern for our reactions, his demeanor showed his decision was made. I loved this man and trusted him with all my heart and if he was willing to give up his home and business to follow a vision from God, then I should be able to give up my selfishness. I would even be able to get a map and look up Westerly."

    Later that day I called my oldest daughter Allison in New Jersey to inform her of my decision. She had recently transferred to Rutgers from Northeastern University in Boston, where she was majoring in engineering. Allison, probably because of her training, appeared to be less surprised than anyone else as she mused about the happenings of that day. She remarked, "As I reflect back to the time when I found out about your decision these are my thoughts … phone rings … Hi Al, I just wanted to tell you about some decisions that I've made. We had a family meeting today and I told them all that they could make up their minds and do what they wanted to do. I told them they did not have to follow me but I was going to go to minister in Westerly [Westerly, where's that? I thought]   I feel that God wants me to go into the ministry there. Rev. McGhee asked me to come to Woonsocket with him but I really feel that God is leading me to Westerly. [Ok, but where's Westerly?] Do you have any thoughts or questions that you need to ask me? [Questions? What is there to question? It's about time! He knew God was leading him into the ministry for a long time. I don't even understand anyone's discussion or aversion to it. Plus, who am I to question God's will, I believe in those not so random lightning bolts showing up.] I say, Good for you! . . . Wait! I do have one question. Where's Westerly?" Allison has since made her home in Rumford, Rhode Island. She is an admissions officer at The Wheeler School in Providence, Rhode Island, a co-educational, N-12 independent day school. Allison now attends St. John's Episcopal Church in Providence.

Wesley, my only son, who often looked to me for guidance, was also a member of Pond Street Baptist Church. He did not appear to be as emotionally impacted or distracted as I thought he would by my decision to leave Providence. At the time he also attended Olney Street Baptist Church where he sang and played the piano for the youth choir on occasion. He had been seeking a niche for himself and was reaching out to find his own place in the family and church, and it wasn't until later years that I found out his true reaction to my move. Wesley remembers, "You didn't put any pressure on the girls or me to leave Pond Street. In fact, I don't remember you putting any pressure on Mommy either. I believe that you said this is what God wanted you to do regardless of what anyone else did in the family. I also remember that you had a better ministry opportunity at St. James Baptist Church under then Pastor Hugh McGee. Yet, you chose to become an associate under Pastor Harold Lambe. After you left I continued to live in Providence with Allison until I went off to law school in 1983. After law school in 1986, I started attending Pleasant Street sporadically without any real commitment, but during one Sunday morning service in the fall of 1988 everything changed. That was the day God became so real to me. When I heard the invitation to allow Jesus into my heart as Lord and Savior, I came forward running, not walking. The rest is history!" Wesley was the former general counsel for NICA, an association of self employed and independent contractors, headquartered in Braintree, Massachusetts. His present position is Executive Director of NICA Legal Institute. Wesley is also an adjunct Professor of Legal Studies at Suffolk University. Along with this, he is a lay minister at Pleasant Street Baptist Church, and he still finds time to sing and occasionally play piano for one of our choirs.

On the other hand, as expected, my wife Ida was very angry with me. To say the least she was always skeptical and suspect when I called a family meeting. This one was no different, and as she soon learned, her fears were justified. This was not the first time she had been uprooted from comfortable surroundings and forced to consider a radical life change. The first was when I left a secure position at William Bloom and Son to pursue a dream of having my own business. Next and probably what proved to be the most dramatic, was when I stayed home from Philadelphia and saw the vision of the Lord's heart, and upon Ida's return announced to her I was giving up my life in Providence to devote myself completely to God for the work of the ministry. I know Ida didn't marry a minister, but now what? What to do? Again I was proposing to abandon a comfortable home and friends in Providence for the uncertainty of moving to a small church in Westerly to be an Associate Pastor. And not only that, the day was just a few years distant when I would turn the key in the lock and close the doors of my businesses for the last time. And now, my wife said to me in no uncertain terms, "You go if you want; I am not going to Westerly." It was three months after my departure that Ida reluctantly appeared at Pleasant Street Baptist Church one Sunday morning, and said to the congregation, "I do not want to be here but since my husband is here I felt obliged to come."

A Friend In Need

The first five years at Pleasant Street Baptist Church under Pastor Lambe was a time of healing for me. Harold was a very gracious, confident, unassuming man, comfortable with me at his side and eager to provide the atmosphere for my growth and healing. Not only did he become my mentor, but more than that, he was a caring, unselfish friend. When I arrived at Pleasant Street Church and asked him what he wanted me to do, his response was filled with much grace and understanding, seemingly aware of my need for healing. He said, "Josh, I want you to feel free to do what God has called you to do. I want my people to appreciate your ministry as much as mine." It wasn't until many years later that I came to understand the significance and importance of those words. I was pleased to work under Harold Lambe, for it afforded me an opportunity to use my many skills and allowed me the comfort of doing ministry without significantly disrupting my life and business. Since I entertained no personal goal of pastoring a church, I naively hoped things would not change for me.

Harold and I became very close, and I tried to help him in his ministry in every way I could. I interceded for him during some of the times he was taken to task by a powerful, disrespectful group of trustees who saw themselves as the religious guardians of the church charged with maintaining the status quo. They openly demonstrated their lack of respect for their pastor by making it clear to all that they ran the church, and anyone who disagreed would be moved aside or trampled underfoot. They informed Harold that his job was to preach and not interfere with their activities.

The trustees made the major decisions in the church. At times they deliberately held back Harold Lambe's pay. They openly challenged his authority in front of church members; they refused to allow him to make any changes in the church [even to the point of where pictures could be hung]. In general, they felt it necessary to keep Pastor Lambe in tow.

For the most part they ignored me because I had no authority or power to concern them. A few notable things I was able to accomplish during this time included a long overdue by-law review and revision, and the installation of sound equipment to record the worship services. During my tenure working side by side with Harold Lambe, I received a small stipend from the church, just enough to pay for my gas to and from Providence.

CHAPTER TWELVE

IT'S NOT SUPPOSED TO HURT

"As far as I am concerned, God turned into good what you meant for evil. He brought me to the high position I have today so I could save the lives of many people."
Genesis 50:20

In the fall of 1982, while at Pleasant Street Church, I continued my preparation for ministry. I was approached by Dr. David Kilpatrick, pastor of the Greenville Baptist Church, in Greenville, Rhode Island, who suggested I seek ordination under the auspices of American Baptist Churches of Rhode Island. Dave was the immediate past chair of the Standing Committee on the Ministry and my tutor in three courses of the Certified Lay Ministry Program: Preaching and Worship, Pastoral Care and Baptist History and Polity. In our time together, he had shared his experience of a personal life changing encounter with the Holy Spirit, and I became enthralled with the prospect of a deeper presence of the Holy Spirit in my life. Dave invited me to become part of a group of people from his church who were involved in "The Life in the Spirit Seminars." Their goals were the same as mine: to allow the presence and power of God's Spirit to infuse my whole being. In the fall of 1977, I had traveled with Dave and some of his church members to Green Lake Baptist Assembly, in Oshkosh, Wisconsin, to attend the first American Baptist Conference on the Holy Spirit ever held at Green Lake.

A short time later, Dave informed me that there was a track to ordination, based on experience, under the standards of the American Baptist Churches USA, and I should apply to the Standing Committee on the Ministry of ABCORI to begin the process of ordination. I was in my final year of biblical studies at Barrington College, and coupled with my past ministry experience, Dave Kilpatrick assured me there should be no reason for the committee to turn down my request to proceed toward ordination. Little did he or I know there was a huge fly in the ointment in the form of the new chair of the Standing Committee on the Ministry. He was an educational elitist who was determined that no one would get by him without the standard four years of college and three years of seminary. Any pain and struggle I went through previously would be dwarfed by what was about to happen to me and the lingering effects it would have on my life some twenty years later.

The chairman, along with the committee, listened to me recite the details of my vision, and they heard my request to give sanction to the ordination process. After listening to comments from the committee the chairman stated, "We appreciate all that you have presented to us and we are aware of your accomplishments in ABCORI [president and also ABCORI Man of the Year in 1980]. However, we feel you need seminary education. We will rewrite the specific standards that you must meet here in Rhode Island." They ignored the fact I had applied to commence the process of ordination under existing standards of American Baptist Churches USA, which were designed for experienced, highly qualified individuals who did not have previous seminary experience. I left the meeting that day disappointed, discouraged, and infuriated by the elitism displayed by the chairman and a few other committee members. I had been rejected because my experience and background in ministry and administration did not meet their standards, and they were the guardians to the gate of ordination.

Before this, candidates for ordination were recognized under the education prerequisites as adopted by the American Baptist Convention in 1961. The Standing Committee on the Ministry decided they would no longer abide by their previously adopted rules and would write new standards for ordination. I would have to reapply once the new rules were completed. Indeed, they took several months to change the rules capping the maximum experience credit at two years instead of the previous three years. After a second request was again refused, the chairman decided to appoint a special committee to look into my unique qualifications and report back. The committee was headed by Dr. Ralph Patterson, pastor of the Norwood Baptist Church in Warwick, Rhode Island, and included a young pastor, new to the state. After several weeks, the report of the committee came back. Dr. Patterson reported, "I have never met a person more prepared for professional ministry." However, the Standing Committee on the Ministry of ABCORI, led by its resolute chairman, once again deferred my request for recognition of ordination.

Divine Approval

Pastor Harold Lambe and the members of Pleasant Street Baptist Church made it clear that, "Enough is enough; we will proceed to ordain without their sanction." And they did. On September 9, 1984, I was ordained to the Christian Ministry by the Pleasant Street Baptist Church. It didn't matter whether the Committee on Ministry approved my ordination or not, for their affirmation under any circumstances would be merely symbolic. God's approval was all that mattered. The ordination had to be held in Central Baptist Church, Westerly, because Pleasant Street had never seen such a "great cloud of witnesses." Some 300 to 400 people filled the church to the balconies, and it is unlikely any ordination of an American Baptist minister in Rhode Island attracted so many dignitaries. Though SCOM withheld their approval for the church to proceed with ordination, their decision was made less relevant by those church leaders who gave overwhelming assent by their physical presence. The guest preacher for the event, Rev. Earl W. Lawson, Pastor of Pilgrim Way Baptist Church, Hartford, Connecticut, preached a powerful, emotionally charged ordination sermon, in which he declared with great passion, power and sobriety: "God calls somebody to preach when nobody is around. It doesn't matter what the pulpit committee says. Ordination is from above." As I knelt in prayer for the laying on of hands, my only thought was of the mercy of the God who had called me. I was so humbled, and felt so unworthy to be in the presence of such a gracious God. During the Prayer of Ordination I recalled the words of Jesus,

> "You didn't choose me. I chose you. I appointed you to go and produce fruit that will last, so that the Father will give you whatever you ask for, using my name." [John 15:16]

God's Plans Cannot Be Thwarted

Though the religious institution tried to halt my progress toward ordination, God had the last word. Some twenty years later, in January of 2004, the American Baptist Churches of Rhode Island Standing Committee on the Ministry confessed their transgression and granted me professional standing in the Registry of Ministerial Leaders of the American Baptist Churches USA. This action was triggered by the fact that the God's vision of ministry given to Pleasant Street Baptist Church was coming to fruition before their very eyes. It was hard to continue to ignore a church experiencing such renewal while continuing to extol the virtues of churches merely conducting weekly memorial services. Pleasant Street Baptist Church has emerged as one of the most exciting, vibrant, dynamic churches in ABCORI, and after nearly twenty years of pastoral leadership, it would be difficult for them to ignore me as the pastor.

Dr. Paul Schoonmaker, writing in the 2003 winter edition of "*Interaction*", an ABCORI publication, noted that "Pleasant Street is a growing congregation that includes people of all races and backgrounds [it was originally founded by and for Native Americans]. There are many other dimensions to the ministry God has raised up in Westerly, but if one word could be used to describe this multi-faceted ministry, it would be 'alive'. The path may be different for the rest of us, but what is certain in every case is that when there is a vision from God and when we are obedient, our churches will come alive. The Rev. Joshua McClure and his congregation can echo the words of Paul, "*Whereupon, O King Agrippa, I was not disobedient unto the heavenly vision!*" [Acts 26:19 KJV] May it be so for all of us!"

A Blip On The Radar Screen

During the years leading up to the recognition of my ordination, I ran the script through my mind many times trying to find answers to the question: Why?Why was it necessary for me to be put through such pain and anguish while trying to prepare for what God had directed for the future? Why was I the recipient of such open and outright disdain from some members of that committee? Only recently did a picture begin to emerge which might explain the actions and attitudes of The Standing Committee on the Ministry towards me and my request for ordination in May of 1982. Their personal response may have been triggered by an incident that happened back in 1977, near the commencement of my studies for the lay ministry. One Thursday, my pastor at Pond Street Church approached me and asked if I would preach at a church on Smith Hill in Providence because the pastor had to leave town that weekend. The pastor of the church was the wife of the chairman of the Ministry Committee. This turned out to be one of the most regrettable of all the learning experiences of my young ministry. I found this church to be a very small congregation of mostly elderly people, barely responsive to the message of the gospel and appearing to be quite detached from the worship service itself. I was confused and having had little experience in preaching and worship outside of Pond Street Church, I was at a loss how to enliven them until I remembered a phrase my pastor often used to perk up an unresponsive people. He would say, "Anything that is dead should be in the graveyard." Frustrated and confused by the lack of response, and thinking it would help the situation, I repeated the words I had heard my pastor say in like or similar situations. In this instance it was to no avail, for not only did I not get the desired response of changing the dull atmosphere, but it seemed to drive the people deeper into a stupor. I left there that Sunday little realizing what harm I had done.

    A few weeks later, my pastor approached me and asked, "Did the pastor tell you that on Friday they buried one of the longstanding members of the church?" "No!" I replied, "She had not." At that moment I felt a deep sorrow for my actions. I was made aware of the deep hurt and pain one can lay on those in his care, and I sensed the conviction of the Holy Spirit in my heart. I learned a very valuable lesson for my future ministry; I should be a man of deep compassion, observant, caring and loving to God's people and I must not try to mimic the action of others no matter how successful they appear to be. The fact my pastor was a close friend and classmate of the pastor of this church helps me better understand the negative attitude of the Ministry Committee and why he gave me little support or encouragement in the ordination process. To this day, over two decades later, this incident remains a very humbling and defining moment in my life and ministry.

CHAPTER THIRTEEN

When You've Lost the Star

"No longer will you need the sun or moon to give you light, for the Lord your God will be your everlasting light, and he will be your glory."
Isaiah 60:19

The year 1986 was the commencement of my call to be pastor of Pleasant Street Baptist Church, and it proved to be the launching point for the vision I had received ten years prior. In May, my pastor, Harold Lambe, accepted a call from The First Church of God, Peacedale, Rhode Island, to be its pastor and to succeed its long time beloved leader, Rev. Kenneth Mars. Before this, I had been approached by a church in New London, Connecticut to ask about my interest in being a candidate for its vacant pastor position and now some members of the church in Peacedale approached me to determine my interest in their parish. At the time, I had no desire in being a pastor. I was very comfortable as an associate pastor at Pleasant Street; further, I was not about to compete with Pastor Lambe for the same pulpit. I did not want more responsibility. I was running a full-time retail kitchen business and manufacturing plant in Providence. I was traveling three days a week to attend Andover Newton Theological School in Newton Centre, Massachusetts, and at the same time serving as Associate to Pastor Lambe at Pleasant Street.

After Harold Lambe's departure for The First Church of God in Peacedale, members of the Pulpit Committee of Pleasant Street asked me to consider becoming their pastor. In spite of all the reasons previously cited, and the fact it would permanently disrupt my life, I knew

God would not allow me to do otherwise. On September 28, 1986, I was installed as pastor of Pleasant Street Baptist Church.

The Star Reappears

Shortly after my installation, I heard a voice confirming this was the place God would have me be. At first I did not realize the significance of the visit. It had been ten years since the vision. Ten years since I had felt God's heart. When I reflected on it, I was impressed with the similarity of my journey to the journey of the Wise Men from the east who came to find the Christ child. Up to this point in my understanding of the birth of Christ, I had believed that the Wise Men saw the star in the eastern sky, and followed it all the way to Jerusalem, and ultimately to Bethlehem, to the place where the Christ Child lay. Upon closer scrutiny, it appears there was a time the Wise Men traveled in darkness without the aid of the star until they arrived at Jerusalem. After their meeting with King Herod, the star reappeared leading them to Bethlehem and to the Christ child. After a query from Herod as to the birth location, the Wise Men replied, "*We have seen his star as it arose, and we have come to worship him.*" [Matthew 2:2b] And we further read [verse 9] "*After this interview the wise men went their way. Once again the star appeared to them, guiding them to Bethlehem.*"

What I have come to learn is that visions must be pursued by faith. Sometimes the star appears briefly and does not reappear for a long time. Sometimes one has to walk in the dark with only faith as a compass. However, even in the dark, faith will light the way. Paul says in his Second Epistle to the church at Corinth, Chapter 5, verse 7, "*That is why we live by believing and not by seeing.*" There was a time along the way on my journey to Pleasant Street that the star was not visible. From December of 1976 to September of 1986, God was silent. For ten years I walked in the dark, preparing for what I did not know. I followed the light of an image seen only once, but trusting the God who gave it. For ten years I followed the direction of the vision until it came to Pleasant Street, and then after ten years of journeying by faith, the star reappeared. In September of 1986, God's voice once again spoke to me, "This is where the vision is to be fulfilled."

Soon after I accepted the pastorate of Pleasant Street Baptist Church, I came to realize two things: first, pastoring this church would be far different and far more challenging than anything I had ever faced in supervising employees; and second, I would need to define my ministry quickly. I had never pastored a church before, and this was to be a defining point in my effectiveness as a leader in the church. I had owned several businesses in which I interviewed people for employment, reviewed their resumes and work histories, checked their references and observed their manner. If I felt they could help the business to succeed, I would hire them. Here at Pleasant Street, I was the one interviewed by the Pulpit Committee. I had been in the church the past five years, so people had plenty of time to observe me. They were cognizant of my work under Harold Lambe, and they asked me to be their pastor. I was not sure if they called me because I was convenient, or because they thought I could help. However, what was clear is that they considered themselves the boss and I was the employee. They were hiring me to do a job for them. If they discovered they made a mistake and I didn't meet their needs, the by-laws stated, "The term of office of pastor may be ended upon at least thirty days [30] notice on the part of the pastor or the church." I was aware of the many conflicts that had existed between the church and Harold Lambe, but one thing I was determined they would know: I would not run; I would leave only when I heard God say it was time. God was the one who called me to a ministry here at Pleasant Street—no person or group hires God's servants. I would stay. I was further aware that difficult times lay ahead for pastor and people, and there was no time for on-the-job training, so I would readily have to share my vision for the future of Pleasant Street.

In my first few months as pastor, I proposed a full slate of ministries and activities which would reach out to all people, ages, ethnic backgrounds, and social classes in the community. This vision made some members angry, and won some over. Yet gradually, with God entering people's hearts and speaking to them, they came to know and understand what His message and intent were.

What did this vision include? It included ministries for men and women and children, with a strong counseling component, providing a service which some other churches only offered as a recommendation outside of the church. It included a strong youth element, even though God had not yet supplied the recipients. The vision included a place for family ministry targeted at couples, singles and young marrieds. There was to be door-to-door evangelism, and in-home Bible studies for the community.

The vision also included a powerful music ministry for all ages, intercessory prayer groups, tape ministry for the sick and shut-ins, and at some point, as God directed, a TV ministry to reach more people. This would require support services such as vans to transport people; a ramp and a bathroom for disabled people; a library and computer room for tutoring; and the establishment of a church nursery. However, this was not the most shocking part of the vision. That would be reserved for the educational component, which proposed teaching high school and college level courses which would utilize other pastors or church leaders. Along with that, the vision included a pre-school for three-to-five year olds, capped, by the building of a fully accredited Christian school from Kindergarten to grade eight.

The vision was not so much sensational as essential. In retrospect, church members slowly came to appreciate that they only had a church, a building, a piece of real estate. I told them a church is not real estate alone. It is people, poor, lonely, in despair, without hope, needing to know that someone cares, reaching out beyond their learned experiences, encouraged by the preaching of God's word which would bring them closer to God. I also reiterated the fact the whole emphasis of the vision would be to establish a ministry complex that would minister to the community far and wide. My role in the ministry would be to proclaim the simple truths of God's word as revealed. My promise to them was to preach the full Gospel so simply that even children could understand it and come to make Jesus the desire of their hearts.

Adding stress to my acceptance of the call to the church was the awareness that I could not be effective here at Pleasant Street, nor could I spend the sufficient time if I added the pastorate to the load I was already carrying. I would open up my business early in the morning, leave for seminary when classes were scheduled, return to the business from school and then go to church to carry out my duties in the ministry. Something had to go now that I had given my assent to the pastorate of Pleasant Street. The decision was difficult, but I decided to forego the last one and a half years of seminary at Andover Newton Theological School, in Newton Centre, Massachusetts, and enroll as a distance student at Trinity College and Seminary in Medwell, Indiana, where

I could continue my theological education. This allowed me to focus much more of my time in fulfilling the role of a pastor. And yet, what I refused to admit was the strain of trying to maintain my cabinet business. I did not want to give up my last bit of independence. Surely, God had captured my heart years earlier, but I had not yet surrendered myself enough to rely totally on His provision. The moment came a few years later, in the summer of 1988, when both heart and mind became one, and I surrendered the building and inventory to the bank to fulfill my mortgage obligations to them. Now armed with the vision and God's promise alone, I moved forward to establish myself as leader of this waiting congregation.

Enduring Leadership

In my role as pastor, I needed the people of Pleasant Street to take me seriously. My first address to the congregation was to inform them I had not come to the church to do maintenance or simply to help them survive. I was here to teach them how to live again. They could no longer be satisfied with the status quo. I came to establish ministries, to grow the church, and the church would be vastly different both physically and spiritually. I spoke clearly and decisively. "God gave me a vision for this church ten years ago, in December of 1976, and I am here to see it fulfilled."

Following my declaration I was approached by a very forthright, stern, no nonsense woman who was chairman of the Trustee Board. She greeted me by announcing that she was in charge and I would do nothing without her and the board's approval. She further informed me with no small amount of bitterness that she did not like Rev. Lambe or ministers in general, and she did not like me. She stated with a certain confidence, and air of authority, that I would be treated the same way that Harold Lambe was treated.

I asked her why she was so angry with pastors, and she reluctantly told me of her experience.

"I came to Harold Lambe with domestic problems with my husband. Lambe didn't listen to me. He took my husband's side, told me I was wrong and gave me some Scriptures to read. We're divorced now and I am still angry about that," she said.

"That is unfortunate and I would like to sit down with you and talk about it." I told her. "I don't want to talk to you or anyone about it." I felt such pain emanating from her, and my heart went out to her. But I also felt a need to say, "That is your choice. However, you will find out that I am not Harold Lambe, and I will not be treated the way you treated him."

I relied heavily on my business experience and my ability to work with people, but I did not know how to handle the trustee. I asked myself, "Am I going to be God's man or the trustee's man?" The answers came quickly. I had no choice but to stand the oncoming assaults and seek God's wisdom and presence in every decision or undertaking. I had to assume leadership under God in spite of resident opposition; however, I believed I held one advantage. In my five years as associate pastor, I had come to know the people of Pleasant Street, but they really didn't know me. I was later to find out how wrong I was. I didn't know them at all. During this time the words came to mind,

> "Be careful! Watch out for attacks from the Devil, your great enemy. He prowls around like a roaring lion, looking for some victim to devour. Take a firm stand against him and be strong in your faith." [1Peter 5:8, 9]

I did not realize at the time how true these words were, nor did I realize my only comfort would be found in the words of the Apostle James:

> "So humble yourselves before God. Resist the Devil, and he will flee from you. Draw close to God, and God will draw close to you." [4:7, 8]

Through An Opaque Lens

During my first five years as pastor at Pleasant Street, I was constantly under attack because the vision demanded change: It challenged the leadership of the trustees; it threatened to break down strongholds that had existed for over a half-century, and it called the church to halt the downward spiral toward the yawning abyss of extinction. I was called on the carpet many times by the trustees for minor incidents, some real and some fabricated. Among other things I was once accused of embezzling funds which I never even had access to. I was accused of falsifying my own personal medical spending accounts, and one trustee had a complaint that was raised at every meeting: "The pastor is making too much money." I was at then at the 70th percentile of ministerial salaries. The physical consequence of these charges seemed miniscule when compared with the pain I was soon to undergo. My naiveté and trust make me incapable of anticipating what was to happen in the summer of 1992. Merely reflecting on it still brings tears to my eyes. It was a devastating betrayal by the church secretary who secretly taped my counseling sessions over the office intercom. She shared the tapes with trustees, deacons and other members of the church. The tapes were to be used as evidence of my alleged indiscretions with a female member of the church. The accusations were false and unfounded, yet they caused some people to question my integrity. In trying to hurt me she placed another person in great danger of bodily harm or worse. This incident and many others caused moments of such great stress that I would at times sit in a recliner at home from dawn to dusk, only leaving the comfort of my chair to go to the bathroom.

I made an appointment with my doctor hoping to get some medication to ease my distress. My doctor refused to give me any medication because it would only mask the problem. He said, "It's up to you to remove the cause of the tension, otherwise it will kill you." On December 11, 1994, I tendered a letter of resignation to Pleasant Street Baptist Church effective January 15, 1995. "The primary reason for my decision is the deliberate, continued, hindering of the ministry, personal attacks on me, and concern for my physical and emotional health. Each incident has been a distraction from the ministry and required enormous amounts of attention, time, and energy. These most recent accusations have brought me to a point of severe stress, and I have been advised by my physician that unless the cause of the tension is removed, it could result in serious injury to my health; so after much reflection, deliberation, and prayer, I have arrived at a decision which I believe to be best for me, my family and the future of Pleasant Street Baptist Church."

On January 15, after I had concluded what I thought to be my final sermon, a group of people entered the fellowship hall adjoining the sanctuary. A young woman, the mother of six children, stood up in the midst of the forty-nine people present and said. "Wait a minute, Pastor is not leaving, these other guys are leaving." She called for a vote on the spot and forty-four people voted for me to stay. Four said I should go.

One left the fellowship hall in a rage, slamming the door hard enough to shake the building, cursing all the way.

When I tried to quit the ministry because of failing health, God stopped me and reminded me of the vision. He promised He would not fail me. It was not time for me to give up. Five days later on January 20, I stated in a letter to the congregation: "What is at stake is the future of Pleasant Street, for you, as members, must decide what kind of ministry you want, what kind of church you want to be, and whether you are now willing and committed enough to confront and take necessary action to ensure a vibrant life, growth, and mission of this church."

Back in November of 1988, I had drawn up and published an organizational ministry chart for the vision. I took several sheets of newsprint and taped it to the far wall of the fellowship hall of the church. The plan called for the removal of the Board of Trustees from its position as the single most powerful board in the administration of the church, and established working boards of Missions, Evangelism, Deacons and Christian Education to administer the "Vision of Ministry" for Pleasant Street Baptist Church. The ministries included outreach, home missions, ministry to disadvantaged, door to door, friendship evangelism, bus ministry, youth and adults, new life orientation for new members, care team ministry for shut-ins and delinquent members, educational ministries, and ministry to sick that included the sending of cards and flowers. This was only the beginning; activities in the following years added many other ministries to the church.

The more I talked about the vision and the various ministries of the church, the more people were sure it was my own personal agenda. However, before too long, the church and community were to see that God had given me eyes to see far beyond what others were able to envision. In the ensuing years, I worked very hard to make the vision come to fruition. I expounded on it at every opportunity. I kept it in front of the congregation, and when people did not respond quickly enough, I scolded them for not trusting the Lord enough. I was so intent on getting people to see the vision I began to use tactics which became burdensome and drove people further away. I was quick to make them feel guilty, pointing out their stubbornness and inability to see. This caused more opposition and inadvertently led to anger, frustration, disappointment and isolation between myself and some people. In its wake, I was about to learn a most valuable lesson. If God truly gives a vision only God can fulfill it. In my eagerness to see results, I had missed this most critical element.

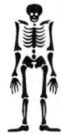

Vision Manifest...

"So one night the King of Aram sent a great army with many chariots and horses to surround the city. When the servant of the man of God got up early the next morning and went outside, there were troops, horses, and chariots everywhere. 'Ah, my Lord, what will we do now?' he cried out to Elisha.

'Don't be afraid!' Elisha told him. 'For there are more on our side than on theirs!'

Then Elisha prayed. 'O Lord, open his eyes and let him see!' The Lord opened his servant's eyes, and when he looked up, he saw that the hillside around Elisha was filled with horses and chariots of fire."

2 Kings 6: 14-17

CHAPTER FOURTEEN

A Meeting of the Heart

"I will put my laws in their minds so they will understand them, and I will write them on their hearts so they will obey them. I will be their god, and they will be my people."
Hebrews 8:10

"It is not the critic who counts; not the man who points out how the strong man stumbles, or where the doer of deeds could have done them better. The credit belongs to the man who is actually in the arena; whose face is marred by dust and sweat and blood; who strives valiantly; who errs and comes short again and again; because there is not effort without error and shortcomings; but who does actually strive to do the deed; who knows the great enthusiasm, the great devotion, who spends himself in a worthy cause; who at the best knows in the end the triumph of high achievement; and who at the worst, if he fails, at least fails while daring greatly. So that his place shall never be with those cold and timid souls who know neither victory nor defeat."

This quote by Theodore Roosevelt at first glance appears to offer great encouragement and much merit to the combatant; however, to the man of God it brings forth criticism, for it is, indeed, the critic who counts no matter how we try. Surely, the credit belongs to God not to men. The writer states [Hebrews 12:5, 6]

"And have you entirely forgotten the encouraging words God spoke to you, his children? He said, 'My child, don't ignore it when the Lord disciplines you, and don't be discouraged when he corrects you.

For the Lord disciplines those he loves, and he punishes those he accepts as his children."

Many times I have been disciplined by God, but during those times of correction I have never felt more loved by Him. From the moment I saw the vision inscribed on the wall of my living room I knew in my heart that to carry out God's commission would require every bit of my knowledge, experience, and wisdom. I envisaged myself behind tinted glasses filtering out all competing rays until the object of God's heart became clear, and the mission field came into view. Since I had enjoyed a measure of success in life, I was confident that my many years of experience coupled with my deepening desire to know the Lord more intimately would be sufficient for the task ahead.

I have since learned that when one answers God's call two converging certainties, one temporal and one eternal, must remain forever linked. God! I am not able and Christ is Lord. How often I thought of Moses' response to God when he was directed to go to Pharoah for release of the captive Israelites. Moses queried the Lord, *"But who am I to appear before Pharoah?* God responded, *"I will be with you."* [Exodus 11a, 12a] Moses then knew his insufficiency would be overshadowed by God's sufficiency.

Calvin Miller in his book, *The Unchained Soul,* speaking of Christ determines, "Those who wish to be conformed to His image only make real progress after they discover their own insufficiency. We are converted the very moment we admit that our own management of life is inadequate. We need to be forgiven and filled with Christ. Does not our greatest need teach us we are altogether incapable?" God simply asks us to link our impotence with his omnipotence and drop the words "I can" from our vocabularies.

The visible manifestation of the ministry for Pleasant Street Baptist Church came alive when I learned this most essential lesson. I was consumed by the vision. The vision was embedded in my heart. It was so much a part of me that every thought, every action, every plan was centered on fulfilling the divine image that appeared to me. My thought was that I could bring it to fruition; however, I had failed to acknowledge or understand my inadequacy and the necessity of God's sufficiency in its implementation.

I am still taken aback by the prophet Isaiah's great Temple vision found in [6:1ff.]When Isaiah saw the Lord sitting on the throne of the Temple, the lofty view of God's Holiness reflected the prophet's own depravity and sinfulness and great need for forgiveness. His view of God stripped him of all hope of measuring up to God's standard. When the Lord asked, "*Who will go for us?*" the prophet humbly assented out of the depths of his emptiness "*I'll go! Send me.*" The vision of "The Lord Almighty" made Isaiah realize that the same God who in the beginning created everything out of nothing would once again be called to create him anew for the work he was being called to.

While living in Providence, I often watched a Christian television program which I found to be encouraging and enlightening, and I deemed it to be biblically sound. More importantly, I found the program had much in common with the vision of ministry God had earlier afforded me. This program, which originated in Fort Worth, Texas, was hosted by a man named James Robison. James was a man of humble beginnings. Adopted by a wonderful Christian pastor as a child, he found the Lord in adulthood. He, his wife Betty, and their family founded and produced this well-rounded program containing Bible studies, music and guests who were, it seemed to me, "theologically sound". I truly admired James Robison's honesty, frankness, deep humility, compassion and his outpouring of grace upon the many lost and disenfranchised people who were in need of healing but were rejected by elite churches. Not only that, I was even more impressed by the fact James Robison changed the thrust of his outreach to become a support ministry to raise funds for starving children in Africa, Angola, Romania and other parts of the world. I trusted James Robison's ministry and I sent several donations to buy high protein beans to make nutritious soup for these children. For $10, these missionaries could feed one child for six months. Granted it wasn't steak and eggs, but to these kids it seemed like it.

One morning as I was getting dressed to go to work, the television was tuned to James Robison's television program, *Life Outreach International.* I was tying my necktie when in the background I heard words coming from James which literally stopped me in my tracks. James said, "I have a confession to make. God spoke to me this morning and admonished me about a vision of ministry He had given to me for the church." James continued, "I tried many times, in many different ways, to make the vision work, but I found nothing but frustration and loneliness and isolation. I even got angry at folk, for not reacting to it."

At this point I sat down, no longer interested in my tie, I was drawn to that television screen as if by a magnet. My ears were wide open not wanting to miss a single word of what James was saying. I was transfixed. I could not have moved if I wanted to. I knew the impending words were for me. It seemed that every word James spoke was what I was presently experiencing. I was hanging on every word and what I heard was life changing. James said, "God told me to stop what I was doing." God said: "I gave you a vision for your people. It is not your vision, it is mine. I did not tell you to make it happen. I did not tell you to push people around, or manipulate them, or embarrass them, beat on them or make them feel guilty. I did not give the vision for you, nor did I ask you to fulfill it. It is My vision and I will bring it to fruition in My time. All I asked you to do is get people to hear My voice. I will put the vision in their hearts. I will draw them to me."

I was so affected by what I heard I began to cry and the tears flowed uncontrollably. My eyes were red, my face and cheeks were wet from the intense flow of tears, my heart was palpitating wildly. I fell to my knees and began to pray. I asked God for His forgiveness and for those I had wounded. I saw a picture of myself and I was convicted. There was no question in my heart God had used James to discipline me. I had done all of the things James cited, and now I could understand why the vision was not being fulfilled. God spoke through James Robison in a wonderful way to chasten me and remind me that I was trying to do what was not mine to do. Changing hearts is the purview of God alone. From that moment on, I vowed to never again interfere with the implementation of the vision. I promised myself I would preach and teach a pure simple, powerful, Spirit-filled gospel whenever and wherever God gave me opportunity. I had been given a clear mandate for my role in the vision. I now knew what God expected of me, and more important, I had the assurance of what I could expect from God. A burden had been lifted from my shoulders. My whole insides were still trembling, but now in anticipation of what God was about to do. I vowed from that moment, to stand in faith and watch God work miracles in Westerly. God was about to bring into view those things I had hoped for and tried to create. The vision was about to explode onto Westerly.

Awakened To Vision

In the fall of 1986, I requested that the church buy a fifteen-passenger van to transport people from Providence to Westerly. As might be expected, my request was met with varying reactions, mostly negative. Some of the trustees were infuriated because they thought I was confronting them to test their authority. Some people felt vulnerable because they were comfortable and wanted things to stay as they were, and then some members were noncommittal, not caring one way or the other. In January of 1987, a special meeting was called to discuss the possible purchase of a van for the church outreach ministries. Some insisted there were no monies to draw from. Others asked, "How can we even consider a van for the church? Why do we need a van anyway? What about service? What about maintenance? How will we pay for it?" Again, I felt the anger of many of the trustees. I reminded them of their obligation of ministry, not survival. I shared ideas with them about usage. Sunday school, choir needs, congregational needs for those without transportation, outreach ministry to Providence.

"This is not about money, it is about faith. It is about trusting God for the results. God is faithful," I told them. I talked about the vision that God was already growing. I noted the new people who were starting to attend church. I was fully aware that it had been many years since the church had been asked to move out of its comfort zone, many years since they were challenged to do the ministry the church had been called to do. Finally, after some heated argument, there was a decided shift in the tone of the meeting, and a few days later, on January 16, 1987, Pleasant Street Baptist Church took its first step in implementing the "vision of ministry" by voting to purchase its first church van. It was a used van discarded by the local YMCA, but it was a beginning—and it was still warm.

Not long after, in early 1988, it became apparent that another van would be needed to transport people from the Groton and New London, Connecticut areas. A relatively new church member named Carolyn Ramseur, who lived in Groton, was proving to be a one-woman outreach ministry in her area. God had placed the vision in her heart, and everywhere she went she would talk to people about Pleasant Street Baptist Church. No one was safe from her witness of Jesus Christ. Carolyn Ramseur witnessed to people in every conceivable place; however, her favorite place of ministry proved to be the public malls. She wanted to be sure that if folk, were shopping they knew what to shop for. The church repeated the same arguments they did with the first request of a van, but now the results were in and opponents had little ammunition left to block a van traveling to Groton and New London. By the end of 1989, it was obvious God's plan was to grow his church through outreach, and the van ministry was instrumental in the early growth of the church.

Confirmation

To say the least, I was buoyed by what was happening at Pleasant Street. However, I must confess I really did not know what to make of the vision. Not having done it before, how could I stay out of God's way? How would the vision be implemented? How was I to begin to grow these new converts to the Lord? What did God want for His church at Westerly? I had many questions but few answers. I was moved by the purposeful and powerful stirring of God's Spirit and the outpouring of grace upon people. What was astonishing was the fact that some of those who had remained unmoved in the church for a very long time were resurrected. Surely God already knew my heart. He had heard the uncertainty in my voice and the fervor in my prayer. The answers and confirmation I sought had already been forwarded to Westerly by divine mail, and it was about to arrive in the most unexpected way.

Confirmation of the vision was to come through a man named Bob Alessio, who assured me in spite of my previous doubts that I was in the place God wanted me to be. Bob was one of the first persons I met in entering the Christian community in Westerly. Bob is a joyful, dynamic Christian man who radiates such a presence of Jesus that it is impossible to ignore him. Bob wears a smile which stretches from ear to ear, and his love and excitement and zeal for the Lord are all-consuming. He is a unique individual, not only because of his great love for Scripture but in the fact that he lives what he professes. I always thought Bob should be featured in *Readers Digest* as a most unforgettable character I have ever met. I recently asked Bob how we met, and his answer was similar to mine, "I don't remember, we just met."

In those early days, Bob was a communicant of St. Clares, a Roman Catholic Church in the Misquamicut section of Westerly. The fact that I was a Baptist minister and Bob was a deacon in the Catholic Church made little or no difference to our relationship; we trusted and respected each other and were both hungry for the Word of God. We permitted no barriers of any kind, secular or religious, to come between us. Bob heard about the Wednesday evening Bible study I conducted in the church. To my delight, he started to attend. When asked what drew him, Bob once said, "When I first started coming to Bible study at the church, I didn't know Josh very well, but the way he articulated his understanding of the church was powerful and it kept me coming back." At one point, Bob and I joined together in leading a group called "Finding New Life In The Spirit" seminars, which had originated in the Catholic Church at the height of the Charismatic Movement. I was familiar with the seminars, so I welcomed the opportunity to introduce them to our church.

I will never forget the night Bob rushed into the Bible Study breathless and excited. Father Jake Randall, pastor of St. Patrick's Roman Catholic Church, Providence, had contacted Bob and suggested he pray about starting a prayer group in the Westerly area. A woman in St. Patrick's shared a prophecy with Father Randall. She revealed that while in prayer the Lord spoke to her heart that the most southern points in Rhode Island would become a powerful witness to the Lord. Bob was aware of the "vision of ministry". He had witnessed God working in the hearts of people in Westerly, and the word he heard excited him. That night he shared with me and others what he had heard. He was excited because his immediate thought was, "It is happening at Pleasant Street." His heart was thrilled and ecstatic that God was confirming His vision for Westerly. Bob said that when he prayed about starting a prayer group in Westerly a word came to him from the Lord, *"Lift up your heads, O you gates: be lifted up, you ancient doors that the King of glory may come in."* [Psalm 24:7 NIV] Bob said, "I needed affirmation so I came to Josh, and through him God gave confirmation."

I love and respect this wonderful Christian man, and to this day, Bob remains a very honored and trusted friend. He has been and continues to be a bright light of encouragement for our ministry in Westerly, and his belief in the vision has never wavered. "If a vision is true it has to be anointed," Bob said.

And indeed the vision given to me for Westerly is true. Bob Alessio surely is confirmation of that fact.

Divine Response

My partiality toward James Robison led me to attend a Bible conference sponsored in the Dallas-Fort Worth area in February of 1990. It was the first time I had attended a James Robison Bible Conference. I was looking forward to it because of my previous experience with James and also because I had some specific needs to place before the Lord. I enjoyed the worship and singing and the anointed speakers James Robison attracted, and I hoped to have an opportunity to meet him personally. As I checked into the Red Roof Inn late that Tuesday afternoon, I was excited. I felt somewhat anxious but expectant, hoping that God would answer two specific prayers I had jotted down and brought with me from Westerly. Lately I had been feeling a greater need for prayer, more so than ever before. I wanted to understand how to lead my people to greater intimacy with the Lord. I wanted to know how to help them grow stronger, so I asked God to provide me with a prayer partner during my time at the conference. My other request was for direction and insight into the vision for the people at Pleasant Street. One of the main speakers at the conference was a man named Malcolm Smith, an author and teacher on how pastors might avoid spiritual burnout. I had heard much about Malcolm's insights into the word of God, and I was anxious to see him. About six that evening, after I unpacked, I decided to go downstairs to have dinner. I was feeling a little lonely and apprehensive about the proceedings the next morning. I didn't know anyone at the hotel, so I sat over near the low rail that afforded me a view of people who were checking into the hotel.

I was roused from my reverie by the sight of two men who entered the dining area and seated themselves at a table far across the room. Barely had they sat down when they looked my way. They sat for what seemed like only a moment, then both of the men got up from the table carrying their trays, and before I realized it they were standing in front of me with trays in hand. One of the men asked, "Are you alone?" "Yes," I answered with some reluctance. "May we sit down?" he asked.

After they sat down, they introduced themselves. They told me they were from Freeport in the Bahamas, and this was also their first Bible conference.

The next words spoken by one of the men caused my eyes to well up with tears and made my heart leap with joy, for I knew God had heard my prayers. The man said, "We have been praying since we left home that God would provide us with a prayer partner when we arrived here. Would you like to pray with us?" After our meeting we met each morning from 5:30 A. M. until 6:30 A. M. My two new Christian friends and I spent much time on our knees in the presence of the Lord seeking His will for our lives. My first request had been answered, and it was a harbinger of more. How like God! –and He was not finished yet. Friday night marked the end of the conference and all of the conferees had been warned to be in their seats before 7 P.M. or they would have difficulty finding places. That night

The Dallas Convention Center was filled to near capacity. I usually like to sit closer to the podium but when I arrived, the auditorium was already quite full. Therefore, I was pleased to find a vacant seat in the third row, far to the right of the stage. After sitting and waiting for about twenty minutes, I was feeling quite alone because I could not locate my two prayer partners. I happened to glance down in front, and I noticed a woman in the first row holding a folded piece of white paper in her hand. She turned and motioned to the woman behind her and leaned back whispering something to her. Then she placed the paper in the woman's hand. I turned away for a moment trying to appear disinterested, until I heard the words "This is for him." I was unaware of who "him" was until the woman now holding the paper reached behind and held the paper out for me to take. I heard my self ask, "For me? Are you sure?" I was mystified, for I didn't see who gave the note to the woman in the first row. I took the paper from the woman, still believing a mistake had been made. However, the moment my eyes fell upon the few words contained within, I knew it was for me. It was an answer from God, simple and to the point, "I have heard your prayers for your people, and you will have an answer."

Once more, God confirmed his vision to me. He would supply the necessary direction in His time. I then recalled the words of Malcolm Smith that very morning; "Faith is a response inside of you to God's promise. Real faith does work. Faith causes God to intervene in situations, when we believe, God works. Faith comes directly out of the heart of God." There was no question that what I experienced in Dallas was the result of a living faith. Is faith not, *"the confident assurance that what we hope for is going to happen."* is it not, *"the evidence of things we cannot see?"* [Hebrews 11:1]:

After returning home, I wrote in my pastor's report of April 20, "Upon leaving Westerly for the Bible conference, I realized we were at a transition point. Because of the many changes in our church, I had some very specific prayers to place before God, most important of which was for divine direction for us for the next several years. God responded in a wonderful way, and I am still sorting out the answers, but what was most revealing was the answer that God has anointed this church, and He will give increase to the vision as we are faithful to what He has already given us. I believe His clear statement to me was, 'I will build My church – and He is doing just that. I see many exciting things in our future such as building expansion with plenty of parking. I see expanded youth ministries, singles ministries, handicapped ministries, senior citizens and elderly ministries; an expanded music ministry including our young people, a renewed thrust towards evangelism, and outreach and a heightened awareness of the Holy Spirit's empowering presence in this body for witnessing and healing of the whole person, body and soul. I do not believe we will have to wait long, for the future is now upon us. Further, I am well aware this can only happen if you, as a body of believers at Pleasant Street, grasp God's vision and make it your own." God had answered my prayers. He opened my eyes to a vision of His heart far beyond what He had enabled others to see. The unfolding of the vision was not far behind.

CHAPTER FIFTEEN

Miracle in Our Midst

"God publicly endorsed Jesus of Nazareth by doing wonderful miracles, wonders, and signs through him, as you well know."
Acts 2:22

In 1986, Billy Graham wrote a book about angels. In it, he recounts a most amazing story about John Paton a missionary in the New Hebrides Islands. One night, the warriors from one of the local tribes surrounded the mission headquarters, intending to burn the Patons out and kill them. As you can imagine, John Paton and his wife were terrified and prayed all through the night that God would save them. When daylight came they were astonished to see the warriors leave without attacking them.

A year later, the chief of the tribe became a Christian. During the course of their conversations John Paton asked the chief about that night. What had kept the warriors from burning down the house and killing them? The chief asked, "Who were all those men you had there with you?" Paton replied, "There was no one other than my wife and I."

The chief told Paton that he and his warriors had seen hundreds of men standing guard around the mission headquarters, men with shining garments and holding drawn swords.

A miracle? What are we to believe? Do we question whether miracles exist today? Do we ask as did Gideon in the book of Judges? *"And where are all the miracles our ancestors told us about?"* [6:13] Surely, miracles are rare. That is why we call them miracles. Yet, are they rare because like the spotted owl, they are an endangered species, or are they rare because finding people who have faith and who are willing to participate in a miracle are rare? Receiving a miracle is dependent on us putting things in God's hands. When we keep things in our own hands, the outcome is predictable; when we put things in God's hands, who knows what can happen? ... Maybe miracles. Yet, it is more than putting things in God's hand; it is putting ourselves in His hands.

Miracles

In 1972 my son Wesley, then 13, was out riding his new bicycle with a friend. It was about 6:30 in the evening when he was struck by an automobile just after leaving the neighborhood playground. The collision threw him against the windshield of the car and then propelled him several feet into the air. On the way down he struck the car again before he landed on the ground. The bike was found a distance away twisted like a pretzel and hardly recognizable: the front and hood of the car was dented and its windshield so shattered that it could not be driven. When the ambulance arrived to transport Wesley to St. Joseph's Hospital in Providence, the driver looking at the condition of his car remarked, "You are lucky to be alive." At the time of the accident I was in a prayer meeting at Pond Street Baptist Church, Providence. When word came to me that my son was hit by a car and was in the hospital, I simply said, "I will be there." I felt no compulsion to rush to the hospital at that moment, because in my heart I had an assurance that he would be all right. When I arrived at the hospital later, I found Wesley sitting up on the bed smiling and talking, and I was told by the nurse he had no cuts or physical injuries. I later learned there was not even a drop of blood found at the accident scene. As Wesley related the details of the accident, I knew why he was able to walk away from almost certain death, and I also knew why the assurance in my heart. "I spotted the car just before it hit me and I knew I was in trouble, so all I could say was, 'Lord, save me.' For an instant I saw a bright light, and then I felt as if I was floating on air. God answered my prayer," he said. The face of the driver of the car registered utter disbelief when Wesley got up from the ground. He said, "I thought I had killed that kid." Wesley left the hospital that night with a slight fracture of his left foot.

More recently in September of 2002, during Sunday prayer time a woman in our church recited her deep concern over a suspected growth in her stomach. The woman, a Native American mother of seven and grandmother of twenty-three, had been a member of Pleasant Baptist Street Church for around fourteen years. She readily confessed she knew far less about the Bible than she would have liked, but at the same time she passionately held to an unwavering faith in Jesus Christ's death on the cross, noting Peter's words [1 Peter 2:24b] *"You have been healed by his wounds!"* This woman had been experiencing a burning sensation in her stomach so she went to see a gastroenterologist. She went to the Lawrence and Memorial Hospital in New London, Connecticut, for tests; three sets of x-rays were taken, along with an ultrasound of her stomach. After the tests her doctor confirmed there was a dark spot about the size of a half-dollar visible in the stomach area. He suspected it might be a tumor, and he made an appointment for the following Monday to give her his final determination. She called her family together to inform them of the doctor's findings and to seek their comfort and support before returning to the hospital. Members of her family were concerned because they feared the worst that the suspected growth might be cancerous and malignant. When the woman reported the doctor's suspicions to our congregation that morning I decided her condition warranted that the entire church body pray specifically for the removal of the growth in her stomach. Somehow I sensed that God would answer this particular request. And He did. When she returned to the hospital the following Monday morning, a further x-ray found nothing; the dark spot had disappeared. Yet the previous x-rays prove there had been something there.

On August 29, 2005, Hurricane Katrina smashed into the Gulf Coast leaving a heavy loss of life in its wake. There was great devastation of homes and property and massive flooding in Louisiana, Mississippi, and Alabama. Pastor Alan Jenkins of the First Missionary Baptist Church, Bay St. Louis, Mississippi, tells his story: While surging storm waters deluged a house not 20 feet away and 18 inches higher, not a drop of water crossed the threshold of the church. A miracle? Jenkins says, "It's a miracle, that's for sure." One church leader had been previously heard to say, "I'm looking for a miracle, I expect the impossible, I feel the intangible, I see the invisible." Isn't that what miracles are made of?

Could the prelude to miracles simply be to know the God who comes to us in time of need? Does our expectation for miracles not coincide with the magnitude and relevance of our God?

Webster's *New World Dictionary*, Third College Edition, defines miracle as "1. An event or action that apparently contradicts known scientific laws and is hence thought to be due to supernatural causes; an act of God. 2. A remarkable event or thing; marvel." In simple terms, I take that to mean: A miracle is an event or action that is totally amazing, extraordinary, or unexpected. Is that why when we see a miracle unfold before our very eyes we want to be sure some credible witness affirms the whole thing happened? Can we not trust our own eyes? Can we not trust the God of miracles, or are we so dubious because we have so domesticated our Lord that He is incapable of doing more than showing up at Sunday school? Once the mystery of God is removed from miracles, what is left to believe, since in each miracle there is mystery? Even so, I firmly believe the vision of ministry God ordained for Pleasant Street is a miracle. What will you believe?

Calvin Miller is a professor of preaching and pastoral ministries at Beeson Divinity School at Samford University, Birmingham, Alabama. He is author of more than thirty books, including the classic, *The Singer Trilogy*, an allegory of the life of Christ, and recently he completed a new book entitled, *Miracles and Wonders*. Miller states: "It has been said by many researchers that ninety percent of Americans believe in God and eighty percent believe in miracles. Why? It would seem we are in need of a God who is bigger than we are. We need a God behind us who can take our hopeless situations and fill them once again with hope. We want to be mystified and enthralled by a God whose every movement is larger than our problems. Give us no weak God who wants to avoid our predicament. Give us instead a God who does wonderful and impossible things—real things—miracles! We want a "pro-me" God who can—If need be—set science and logic to one side and act above such rational confines."

He further says, "Logic is the foundation of knowledge but miracles are the foundation of faith. Only when a dead man lives again is there any point in believing." That being the case, is there a greater miracle than the new birth? Is conversion not the grandest miracle of all. I personally know this miracle. I have experienced this miracle. It means I have arrived at a new and glorious sense of my significance. I have come to know who I am and why I was created in the first place.

Since miracles are the foundation of faith, isn't Miller saying that we can only believe them by faith? And since we are the greatest miracle of all, we can rightly believe miracles indeed exist today. The vision of ministry at Pleasant Street Baptist Church confronts all of the above queries, and challenges modern Christianity to ascertain why the church today is so pregnant with empty hope, rather than faith in what God can do. In the midst of admitted church decline and stagnation, the growth of the church and ministry at Pleasant Street Baptist Church is a modern miracle and belies the notion that miracles are no more.

More Miracles, Wonders, And Signs ... The Vision

Many things at Pleasant Street are indeed amazing, extraordinary, and unexpected. The fact that God would look to the southernmost town in the state of Rhode Island and select one of His smallest churches with few assets and diminishing resources, and use them to glorify Him is in itself a miracle. The fact that God would prepare me, a most unlikely, unsuspecting man for forty-five years before sharing his vision for Westerly with me is *simply extraordinary*. The fact that I would possess God given skills to fashion a communion table of wood as a memorial, and this table would be the only survivor of a devastating church fire, and some 27 years later I would serve the Lord's Supper at this very table—coincidence. Or a miracle?

Was it not *totally unexpected* that this small church unveiled the largest hands-on outreach ministry in Westerly? Was it not a miracle that this little church in Westerly, with little money or resources, came to acquire five houses resting on almost two acres of land in support of God's vision? Was it not amazing that God called and is calling people from all walks of life with varied talents to support this *"vision of ministry"*. The things God has provided for this little church in Westerly is in itself *extraordinary*, but the miracle is not about what God has done, as much as it is about who God is and who He reveals himself to be. God has made Himself available to this little church in Westerly because the people realized early on all they have is God, and that in itself is enough.

After acquiring vans for our outreach ministry, we would ride about the neighborhoods of Westerly on Saturday mornings passing out brochures and tracts, introducing the ministry and sharing the Gospel of Jesus Christ. There were few noticeable results, but seeds were planted in remote places in Westerly. Not long after, we began Bible studies in the church and in homes, and slowly but surely people started to respond.

On a Wednesday evening in the summer of 1995, a middle-aged couple came to our Bible study and prayer meeting. They mentioned they had a summer home in Charlestown a seaside community bordering Westerly, and had inquired where they could find a church that was alive and active in ministry. They were directed to Pleasant Street Baptist Church by someone from a large local Episcopal church. After their initial visit to Pleasant Street, they made the decision to go back to Pittsburgh, sell their home and move into their residence in Charlestown to be near their new church family. Enter Bill and Joan Ewart.

God's promise to place His vision in the hearts of people was confirmed in the Ewarts, as they confessed that God prompted them to be a part of the vision of ministry at Pleasant Street. During plans for our next stages of the growth of the ministry, Bill and Joan immediately got down to work. Bill was a very distinguished looking man, tall with a shock of white hair, an avid tennis player, caring and fiercely loyal to the work of the Lord. Joan, on the other hand, was slight, insightful, intuitive, and a deeply spiritual person. She was an organizer, and a woman who listened intently for that still small voice. Joan was acting coordinator of RI for the Lydia Fellowship International Ministries, a women's prayer fellowship, trans-denominational and international, begun in England in 1970. Joan volunteered to become chairman of our building committee and later became Sunday school superintendent. Bill, a former executive in the steel business, became chairman of the board of trustees and a Sunday school teacher. Bill and Joan quickly became proponents of the vision of ministry at Pleasant Street. During their tenure at the church, a plan was developed which included renovations to the present church facility to support an expanded congregation and increased outreach ministry to the community. An alternative Christian school and day care facility were also to be added to the ministry complex, as well as ample off street parking, a school yard and ministerial housing. It was a good plan; however, there was one huge problem. The church had no money and meager resources. In most circles this would be a sure combination for despair and defeat, however, Pleasant Street had the equalizer—it had a vision and the surety of God's promise.

By May of 1996, members of the church had heard enough about the vision because God had been confirming the vision in their hearts. They weren't quite sure what it all meant, but they were willing to try God to see where He would lead. It became apparent that it was time for us to see if people were ready to undertake the next step of setting up a fund raising campaign. Under the leadership of Bill Ewart we called in a professional fund raising consultant to do a preliminary evaluation of our potential as a church. After some research and several recommendations we chose Franklyn Cook, of Fund Consultants, Lincoln, Rhode Island. Frank Cook was a Christian and very familiar with raising money for larger churches. He came to our church and found it to be quite different than he had imagined. He first researched the members of our congregation. He noted the small numbers of potential givers, the fact that many of the members were from Providence, Groton, and New London, and few were from stable two parent families.

He later admitted his initial conclusion was there was no way this church would be able to begin a capital funds campaign. All members of the church were subsequently invited to meet with Frank to do the preliminary evaluation.

On May 16, Frank and sixteen members of the Pleasant Street Baptist Church gathered in the fellowship hall of the church to find out if this, indeed, was a vision ordained by God. I opened the meeting that night by reviewing the vision and what I had heard in my heart from God. Then Frank explained his process and what he was looking for to help him arrive at a decision of our chances for success. People were asked to put on paper what they would commit to the vision over a five year period. When the papers were collected, tabulated and handed to Frank his countenance took on a strange look. He hesitated for a moment, and then slowly and haltingly without taking his eyes off the tally sheet said. "I can't quite believe this." Based on what Frank Cook now saw on paper he said, "You have pledged over $90,000. I would encourage you to not delay any longer."

One year later in May of 1997, fifty-one giving units in the church pledged $250,000 toward the vision of ministry, the money to be due on or before May of 2002. A miracle at Pleasant Street Baptist Church had now become sight. Our God-given vision had become real for all to see. We could now move forward with the vision.

The first property purchased, at 31 Pleasant Street, now borders the east side of our ministry complex. This house was acquired in February of 1998. It has two large apartments with three bedrooms and bath, and serves as the church parsonage. What was significant about this purchase was that previously, upon sharing the vision in Westerly, I was told it would be near impossible to buy property in the neighborhood. Most of the properties were longstanding Italian family homesteads and the residents had kept the property in the family for generations, and it was expected they would continue to do so.

Early one morning in the fall of 1997, I was standing near the front of the ramp alongside the church when I was approached by an elderly Italian man, who asked in heavily accented English: "Are you the Father?" At first I didn't know how to respond because I had never been addressed as "the Father".

Then it occurred to me that since this was a very heavy Catholic area; most people looked on ministers as they did priests, so the name Father was plausible. I regained my composure, and then answered the man. "Yes, I am the Father." The man's next words brought joy and thanksgiving to my heart, "Would you like to buy my house?" I thought to myself, "God is faithful." And on that day, the land and buildings needed to support the vision of ministry had now become sight. *"What is faith? It is the confident assurance that what we hope for is going to happen. It is the evidence of things we cannot see."* [Hebrews 11:1] The man standing before me was the evidence of faith.

Approximately one year later in early 1999, a house at 33 ½ Pleasant St. was purchased by Bill and Joan Ewart. Since the church did not have available funds, the Ewarts decided they would own the property to provide space for living quarters for staff and family. The church could later purchase the property when funds allowed. Next door to the church, at 35 Pleasant Street, the piece of property once owned by the church became available for purchase. The owners were leaving town to live in Florida and could not be responsible for maintaining a four unit complex in Westerly. The building could be used for families in crisis and for expansion of the church ministries. The ministry was growing and there would be a need for additional land space. In late 1999, the church once again became the owner of the property at 35 Pleasant Street—at a considerably higher price than it was earlier sold for. It brought to mind the words of Solomon *"Where there is no vision, the people perish.*" Repurchasing the house was symbolic of the church now having the blinders removed from its eyes and being snatched back from the brink of disaster.

By the year 2000, plans for the ministry complex had begun to take shape, and it was determined the educational piece would feature a fully accredited Christian school, kindergarten through grade 8. There would also be a pre-school to prepare children for kindergarten. To do this, two more pieces of property would be needed: 33 Pleasant Street, the key property joining 31 and 35, and 31½ Pleasant St, which would serve as our pre-school. These properties would complete the west and north boundaries of the ministry complex. Together they totaled approximately 1. 8 acres of land in a place where many thought it to be impossible to acquire any land. Up to this point I had not expected to solicit any of the owners of the acquired properties. God had said "I will place the vision in their hearts." If God wanted us to have these last two pieces, He would have to touch the heart of these owners and direct them to sell to the church.

I prayed much about what to do next, seeking God's direction in the upcoming process. Soon the answer came just as clear and decisively as at any time before. Thirty-three Pleasant Street appeared to be the biggest problem because it was a necessary piece of property, and the owners had recently said they had no interest in selling. In fact, they told our real estate agent they would not entertain an offer to purchase their property. Fortunately, I was not listening to them but to God, who in turn told me how to acquire the property for the ministry. The family was caring for an 84 year-old aunt, who had lived in the house most of her life. They feared for her health if they even suggested she move elsewhere.

Our real estate agent had recently spoken to the woman's nephew, and he was adamant about not dislodging his aunt. Yet at the same time, God was speaking to me, telling me to make them an offer for the house and land with the stipulation their aunt could remain in the house as long as she wanted. It did not appear to bode well for the church that it would not be able to develop the property until she died or left voluntarily. On Saturday, I met at the office with my realtor and told him what God said to me about letting her stay, and quoted him the exact offer to be presented. He argued with me for about an hour, repeating his conversation the previous day with a nephew who also was the family attorney.

After I insisted he follow my wishes, the realtor concurred, but asked if he could wait until Saturday the week following. He then left the office visibly upset muttering to himself, all the while insisting it would not work. During the week I prayed even more to be sure I heard God right. I wanted to make sure it was God's wishes and not mine. The next Saturday the realtor approached the family with the offer and they accepted it. Six months after closing, the family moved out. My real estate agent is still shaking his head over that transaction, but he has gained deep respect for what God is doing here at Pleasant Street.

After the purchase of 33 Pleasant St. Bill and Joan sensed a need to return to Pittsburgh. They turned the property at $33^{1/2}$ over to the church to assume the remaining liability on the mortgage. Following the Ewart's suggestion, the house was named "The Love Freeman House" in honor of Love Freeman, a longtime member and former chairman of the Deacon Board at Pleasant Street Baptist Church. The property is now an integral part of the vision of ministry. Our plan is to use the home as a retreat house for ministers and missionaries. Bill and Joan Ewart are synonymous with the vision of ministry unfolded at Pleasant Street Baptist Church. Though their stay at the church in Westerly was short by human standards, their imprint on this church and community is sealed forever in eternity.

Thirty-one and one-half Pleasant Street presented a different kind of problem, for after two years the owner had not responded to phone calls from me or our real estate agent. They had not acknowledged the cards or notes stuck in the door. I continued to pursue the property until the answer from God came one night as I stood before the Town of Westerly Zoning Board to get final approval on our plans for the ministry. I needed a variance to complete the ministry complex as outlined. To get the Board's approval all neighbors within a radius of 200 feet had to be notified. The purpose of the notification was to give all neighbors opportunity to file objections before the Board made the decision.

All went well until the chair of the zoning board asked if there was anyone who had a reason why they should not approve the church's plan. At that point, a man raised his hand and was asked his name and his particular objection to the plan. When he stated his name, I knew this is the man we had been trying to contact; it was my silent neighbor at 31½ Pleasant Street. I feared for what he might say. "I have no objection, but I would like to know what the plan entails," he said. After a presentation of the architect's drawings and an explanation by our attorney, the man was satisfied. Once the proceedings ended, he approached me indicating a desire to talk about the sale of his property. In 2002, the final piece of the administrative subdivision supporting the vision of ministry was in place. The physical aspect of the vision was now sight.

CHAPTER SIXTEEN

VISIONS IN THE HEART

"Your sons and daughters will prophesy, your young men will see visions, and your old men will dream dreams."
Acts 2:17b

The morning I first met "The Fisherman", I was about to cross the driveway between the church and the adjacent building that housed the church office. Preoccupied with reading my mail as I headed down the ramp, I was brought to a halt by the loud reverberations of a motorcycle engine. No sooner had I stepped onto the gravel surface of the driveway separating the two buildings than a highly revved motorcycle swerved into the narrow space of the driveway, its wheels stopping abruptly at my feet and the bike blocking my further progress. Startled by the roar of the engine, I turned to face an imposing looking man on a black motorcycle, dressed in a black leather jacket and pants, with a black helmet hiding his face. His first action was to remove one of his black leather gloves.

The man was so close to me I had little room to run, and I must confess that was my primary inclination. For a moment, I felt threatened by his appearance owing to the cultural bias that black is evil, and anyone dressed in black riding a motorcycle is suspect. The man lifted his helmet, and before me was a total stranger. He looked me over, then raised his eyes and I heard what I perceived as a challenging query, "Are you the minister?" At that moment I wasn't sure I wanted to admit to him who I was, but I haltingly replied, "Yes, I am the minister." He then said, "I read about what you are doing around here, and I want to help." He then reached into the pocket of his black leather jacket and pulled out a brand new, crisp one hundred dollar bill. He handed me the money and immediately began turning the motorcycle around avoiding any other conversation. I thanked him and asked, "What is your name? Where are you from? I want to acknowledge your gift." While steadily moving towards the street he waved and said, "No need to do that, just remember me as The Fisherman."

Watching him speed off on the motorbike, my impression was reminiscent of Clement Moore's jovial character in the Christmas classic, "Twas The Night Before Christmas: But I heard him exclaim, ere he drove out of sight, "*Happy Christmas to all and to all a good night!*"

Within a year, "The Fisherman" returned two more times, repeating his former gift of crisp one hundred dollar bills, and again quickly riding away. All I could do was watch him speed off down the road. That was the last time I saw him until the summer of 2003. On that occasion, I was standing in front of the church office when a red pickup truck came down the street, and the driver abruptly pulled into the driveway directly across from the church. He stopped, jumped out of the truck, and made his way diagonally across the street toward where I was standing. He was a tall man, standing six foot three inches. He had black hair and wore a dingy red baseball-style cap on his head. He had very pleasant features, and as he approached there was something familiar about him. There was a calm, self assured way about him, and as he drew nearer. "You don't remember me, do you?"

I had to admit I did not recognize his face, nor was his vehicle familiar to me. I previously had no opportunity to be close enough to him except when he was wearing his motorcycle gear.

"I am The Fisherman."

In his hand he held a brand new, crisp one hundred dollar bill. He placed it in my hand and quickly turned and left. To this point he has contributed a total of $850.00. When I finally got the chance to talk to him and thank him, I had many questions, and again he seemed to want to avoid lengthy conversation. What he revealed was that he lived in Pawcatuck, Connecticut, and he was, indeed, a commercial fisherman for scallops. During our conversation, he insisted, "My name is not important. I was reading in the paper about what you are trying to do here. I was raised Catholic and I don't even know why I am doing this, but I have to do it. I really don't know why."

"I know why!" I told him. "God promised me, if I would be faithful, He would place His vision in the hearts of people. God has touched your heart to see His vision." The fisherman fixed his eyes on mine and responded with philosophical resignation, "I don't know about that, but I am here." What I knew for certain was that God had captured this man's heart, and his witness of the vision for Pleasant Street was testimony to God's faithfulness. All the while God was confirming His vision in the heart of The Fisherman, Joseph Toscano appeared to prove this was not an isolated incident.

Joe Toscano is a civil engineer, well known and highly esteemed in Westerly. In 2001, just before Christmas, I was riding an exercise bike in the lower level of the Westerly Pawcatuck YMCA, when I was approached by a man I had seen a few times, but had not formally met. He appeared to be in his early forties, dark wavy hair with a tinge of gray. He wore thin rimmed glasses nestled on a pleasant face which was etched with the brightest smile I had ever seen. Joe crossed the room to where I sat, and he stopped in front of me. "Josh, I heard about the vision, and I want to do something to help. I got a bonus from one of my clients, and I want to give it to you."

He was holding a small white envelope in his hand. He then held it out to me and said, "I have here $140.00, and I want you to have it." Joe handed me the money. I thanked him. "God bless you." He turned with that wonderful smile and left. I must admit I was completely taken by surprise, but then I recalled God's words on that chastening morning while watching James Robison on television. "All I asked you to do is get people to hear my voice. I will put the vision in their hearts. I will draw them to Me." Here at the YMCA was an unsolicited confirmation of God's faithfulness through this wonderful Christian man; however, I was soon to learn God was not finished yet.

Approximately a year later, I was approached by Joe Toscano again. This time there was no envelope, but the same engaging, captivating smile. At first there was a hint of sadness in Joe's voice as he explained his desire to repeat his actions of the previous year but he did not receive a bonus, hence he had no money to give. This man's heart had been so touched by God that he said, "Maybe I can donate my time to help with the land surveying of your properties." I had no idea what all of this meant until a year later when we stood before the Westerly

Planning Board and subsequently the Zoning Board with plans for the ministry complex, which we would not have been able to pay for except for Joe Toscano's generous contribution to the ministry. I tried to express my appreciation to Joe for what he had done, and his donation to the vision. Joe's reply was, "This is what I wanted to do."

Recently, I had occasion to stop at Joe's office and while there I spoke with him about the vision and what an important part he played in it. Joe reacted with complete surprise that I held him and his contribution in such high regard. He folded his arms across his chest, looked at me with that wonderful smile and sparkling eyes and said with such resolve, "Josh, our relationship is different from any other. With you I never wondered what I was to do next. I just did it. It's like just putting one foot in front of the other." I smiled as I recalled God's words to me. "I will put the vision in their hearts. I will draw them to me." Standing before me in the person of Joe Toscano was the evidence of God's faithfulness.

How could I ignore the truth that was manifest before my very eyes? How could I doubt the God who gave me eyes to see beyond what others could see? Had God not fulfilled His promise to me? Two men, unknown to each other and previously unknown to me, both of another religious persuasion, and neither understanding what it all meant, found themselves compelled to follow a vision of God's heart for a small, unpretentious church. How could I do less than trust God completely for fulfillment of the vision for His church at Pleasant Street?

I would be remiss if I did not mention that this was the point my heart began to fully realize the vision was God's alone to implement. I stood in awe as each succeeding step unfolded, and God raised up visionaries to accomplish his purposes. In fulfilling His promise, He placed his vision in the hearts of people previously unknown to me, and He used them in marvelous ways to bring His vision from faith to reality. Some of them made contributions which validated the miracle in more visible ways, while others made lesser contributions with just as great an impact on my heart, and proved to be most encouraging to me. Every involvement, no matter what the magnitude, added to God's plan for His church and people.

I first met Russell Jeffrey through Frank Vitale, former vice principal of the Babcock Middle School in Westerly. Frank is a Christian man who was genuinely interested in youth education, but because his work at school limited his outside participation he contacted Russell. A few years previous, Russell Jeffrey and his wife Carey had done all of the necessary research to start a Classical Christian school, but abandoned their plans due to burdensome regulations. When Russell heard about the vision and the fact it included a Christian school he contacted me. We met and talked about my vision for youth education and my concern for youth in general. Russell was a very distinguished, good looking young man who had made a great deal of money in the investment field. Though he was prominent in his field, he had a very easy air about him and when we sat down to talk he displayed an aura of humility.

Russell Jeffrey was a man who would look you in the eye when he talked, and you could believe what he was saying. He never bragged about his accomplishments, but simply gave all glory to God. He had a very young family consisting of a wife and three boys. He tells the story that his wife Carey had been a Christian long before him, and it was her influence along with that of his youngest son that led him to Christ. At one time, his son was very sick and Russell was extremely worried about the outcome of the boy's illness. His wife prayed for her son and trusted him to God. Russell had difficulty trusting the boy to God, but what opened his heart to the Lord was when his son said to him, "Don't worry, Daddy, everything will be all right." It was more than Russell could take. If his son had such faith in God, then he wondered why he should not embrace the same God. Soon after, Russell gave his life to Christ.

Russell was a very generous man. He made a monetary commitment to the vision, but what was more important to me was his wisdom and the encouragement he brought when I was struggling with the direction in which God wanted me to go. I had a group of influential people around me who were knowledgeable about raising funds and wanted to help with the vision. I listened to many of their thoughts and ideas about what to do, but the clearest voice of wisdom was that of Russell Jeffrey who continually reminded me that I should be faithful to what God had placed in my heart. He and Carey donated a like-new 2000 Toyota Seneca seven-passenger van for our youth ministry. When we had an opportunity to purchase a much needed fifteen-passenger van for youth programs and for our children's choir, Russell gave a sizable gift to help purchase the vehicle. Words cannot express my appreciation for Russell

Jeffrey, his wife Carey and their family. God had spoken to this man's heart and he enlisted his family in supplying unwavering support for the vision of ministry.

Gary Engler is a former teacher and administrator in the Stonington, Connecticut, school system. He is active in the Central Baptist Church in Westerly and has served as church moderator, and presently teaches Sunday School. Gary is in his late sixties, a quiet, humble man, soft spoken and willing to do anything that would advance the cause of Christ, especially in the field of education. I met Gary through his wife Linda, who I had known for several years. When Gary heard about the vision and our plans for the school, he volunteered to help. He pitched right in gathering information from the Rhode Island Department of Education and other sources. Gary evaluated the information and has been working diligently with the appropriate authorities to help put together a working plan for our pre-school and Christian academy. Gary serves on our school board and has contributed in so many ways. Most importantly, he has been a friend and encourager, always there when needed.

Another wonderful friend and supporter of our ministry here in Westerly is Jean Stenhouse, a former chairperson of the Westerly School Committee, who is now community liaison director at the Wal-Mart Supercenter in Westerly. Jean is blessed with a wonderfully intuitive mind. She is quiet and warm, and when she smiles she lights up a room; when she speaks people listen. Jean was an early supporter of the *vision of ministry* at Pleasant Street Baptist Church and currently her work at Wal-Mart has made it possible for our outreach ministry to extend far into the Westerly community. In particular, she has done much to enhance our ministry to youth. Each year Wal-Mart sponsors a day where a percentage of the profits is given to non-profit community groups helping to feed, clothe and assist those in need. Several times we were recipients of this generosity, and it made a measurable difference in impacting the lives of many children and families in our community. Her donations of food around the holidays have helped us to feed many people, and she has also initiated events for seniors, such as Grandparents Day. To show our gratitude, our children's choir "A Little bit of Love," has been singing Christmas carols at Wal-Mart during Christmas time consecutively since 2000. Jean has offered sage advice to me in the early years of the vision, and I value her friendship and support.

When we had finished purchasing all the necessary properties, we were faced with the prospect of bringing them together to form an administrative sub-division. Before we could proceed with any construction we needed to get approvals from the town. Regulations required us to meet with the Planning Board, Zoning Board and the tax assessor. William Nardone, a prominent Westerly attorney approached me. "Josh, when you go before the town on these issues I would like to represent you—obviously, at no cost. I believe in what you are doing and I want to help."

William Nardone has been our legal representative in all of these matters, and more. He is from a very prominent law firm in Westerly, and his family has been an integral part of this community for generations. His expert assistance in these matters has made an enormous difference in preparing us for the next phase of the vision. His belief in the vision and his presence has added momentum to the vision of ministry and the trustworthiness of God's promise to share His heart.

In the winter of 2003, a very attractive middle-aged couple attended our Sunday morning worship service. Their first thought was they came by default, but they soon learned it was by God's design. Previous to this, Lorri and Joe DeFelice had been visiting different churches each Sunday, but this Sunday because of a late start they opted for the 11AM worship service at Pleasant Street Baptist Church.

Lorri remarks, "Soon after arriving at the church I knew this was the place God wanted us to be." During the week, while Joe was working, Lorri got involved in the church ministry, attending Women's Bible Study, helping children with reading, tutoring them in various subjects, and volunteering to do the most mundane of tasks. On Sundays, they faithfully attended study and worship together. Their stay at Pleasant Street, however, was far too brief because their plans included going back to the West Coast. In preparation for their return to the state of Washington, they sold their home and other belongings and tithed ten percent of the proceeds to the vision. God had once again fulfilled His promise to place the vision in people's hearts.

There were many others who were touched by the vision: An attorney in Quincy, Massachusetts, Jerry Phelps, offered to do all the necessary legal work for our Christian school. A local certified public accountant, Steven Greene, volunteered to change our whole accounting and bookkeeping system to QuickBooks. Steve computerized all accounts and made himself and his staff available for hands-on instruction to operate it efficiently. For Steve, it was a labor of love and he remarked that he was honored to be a part of the ministry. Little did he know that through him God was fulfilling His promise. A recently graduated attorney, Paul Kuhn, wanted to give something back so he offered to help people in need as a service. Paul proposed that his helping people would be his contribution to ministry in support of the vision. There are many more people, old and young, who God has raised up and imprinted Himself on their hearts. I could not list them all; however, none are unimportant, nor are their contributions less appreciated. Each one of these persons has a special place in my heart, but more importantly each of them has a place reserved in God's heart. They are visionaries all.

But what about the future of the ministry? How is the vision perceived today? What I have come to learn is that God does not rest in the glory of the things He has previously wrought. He steadily and resolutely moves toward the time of fulfillment and continues to draw visionaries to Himself. In April of 2003, a young woman named Connie Kowal responded to an ad placed in the *Westerly Sun* for a secretary/bookkeeper who was familiar with QuickBooks. Soon Connie came to work at Pleasant Street and proved to be a wonderful, competent and efficient addition. What Connie did not know was her work at Pleasant Street would include far more than taking care of QuickBooks.

A little over a year after she arrived, something happened to Connie. I noticed she had a far away look in her eyes; her reservations had disappeared and they were replaced with a focus and determination and energy that I had seldom seen before. God had touched Connie's heart, and she was now captured by the vision of Pleasant Street. Her eyes were opened to see far beyond the mere physical presence of the church buildings, and her heart was consumed by the ministry. When she went home and shared her new-found excitement and passion with her husband Henry, he, too, joined her in pursuing God's heart for people. Today, God's vision for hurting people is being wonderfully fulfilled in the church by Connie and Henry. The fulfillment of His promise to meet people's needs is not halted by narrow denominational lines, as Connie and Henry are communicants of the Church Of The Holy Spirit, an Episcopal church in Charlestown. Surely God's vision touches the lives of the targeted recipients, and what I believe is even more telling is the effect it has on the lives of the visionaries.

I am again reminded of God's words to me, "I will put the vision in people's hearts. I will draw them to Me."

CHAPTER SEVENTEEN

Seven Bassinets

*"And anyone who welcomes a little child like
this on my behalf is welcoming me."*
Matthew 18:5

The "umbilical cord" of Pleasant Street was severed one Sunday morning as I was standing in the pulpit preparing to deliver the morning sermon. I cannot remember my sermon topic that morning, nor do I know for sure what happened. However, I believe it was one of the frequent moves of the Holy Spirit that directed my eyes to look towards my left into the fellowship hall that adjoins the sanctuary. At first I did not comprehend what I was seeing. There were three, eight-foot long tables positioned on the right side of the fellowship hall near the windows. I wasn't sure why my attention was directed toward the hall because there didn't appear to be anything unusual or out of place, but suddenly, I saw it. Suddenly, I realized why God directed my eyes toward those tables: I was about to see His vision.

There were seven bassinets atop the tables. Seven new births, seven babies, seven children of God, seven who would model the Kingdom.

Then, as clear as the peal of a bell on an autumn morn, I heard the voice of God: "There's your church." Immediately I shared with the congregation what I had just seen and what God had said. What I realized at that moment was, these seven bassinets would be the means to define our youth ministry. The distinction for me was, God did not say, "Here's your children," No. He said, "Here's your church." I then understood Jesus' words, *"Let the children come to me. Don't stop them! For the Kingdom of Heaven belongs to such as these."* [Matthew 19:14] Their simple faith would lead this church in sincere, humble, childlike faith in God. And indeed it has.

Our children's ministry has been among the most exciting to emerge in Pleasant Street Baptist Church. When I first laid out the vision of ministry for Pleasant Street in 1986, there was embedded in the vision a component of youth ministry. In my outline it did not show to the extent of some others because it was not clearly defined in my head how God wanted us to go about offering ministry to youth.

In general, I talked about youth evangelism, youth Bible Study, children's church, a nursery and a fully accredited Christian School without realizing that God had much more in mind for our church and in His own time he would reveal His heart for our children.

Education was always a large part of my personal agenda because of my own background, so I struggled, trying to find a way to make our youth a more visible, more informed, more integral part of the church. I felt a deep connection between Jesus' words to his disciples concerning children and yet, I must confess I did not fully understand what it all meant until Jesus pointed out to me their connection with the church.

I then realized, in His words Jesus did not mean that heaven is only for children but that all people need sincere, humble, childlike faith in God. He showed that the receptiveness of little children was a great contrast to the stubbornness of the religious leaders, who let their education and sophistication stand in the way of the simple faith needed to believe in Him. Only then did I begin to understand the role of the children in the vision of ministry He had given me.

In 1981, the Sunday School at Pleasant Street averaged around twelve children, most of whom belonged to the few families in the church. As the vision of ministry began to reach out to people, more children were attracted to the church. However, it wasn't until the early part of 1997 that the children called by God to a place of ministry in Pleasant Street Baptist Church burst onto the scene.

Today our ministry to youth has literally exploded onto the Westerly area, touching lives of many children, inside and outside of the church. Outreach Youth activities include: leading Bible Study clubs in the Westerly High School, and then Babcock Middle School; forums for teenagers on contemporary subjects such as dating and relationships; girls groups, boys groups; combined activities; Bible studies in Providence, Westerly, Groton and New London; tutoring for students; crafts, sewing, cooking, sports, youth and children's retreats.

To support our youth ministries we have converted a building into a Family Life Center, which has a meeting room, conference room, computer room, and library.

Along with this we have two vans, fifteen and seven-passenger, with "Youth Alive Ministries" emblazoned across each side.

Our Youth Alive Ministries leaders are now involved in an after school program with the YMCA for middle school girls. We also have a comparable program with third, fourth and fifth grade boys. We are conferring with another non-profit agency in Connecticut to coordinate efforts to reach other youth. Our youth ministry is alive and seeking to awaken other youth to Jesus Christ as an option to what is offered in the world. The church also operates another fifteen-passenger van for outreach ministries. And yet the most direct result of the "seven bassinets" is our children's choir, some whom rested in those bassinets on that Sunday morning in 1997.

The children's choir sang for the first time at Pleasant Street on Easter Sunday morning in 1999. They were directed by my daughter Allison McClure-Davis, who also was director of the adult Sanctuary Choir. Allison was assisted in directing the children's choir by Deirdre Dorn, a mother who had tragically lost her six year-old son to injury several years before.

The ages of the children were from three to eight, and they numbered approximately twelve to sixteen children. They loved singing so much, and touched so many lives that they became a part of everyday church worship, singing each fifth Sunday. Soon after, Allison stepped down, and Deidre Dorn became the children's choir director assisted by Yvonne Robinson, grandmother of several of the children in the choir.

The next thing was to name the choir. Many different names were suggested, but to no avail. None seemed appropriate until one day, as I was gazing upon these little children, a name rose up in my spirit and I knew it was from God. They would be called "A Little Bit of Love" and from that moment they have shared "a little bit of love" wherever they went—to churches, nursing homes, parades, Christmas caroling in front of downtown Westerly stores, concerts and department stores. Everywhere they go they share the love of Jesus and bring hope to a dying world.

Today the group numbers approximately forty-four children, many from broken families, group homes, and foster homes. They represent all races, colors, nationalities and income levels. Several of these young children between the ages of eight and nine have made real heartfelt commitments to Jesus Christ as Lord, and they share that witness in song. Once, while singing at a sister Baptist church in Westerly, the pastor leaned over to me. "For those kids to be so on fire for the Lord, you must be doing something right."

Little did he know I had nothing to do with what he was seeing; it was God fulfilling His vision of "Seven Bassinets".

When "A Little Bit of Love" sings, the whole church is moved and is often left standing in tears. It reminds all of Jesus words, *"Let the children come to me. Don't stop them! For the Kingdom of Heaven belongs to such as these."* Today some of the older children have started another singing group. Not wanting to leave their former children's choir, but feeling a need to move on, they have simply titled themselves "More Love". The heart of the vision lies within these children. The heart of Pleasant Street and the surrounding communities does also.

This is evidenced in a recent letter written to the editor of the *New London Day* newspaper. "On Dec. 17 in the Williams Park Apartments, the residents were treated to a wonderful Christmas experience. The tenant's association had a Christmas dinner that through the joint efforts of the Police Benevolent Association, staff of the Housing Authority and New London City Council members, was something that the residents will remember for a long time. We had carolers from the Pleasant Street Baptist Church in Westerly. These children helped me to keep Christ in Christmas."

CHAPTER EIGHTEEN

LIFE AT PLEASANT STREET

"Whatever we do it is because Christ's love controls us."
2 Corinthians 5:14

In an earlier chapter I related my initial resistance to ministering in Westerly because Pleasant Street Baptist Church was not what I had in mind for me. I wanted to launch my ministry at a bigger church in Woonsocket in front of a large congregation. Like some of my younger colleagues in ministry today, I had been bitten by the mega church bug. I was captivated by the outsized church, which by its very nature smelled of success. I was convinced that the bigger church would offer me increased visibility, a more diversified ministry, a larger audience to preach to, accelerated growth and the opportunity to be exposed to many more people. All of these things, I reasoned, would enhance my ministry. However, my strongest argument was not based on the fact that I had earned a larger stage or even deserved instantaneous recognition. The impetus for my thinking was the fact that I was approaching fifty and could not imagine that I would have the strength or energy to pastor a church after years as an associate. I hardly considered the fact that God had already inserted my age into His divine calculator, and all that was necessary for me was to commit myself to faithfully follow the future plans He had for Pleasant Street. I was certain coming to Westerly would afford me little or no opportunity to realize my desires for a large church with more opportunity for growth, so any thought of Pleasant Street over Woonsocket was difficult to accommodate in my mind.

This initially made my transition to Westerly more difficult, until I realized the best kept secret in Christendom is the uniqueness of the small church. National averages of major denominations suggest that seventy-five to eighty percent of churches have a normal attendance of fewer than one hundred fifty members on Sunday. Hidden in this statistic is the fact that these churches are housed in buildings of all sizes. It makes me realize that the determining factor for church growth is not how big the church's size but the size of their God. Churches large or small must have a God beyond human expectation.

After yielding my preconceived self-aggrandizing notions about the church and faithfully confronting the call of Christ to nurture His people, I was transformed by the mysterious working of the Holy Spirit in my life. It was then I recognized that the Pleasant Street Church atmosphere is exactly what the large churches are trying to establish in their small groups or cell groups.

Undeniably, there is a certain honor in being called to pastor a large church. However, there is even a glory in being called to serve a church of lesser size. This is not to make a comparison between the two, but simply a realization that God pours His Spirit out on the church in equal measure regardless of size. This truth is evidenced by an aura hard to explain in our emerging ministry at Pleasant Street.

Indeed, Pleasant Street Baptist Church is truly a special place. It's like having an extended family. Most of its people are warm, friendly, inviting and unpretentious. People feel at home in Pleasant Street both members and visitors. It is an environment where people know each other and are concerned about each other, and when one is in trouble other members intervene and become involved in helping. What I have found serving at Pleasant Street has afforded me an opportunity for accelerated growth, personally and in the ministry. I have had to use and develop many skills that pastors in larger churches would not find necessary. The people here are, indeed, my family. I am not only their pastor, but also a friend, a counselor, and a "father" to men, women and children. The ministry emergent here is more hands on, more personal, more family oriented, more-one-on one, and I am more involved in people's everyday lives. It is thrilling to see seemingly ordinary people transformed into extraordinary ministers of God as they take to themselves the responsibilities connected with meeting the everyday needs of other members as well as the needs of a hurting community.

There is glory in seeing people from the community drawn to the glory of God in Christ Jesus. Many in our community who were born and raised in church are, for the first time, confronted by the personal call of Jesus through the mysterious working of the Holy Spirit. Some have been awakened and found new life after many years of languishing in a Rip Van Winkle sort of slumber. Some have dared to stray outside of denominational lines to join our fellowship and experience the miracle of the new birth.

The recitation of our mission statement at each Sunday's worship has led to our becoming more intentional and more inviting to people witnessing for Christ. This is manifested in the freedom of people of all classes and colors to unite together under the power of the Holy Spirit. Thus, there is a new enthusiasm to seek more of the things of God in Bible study, prayer and evangelism. I marvel as the gospel infects so many people's lives that it becomes contagious. And I stand in awe as a witness to people coming to the church out of desperation, and one day coming to know Christ through the supernatural power of a changed life. What I have come to learn is, it is not how great the size of the church building, nor is it how many people occupy the pews, but it is how great the faith of the church. It all begins with the love in the pastor's heart for the people God has entrusted to him. In essence, the faith of the church has much to do with how much of the pastor's heart does God have. I have trusted God to fulfill His promise to me and because of that, God has blessed me to watch the Gospel transform men and women into extraordinary people of faith who are determined to live out the Gospel in their lives.

As pastor of Pleasant Street I wear many hats. One of the most satisfying is growing up with the young children in the church. There is no greater joy for me than three, four and five year-olds clinging to my legs saying, "I love you, Pastor." If my personal desires for a larger church had prevailed I might have missed the intimacy of greeting those new lives in the bassinets that Sunday morning. I might have lost out on the joy of watching children just learning to talk, simultaneously learning to sing God's praises. I would have missed the opportunity to be involved in the many children's activities, but, I would have regretted not having been most of all, an integral part of their growth since birth.

On Pastor's Appreciation Day in September 2002, some of our

youth were asked "What does pastor mean to you?" Allow me to share with you a few of the responses from these children.

Marques, 7: "Pastor, you mean everything to me. You taught me how to listen to my dad. You also helped me do better in my school and pay attention in class. You brought me from the wrong path to the right path."

Divonna, 7: "My pastor means a lot to me; he is a caring person. He helped me to have a better attitude from the retreat. All of the retreats helped me."

Adrina, 8: "Pastor means a lot to me, he is the best pastor I ever had. He taught me a lot he tells me the truth all the time. I love him with all my heart. He is the best pastor I ever met. He taught me right from wrong. He taught me how to be a loving person."

Shatajah, 8: "Dear Pastor, you mean a lot to me because you taught me to always remember God."

Fantasia, 12: "My pastor is a generous person, he respects everyone and always listens if you need to talk to someone or have a problem. I love my Pastor and don't want another one."

Keesha, 9: "My pastor means a lot to me because he is an experienced person of God. He can bring you from relying on drugs to relying on God. He is a love person because if you're sick he will pray for you and God will bring that prayer up and put it on that person. That is what my pastor means to me."

Chanel, 10: "My pastor means a lot to me because he turned my life around. He put Jesus into my heart and taught me to do right instead of wrong. Since you turned my life around I do better in school and at home. My pastor is honest, loving, caring, patient, and thoughtful. He teaches us lessons about Jesus and how he wants us to act. He tells us that we should be thankful to Jesus because he saved us from our sins. If he can do all of these things which he does there aren't too many words to describe what my pastor means to me."

A typical Sunday at Pleasant Street is illustrated by what happened on the third Sunday in October of 2004. It was a day on which one of my licensed ministers was scheduled to preach, so I arrived at the church at approximately 9:20 A. M., a little later than I normally would. Sunday school classes begin at 9:30 and morning worship at 11A. M. Upon entering the church I found waiting for me a mother accompanied by one of her sons. She wanted to speak to me about her other son who had been arrested the previous evening for felony assault. The boy assaulted his grandmother. His mother came to inform me he would be missing from church and the reason why. She also wanted me to know that she was the one who called the police. Both of her sons were members of the church. I spoke with the mother for about twenty minutes then informed her I would look into it the next day. If I was scheduled to preach that morning I would have insisted she wait until after the worship service. A few minutes later, I had a conversation with the chairman of our Vision Building Committee. We talked about the strategy we would use to secure a bank loan to finance our planned church renovations and pre-school. I then prepared for the worship service which concluded around 1P. M.

Before I could leave the sanctuary, I felt someone bump up against my leg. I looked down to find an eight year old boy who asked me to pray for him. He told me he had an anger problem and stuck a pencil in the hand of one of the young girls in his school. We sat down on the front pew and talked about his anger and the need for him to take responsibility for it; then I prayed with him. After praying I told him I would have his mother bring him in to see me so we could talk further about his anger.

Leaving the Sanctuary, I came upon a young woman who was crying. Inquiring about her tears, I found she was very angry and hurt because her mother was telling people things she had previously done in her life before she had made a profession of faith in Jesus Christ. Her mother refused to admit her daughter's life was radically changed—but indeed it was. I asked her if she knew her life had been altered by Christ. I asked her about her relationship with the Lord. When she assured me of her new status in the Kingdom of God, I told her it wasn't important what her mother or anyone else said about her, what was important was that she knew who she was in Christ. Her tears changed to a smile. She left thanking me for reminding her. It was almost as if I could hear my mother's voice, "No matter what anyone says about you, it won't make you any better or worse than you really are."

Standing nearby was another young woman who recently gave her life to Jesus Christ. I had been encouraging her, since her conversion, to reconcile with her father and tell him just how she felt about her life change. Her father was a strong, sometimes rigid, man and she was afraid to talk to him, feeling she was not yet living up to his standards. She didn't know I had previously counseled her father and convinced him his daughter needed his help to grow, and it had to start with his forgiveness of her past. Since she was afraid to approach him, I took the initiative and asked her if it was alright if I intervened. After some reluctance, she agreed. I then took her by the hand, summoned her father and the three of us went back into the sanctuary and talked. I talked with them and prayed with them and left them to be alone. Looking back I saw they were embracing and crying. His little girl once lost had now been found. His daughter had come back home.

When I finally exited the Sanctuary, the mother I had spoken to earlier had returned with her son. This time she had another problem. She was very disturbed because her son who had been arrested had been living with his grandmother, as he and his mother did not get along. The grandmother made some comments about the boy's medication at odds with the mother's account. Because it happened during morning worship, she brought the problem to me. I convinced her very few in the church heard what had been said by the grandmother. I advised her that no one even inquired about it nor was it mentioned by anyone after church, so it would be better not to give power to what her mother said by bringing it up again. She agreed and left the church satisfied.

After that meeting, my director of youth ministries approached me very upset. "Pastor, I must talk to you as soon as possible." When I saw the distress on her face, and heard the urgency in her voice, I said "Let's go into the office and we will discuss it now." We had recently completed plans for an after-school program, in conjunction with the YMCA, for middle and high school girls. The program was to kick off at the YMCA on Thursday of the coming week. A few women who had committed to help informed her they were no longer available. She needed help and didn't know what to do. I suggested we try to find someone else, including a few of the men, to help I offered to help fill in if necessary, until we could find others willing to share in the ministry to these young women.

Stepping out of the office I motioned to a man who had been waiting for me since the worship service concluded. He was clearly frustrated over his relationship with his estranged wife and had asked if I would talk with him after the worship service. I had previously counseled him and his wife and suggested some things that needed to be initiated in their relationship. Using Ephesians [5:21-33], I pointed out the need for him to understand what it meant for a husband-and-wife's relationship to replicate that of Christ and the church. When his wife later talked to him about it, he could not fully understand what it meant for him to give himself rather than material things, so he came to me for clarification. After we talked and I cleared up some things for him, he left vowing to put his new understanding of his role as a husband into practice.

I then gathered up my hat and coat, secured my briefcase from the office and started toward my car. Before reaching the door to the outside of the church, I passed by the kitchen door. The light in the kitchen was still on and I heard voices. I found two women who were left to clean up the kitchen, talking to a man and trying to comfort him. Upon seeing me, the man ran over and said, "Pastor, I am hurting." I stopped, and he told me he had of late no communication with his wife of seventeen years and he suspected she might have found a male friend outside of the home. I spoke to him for a short while and then I suggested he call my secretary on Tuesday for a counseling appointment. He readily agreed. "I'm really hurting, I'm really hurting, I need to talk to you," he said. The church office is not staffed on Mondays. All day Tuesdays and Wednesday mornings are the times set aside for counseling. I left the church for home at 2:38 in the afternoon, hoping I had made a difference in some lives. I was tired, but elated that God trusted me with the lives of his people; even more than that I thrilled that the Gospel could wonderfully be applied to any situation. I hoped I had helped someone to see Jesus.

No longer does my heart yearn for a bigger church and a bigger stage. I could not imagine myself being anywhere but where I am. I thank God for calling me to this place. I thank God for these wonderful people. I thank God that through His hand I can make a difference in peoples lives. The next time He calls and queries, *"Whom should I send as a messenger to my people? Who will go for us?* [Isaiah 6:8] I will not insist on my way. I will not selfishly seek my own good; rather I will seek His will for me. I will trust His wisdom. I will bow before Him and simply say, Lord, if you can find anything you can use in me, I will go wherever you want me. *"Lord, I'll go! Send me."*

The ministry at Pleasant Street brings to mind Henri Nouwen's book, *The Wounded Healer*. The Nouwen book provides a paradigm for ministry in the modern world. I have learned that if we are to reach people today we cannot merely stand on the sidelines and call them out of their pain, but we must enter into their unstable, often disorderly lives, and allow our own brokenness and weakness to touch their pain and in the process lead them to healing through the power of the Holy Spirit. Often I have counseled people in trouble armed with only a prayer [which is more than sufficient], and more often than not the Holy Spirit has pointed to some of my own pain and shortcomings as the means to relate to the person's needs.

Here I must add a caution against anyone thinking our ministry here has come about easily. It takes work. Hard work. It takes patience, endurance, thick skin, humility, but most of all it requires unshakable faith that God will accomplish all that He has promised. It is believing unequivocally that God will supply. One of my most encouraging songs is, "Great Is Thy Faithfulness." Especially do I find encouragement in the third verse, "Pardon for sin and a peace that endureth. Thine own dear presence to cheer and to guide; Strength for today and bright hope for tomorrow, Blessings all mine with ten thousand beside! Great is Thy faithfulness! Great is Thy faithfulness! Morning by morning new mercies I see; All I have needed Thy hand hath provided—Great is Thy faithfulness, Lord unto me!"

For me, ministry at Pleasant Street has been a walk of faith. When I came to Pleasant Street Church I had little to offer the people here except my own pain and brokenness and a sure promise of God borne on the wings of a vision for the church and community. Since my arrival He has provided me with the strength of character and an abiding faith equal to the task. To say there were not disappointments would be deceiving; especially when I look back on the frustrations caused by my own impatience and desire to please God. In all things God has prevailed. He has taught me that if I stood in faith He would manifest Himself in my life and in this congregation. He promised His glory would be seen.

Without question, the one thing that has shone brightly above all else has been the vision. The times when obstacles appeared to block the way, when the direction was in question, when funds failed to appear when needed, when the disappointment of people leaving the church unexpectedly occurred, the vision remained in view. I can testify today without wavering that the words of wisdom dispensed by Solomon, have kept me focused on the goal. *"Without a vision the people perish."*

In the past few years I have received two very significant words from the Lord for our church. First, God promised He would take His church at Pleasant Street deeper into His word and He would reveal Himself in a more profound way. Secondly, He said He wants me to be more intentional in teaching them to understand His word more clearly, so as it can have a weightier application to their lives.

He has given me the strength to carry out His will, and He has supplied the vigor and staying power to endure in difficult times. He gave me the daring to forge ahead in spite of the naysayers. He gave me the audacity to forcefully proclaim His will in the face of opposition. He gave me eyes to see beyond what others were able to see. He gave me boldness under trial. He gave me a new heart to love all of His creations as He loves them. But, what has made the difference, beyond measure, is He gave me assurance that if I relied on him in prayer what He promised would be done according to His will.

Confirmation came on the morning of Sunday, February 25, 2001. That morning I had scheduled a child dedication for my granddaughter Charity, who was then four months old. My son Wesley and his wife Vanessa had selected a young Christian couple from Riverside, Rhode Island to be the godparents. I met Jerry and Jan Bradley that morning for the first time when they arrived at church for the dedication. During the ceremony, Charity's face was angelic. She was quietly serene in her beautiful white dress with ruffled bottom, and a bit of lace adorning. It was almost as if we were a bother to her. She hardly whimpered when I held her and offered a prayer of dedication to God on her behalf.

My movements were carefully measured during the ceremony that morning, for just ten weeks prior on December 13, 2000, I had undergone back surgery for Lumbar Spinal Stenosis. The nerve alongside my spine was literally being strangled by the lime buildup of arthritis, causing back pain and severe leg cramping and making it difficult for me to walk. Because of my tenuous physical condition and the fact I was beyond retirement age, I had resigned myself to the fact I would soon have to relinquish the pastorate of Pleasant Street Baptist Church.

When I began to preach that morning I noticed Jan, Charity's godmother, was not really focusing on my message but she seemed to be riveted on writing something. This caused me no real concern for we have a page in the church bulletin encouraging people to write notes on the sermon. After the worship service had concluded and the benediction was pronounced, I left the pulpit and proceeded toward my office. It was then Jan stopped me. "I have something for you," she said. My first thought was that in her feverish writing she had penned a critique of my sermon and couldn't wait for me to hear it. In her hand was a note written on a small sheet of pastel paper. She held it out to me and said, "God gave me something to give to you."

When my eyes fell upon the words, tears began to flow making it difficult for me to see well enough to read the rest of what she had written: The note read, "I have heard your cries. I woke you up many times in the middle of the night. Many times you have tried to quit but I have stopped you. You're not too old. I will strengthen you. I have given you eyes to see beyond what others can see. Take care of the children. You will finish the course."

For three years I carried this note in my Bible. I wanted it to always be close to me. However, early this year I discovered it was gone. I sat and cried, feeling a great loss because I often looked at it when I was feeling low or uncertain as to my future ministry at Pleasant Street. Though it is gone, most of it I still carry in my heart. It was God's promise to me. How often I am reminded of the words of Martin Luther in that great hymn, "A Mighty Fortress Is Our God." "Did we in our own strength confide, our striving would be losing. Were not the right man on our side. The man of God's own choosing. Dost ask who that may be? Christ Jesus, it is He." Pleasant Street Baptist Church today has a glory all its own. After all, what greater glory could there possibly be than to hear Jesus say, *"Well done, my good and faithful servant."* [Matthew 25:21, 23]

Promised Fulfillment ...

"Then the Lord said to me, 'Write my answer in large clear letters on a tablet, so that a runner can read it and tell everyone else. But these things I plan won't happen right away. Slowly, steadily, surely, the time approaches when the vision will be fulfilled. If it seems slow, wait patiently, for it will surely take place. It will not be delayed."

Habakkuk 2: 2-3

CHAPTER NINETEEN

WITHOUT A VISION

*"I had heard about you before, but now I
have seen you with my own eyes."*
Job 42:5

Since this is a book about vision, I will devote this chapter to the magnitude and prerequisite of divine vision for the church. After receiving a vision from God more than 29 years ago, I committed myself to God and vowed to follow Him wherever He might lead. This, in itself, does not qualify me to claim proficiency in what is of the exclusive dominion of God. However, because God has entrusted me with the message of His heart to bring to his people, I feel no less compelled to share my discoveries and personal experience of His leading.

What is a vision?

The simplest most insightful explanation is that, "A vision is a visual form of divine revelation." Vision is the ability to perceive the Kingdom of God and the King who reigns on the throne. Vision is not about a human person. It is about an infinite God who reaches down and touches the hearts of men and women and gives them fresh eyes to see what is possible in the realm of the Spirit. In 1976, God poured His heart into my helplessness and focused my aberrant mind to His divine Kingdom by a new birth of the Spirit. When He touched my heart, He gave me fresh eyes to see vision, and then He announced, "I have given you eyes to see far beyond what others can see." "Why would You do this for me," I asked? "Why me? Am I special for some reason? Is it because of worldly acclaim or physical accomplishments? Why would you reveal Your heart to me?" The answer came back swiftly, "What I did for you

I will do for any man, woman, or child who is willing to be emptied of self, dutifully give up all they hold dear and faithfully follow after Me." When God isolated me that December afternoon He already knew that I was willing to turn from all else and follow Him.

Recently I have taken every opportunity to sit and reflect on my many years of ministry here in Westerly. During these times of solitude, I have thought about the things which helped shape the ministry for nearly a quarter of a century. I ruminated on things both pleasant and unpleasant, hurtful and joyful. I allowed old wounds to be opened and old pain to be resurrected. I celebrated the joy of Jesus' presence in victory and the victory of His presence in the face of defeat. I pondered all of these things and more. Over the years many people have asked me how I have been able to keep things in focus for such a long time. My answer is straightforward: I see through the mirror of the Prophet Isaiah's temple vision of God in Chapter 6. His lofty view of God gave him a sense of God's holiness, greatness, mystery, and power. The more clearly Isaiah saw God's sanctity, the clearer his own sinfulness, powerlessness and inadequacy became to him; it was then he saw his shortcomings, his hopelessness, and the extent of the forgiveness he received at God's hand. Isaiah realized he could do nothing of lasting value without God.

I have attempted to keep that vision of the almighty God in front of me. In so doing I am left with an ever present reality of myself. Since I am constantly aware of how great God is, I cannot ignore the depth of my own sin. It compels me, as it did the prophet, to rely totally on God, and it obligates me to leave everything behind and be God's spokesman. On that memorable day when God revealed His heart to me I heard the Lord ask, "*Whom should I send as a messenger to my people? Who will go for us?*" I could only respond, "*Lord, I'll go! Send me.*" [Isaiah 6:8]

The contemporary church is at a crossroad. It is declining in the grasp of confusion and frustration, groping for anything that points toward a first century Christian lifestyle. As previously noted George Barna's book *REVOLUTION* proposes that believers abandon the local church. He advocates "choosing from a proliferation of options, weaving together a set of favored alternatives into a unique tapestry that constitutes the personal 'church' of the individual." Few people have made such a bold statement, and fewer still have allowed such a dramatic shift in thinking in so brief a time. Barna in 1992 stated in his book, *The Power of Vision,* "Grasping God's vision for your ministry is definitely not an option. It is an absolute must." He reasoned that vision should become the focus of a leader's life work and the heartbeat of the church. In The *Power of Vision,* Barna clearly and powerfully articulates vision for the church; however, his plan to implement vision fails to acknowledge that the fulfillment of vision rests with the one who gives it.

Oswald Chambers writes in his devotional book, *My Utmost for His Highest,* "If we lose the heavenly vision God has given us, we alone are responsible—not God. We lose the vision because of our own lack of spiritual growth. If we do not apply our beliefs about God to the issues of everyday life, the vision God has given us will never be fulfilled ... The only way to be obedient to the heavenly vision is to give our utmost for His highest—our best for His glory ... This can be accomplished only when we make a determination to continually remember God's vision. But the acid test is obedience to the vision in the details of our everyday life—sixty seconds out of every minute, and sixty minutes out of every hour, not just during times of personal prayer or public meetings ... We cannot bring the vision to fulfillment through our own efforts, but must live under its inspiration until it fulfills itself."

In looking back over the many years of ministry, my thoughts turned to the many times I wanted to quit. As I pondered why and how I persisted through nearly two decades as pastor at Pleasant Street, I was reminded of a lesson I had earlier learned from God. Once a vision is seen and accepted there is no human release. Its acceptance is binding upon the human heart. Its implementation is inevitable. It is bound in heaven, and when assent is given only God can change the covenant. There is no turning back, whatsoever the path may hold, or whatever the cost. Under stress and destined for prison in Rome, Paul was risking his life to affirm his calling, declaring to King Agrippa *"And so, O King Agrippa, I was not disobedient to that vision from heaven."* [Acts 26:19]

When churches lack vision they become stagnant. Churches die for lack of the life of Christ to sustain them. They die because they abort the power of the Holy Spirit to ignite them. They die because the Living Word of God is no longer resident in the hearts of pastors. Churches seek meaning and purpose for life in programs and culture-based theology because they lack a clear word from the Lord. Many people in churches today opt for a comfortable, noncommittal and contemporary theology rather than assemble themselves around a particular vision that God has entrusted to a church leader. When the leader surrenders himself or herself to the heavenly vision and stands in faith while exhorting the people to do the same, then the stagnant, declining and expiring church will renew and revitalize itself. These visionaries will produce fruit greater than ever before. It confirms the findings of Solomon, "*Where there is no vision, the people perish.*" Vision defines a church and its ministry. Without a divine vision there is no direction and the people wander aimlessly. Where there is a vision of God, the church is alive.

Today, the average pastor remains three to five years in his pulpit, so my longevity has in itself divine purpose. If it was simply a matter of the strength of my faith measured against the pain and stress I have endured, I would have surely left years ago. However, because I was called to Pleasant Street Baptist Church as part of God's vision for them, I could not leave no matter how severe the pain or how protracted the stress. I recall how it was for me in 1995 when I stepped from the pulpit after preaching what I expected to be my last sermon as pastor at Pleasant Street. Deep down in my heart, I knew it wasn't over. I knew God would provide whatever was necessary for me, because I had yet to hear Him say it was time to leave. In the past I had to wait until God released me from Pond Street. What would be different now? The Scripture says, [Hebrews 13:8] "*Jesus Christ is the same yesterday, today, and forever.*" I waited on God to release me from Pleasant Street. Release never came. On the contrary, God's will was made known when the young woman stood up in the midst of her peers and cried, "Pastor is not leaving, they are." And they did leave under the urging of God's hand.

Visions are not made or created in human minds. Visions emanate from the heart of God. Visions are supernatural to man, but natural to God. Visions are not for any one individual, visions are for the collective good of the people of God, which leaves me at a loss to understand how a church can survive without a vision. People must have a vision of God tethered by His word. A pastor must have a vision of God which is relayed to the people through preaching or teaching. The church must have a vision of God which gives direction for God's people. If there is no vision in the pastor's heart he must remain prostrate before the Lord until God reveals His vision for the church. Otherwise, in the church there is no order, no direction, no power, no miracles, and no great faith, and because of a lack of vision, people will perish. They will be ignorant of the things of God. Their finite minds will try to determine what God desires of them, but try as they might, without the Holy Spirit they will decline and eventually die for lack of divine direction.

The Scripture affirms,

> "No eye has seen, no ear has heard, and no mind has imagined what God has prepared for those who love him. But we know these things because God has revealed them to us by his Spirit, and his Spirit searches out everything and shows us even God's deep secrets. No one can know what anyone else is really thinking except that person alone, and no one can know God's thoughts except God's own Spirit. And God has actually given us his Spirit [not the world's spirit] so we can know the wonderful things God has freely given us." [1 Corinthians 2:9-12]

This passage leads me to understand that without vision we can know only the things conceived by the natural mind. Our capability for seeing is limited. Our physical eyes are dulled. Only when the Holy Spirit opens up our eyes to see revelation is vision possible. Only then are we allowed to see into God's heart. After that we see the things of God: we are allowed to peer into God's domain; we are allowed to see through God's eyes; we are allowed to see God. Isaiah saw a vision of God, and he was changed. Ezekiel saw a vision of God and he was transformed. Elisha's young servant saw a vision of God, and his eyes were opened. I saw a vision of God's heart for people, and my heart was indelibly marked. I saw not with my physical eyes, but with the eyes of my heart. In effect the vision from God transformed me into the realm of His glory, the place where He resides, the place where *"Christ sits at God's right hand in the place of honor and power."* [Colossians 3:1b]

Beholding Vision

In the midst of dispiriting reports of stagnation and decline, professional church leaders must be asked: "Is the place where Christ resides not also the place God envisions for the church today? How can the church, the living organism, birthed and empowered by the Holy Spirit, be in decline? How can the church of the living God whose Spirit gives life to dead and dying souls ever be declared stagnant?" The answer is obvious; there is a disjunction between God's vision of the church and the goals and objectives of today's pastors and church leaders.

I believe the missing element in most human goal setting is the very thing that constitutes the church-people. When I view the church today with its many denominations, creeds, doctrines, operating boards, staff, budgets, programs and lavish structures, I am made to know that what I am looking at is not the vision of the church God had in mind when He sent His Son Jesus Christ into the world to establish His Kingdom.

Christ died for people lost in sin and under the sentence of death. God's heart for people is manifested in His Son Jesus, crucified, buried, resurrected, and ascended. Peter's powerful Spirit-filled message to people gathered at Pentecost was the means to grow the church. "*God has made this Jesus whom you crucified to be both Lord and Messiah.*" [Acts 2:36b] His words deeply moved the hearers and "*Those who believed what Peter said were baptized and added to the church.*" [41a]

What God had in mind was for people to come together to worship, pray and fellowship, and to share their lives, their hurt and pain with or without a building, simply because they love and adore Him.

The church is not chartered to be an institution of the world; rather, it is called to be a living organism birthed into God's Kingdom under the watchful eye of the King. Unless pastors and church leaders have a God-given vision of ministry to people, church growth is not possible, and the result is stagnation or declination.

The prophet Isaiah declares,

> [6:1, 5] "In the year King Uzziah died, I saw the Lord. He was sitting on a lofty throne, and the train of his robe filled the Temple … Then I said, 'My destruction is sealed, for I am a sinful man and a member of a sinful race. Yet I have seen the King, the Lord Almighty!"

Transformation and church growth commences with a vision of the Lord. If real change is to come in the church, pastors, denominational leaders, lay leaders, and all persons of faith in Jesus Christ must have a vision of God's heart for the church.

Recently God has brought me to a fuller understanding of the divine working of vision. This new insight has opened the eyes of my heart to see the all encompassing import of the church and its ministry.

Vision is simply God granting us a picture of His heart and showing us what He is going to do for His people. All we can do is stand in awe and watch as the unfolding of His heart becomes manifest.

The question for pastors and church leaders is how do we implement vision? We don't. We do not implement vision; we share the vision of God's heart with His people. God never gives vision in a vacuum. When God gives a vision it comes already fulfilled. It is required that we are faithful to believe in its divine outcome. Each one of us must pray to see vision. However, we must not pray for vision, we must pray for God to prepare our hearts to receive vision.

The initial steps toward realizing vision are to:

Approach God with nothing in your hand.
Acknowledge your utter aversion for sin and your need for forgiveness and mercy.
Desire to have the veil removed from your eyes.
Long for God's holiness and purity to be made manifest in you.
Yield your heart to God's love, and thirst for His presence to flood your life.
Be open for His life to be formed in you by the Holy Spirit.
Be expectant for *"the evidence of things we cannot yet see."*
Behold vision.

Once vision is realized in the heart the recipient must embrace it, nourish it, and cherish it. It is a gift of God for His people. The receiver of vision must then be isolated from all past experiences, habits, and cognitive knowledge. The visionary's eyes must have a single focus to see what others cannot see: Abraham *"was confidently looking forward to a city with eternal foundations, a city designed and built by God."* [Hebrews 11:10] Moses *"kept his eyes on the one who is invisible."* [11:27b] Isaiah *"saw the Lord, He was sitting on a lofty throne."* [Isaiah 6:1b] Ezekiel says, *"the heavens were opened to me, and I saw visions of God."* [Ezekiel 1:1b] The apostle Paul declares [Galatians 1:11, 12] *"I solemnly assure you that the Good News of salvation which I preach is not based on human reasoning or logic. For my message came by a direct revelation from Jesus Christ himself. No one else taught me."*

When the leader's heart is consumed by vision, the recipient will stand before the people with a far away look in their eyes and cast God's vision of ministry for the church. He then calls the people to follow, all the while exhibiting faithful, courageous, dynamic leadership as God fulfills the vision of His heart for His people. He must always remain in the forefront, teaching the people the benefits and joy of the journey as the vision moves toward God's desired end.

What was once thought to be beyond human thought, beyond human capabilities, now becomes visible to the church. People now have a close up view of God's Kingdom. Their hearts are now under the sanction of the Holy Spirit as God defines for the church His intended ministry to people. Without vision the church would be lost in a parade of churches wandering aimlessly, imitating, emulating, copying, and pirating programs from other dying churches. It is sad to see a church without vision.

No one goes around depositing funds into someone else's bank account, because each person properly has his or her own. So it is that God's vision for each of His churches is unique. Each church must pursue God's heart until He deposits there a vision forged entirely for it. The apostle Paul exults, [1 Corinthians 12:2] *"And God has actually given us his Spirit* [not the world's spirit] *so we can know the wonderful things God has freely given us.*

CHAPTER TWENTY

DIFFERENCE MAKERS

"Therefore, go and make disciples of all nations, baptizing them in the name of the Father and the Son and the Holy Spirit."
Matthew 28:19

Clinton Helligar found his way to Pleasant Street Baptist church 15 years ago, following his release from a Connecticut state prison. Clint is an imposing figure. He is tall, around six-three with a very erect posture which makes him appear even taller. He was once feared by the police and authorities because of his temper and great physical prowess. Today the difference in Clinton's life defies description. In his own words:

"It was the year 1989. I had lost my house in the city of New London, Connecticut, due to my drug addiction. I remember around this time I was crying out for help, but no one seemed to understand my cry, they could only see my condition. I remember one day standing on a street corner and my uncle drove by but didn't stop, and later he told me that he got out of his car and looked at me from afar and all he could see was what I could have been. My cry for help came from my inner self. When I sold some cocaine to two undercover cops, my cry grew even louder. One year to that very day, God used that sale of cocaine to answer my cry by taking me off the street and I landed in jail. I likened that experience to Joseph saying to his brothers, *"As far as I am concerned, God turned into good what you meant for evil."* [Genesis 50:20] He wrote:

"It was this time in jail that God began a good work in me. I received seven years suspended sentence after serving two. I was paroled in six months and want to say those six months were the beginning of a freedom that the bars that surrounded me could not take away. I could relate to Paul and Silas singing in prison because they also knew this freedom. God took me off the streets and put me in jail and gave me a place where I could hear him, and would know that this was done by Him and no one else. He also showed me that His discipline was redemptive in nature. Boy, when I learned this, talk about rejoicing! After being released on parole, my heart had truly turned towards God. I thought I could now control my addiction, but once again, I had a relapse with drugs. I remember one night being locked in my bathroom with a friend smoking cocaine, saying to him that Jesus was our only means to be free of this addiction. God in His great faithfulness would not let me stay in my condition for He had started a work in me and He promised to see it through. At that time my girlfriend Lillian, who is now my wife, was going to Pleasant Street Baptist Church, so God opened a door for me to go with her.

"I began attending Pleasant Street in September of 1989 and by October the Word had fully done its job in me by the power of the Holy Spirit. I remember my meeting with the pastor who is still my pastor after 15 years. Pastor McClure was allowing God to use him to bring a word that was so powerful to me that I could not stay away. Now I must say that Pastor took an interest in me. I thought maybe he just liked me as an individual; NOT SO. What I found was, this man just loved people and had a deep conviction to bring people to Christ. To this day I must say the desire of my pastor has only grown deeper.

"I remember sitting in the back of the church as I usually did when the Holy Spirit moved me to answer the call of Jesus *"Come to me, all of you who are weary and carry heavy burdens, and I will give you rest."* [Matthew 11:28] My search was over; my home was with Christ, never more to roam. My pastor became my friend, my teacher and the one who presided over my wedding. He is now the teacher and the pastor to my grandchildren. I thank God for my pastor being a man sensitive to God's leading. Today my whole family is being saved and growing."

Clinton Helligar's story is a familiar one except for the fact that many of the people who came to Pleasant Street for help are no longer here. No longer do they grace the pews at Pleasant Street. No longer do we have opportunity to minister to their needs. Some have fallen away, but many more have moved on, or moved away. I often wondered what we did wrong. Why could we not retain the many people who had come to our doors for help? If God sent them, why did they not stay?

For some time I had fallen victim to a common human failing: I was unable to see the forest for the trees. It wasn't until I began this book that God opened my eyes to see the reality of the ministry He had called our church to. If the standard for success in the church is to increase numbers of members in the pews, then it would appear our efforts have been fruitless, because our membership rolls at Pleasant Street have increased only marginally over the past several years. The more I pondered it, the more bewildered I was. I could not quite understand why and how this was possible, because we have intentionally taken great care to teach and train young believers in the Christian faith. We have classes before and after Baptism, Bible Studies of various kinds, discipleship classes, church growth Bible courses, counseling one on one, and other activities for growing Christians. When I looked at our church records over the years and compared them to our actual membership, I was, to say the least, discouraged and confused, yet prayerful as to what it all meant. "Where did we go wrong?" I asked. What more should we have done to right this problem of retention?

In the years from 1989 through 1991, we had approximately 70 decisions for Christ and baptized 75 percent of them. Since then, we have averaged ten to fifteen decisions and baptisms each year. It means the last 15 years, we can account for at least 200 people who have made life changing decisions for Christ, and yet if we were to look at our actual membership rolls they do not reflect numbers much higher than 100. A great deal of my time was consumed trying to find the answer for the breakdown, until early one morning God interrupted my sleep to show me the forest. He showed me the full measure of the vision in His heart which resulted in my seeing for the first time the real ministry which He has called us here at Pleasant Street.

It was difficult for me to see the depth and breadth of the ministry God had envisioned for us. So He carried me inside the forest to see an enlarged vision of what was in His heart for our community. I first heard him say the people of Pleasant Street are "difference makers". We are here to make a difference in the lives of people and are not to be distracted by counting the amount of square feet in the building, or the numbers of warm bodies filling the pews. Square feet matter only in the size of the field of harvest for the Kingdom. We are only to be measured by the numbers of warm bodies when we count those sent out to rescue the cold, homeless or lost. We are called to make disciples and do everything we can to populate the Kingdom of God on a daily basis. The only real measure is how small or how large is the vision of our God. Somehow I failed to remember we had added a category to our church list called "Active Non Members." It means there are many whose names do not grace our membership rolls for various reasons. There are people faithful in attendance and in every sense as involved in the life of the church as those whose names are visible. Next, He showed me the ministering community and the nature of the people to whom we are called to minister His grace. We are in the center of a Catholic community, which means many of those who we lead to Christ are members of the Roman Catholic Church, but my desire is not to change people's denomination but their hearts.

There are young families, youth in crisis, transients, and people feeling like outcasts of society, many without hope. For the most part, the Westerly community is too proud and too self-centered to admit these folk even exist. However, they do exist and are very much a part of this community, though they are barely visible. They do not sit with the middle class in our churches nor do they frequent the same places as those more established in the community. Few of them can point to famous ancestors who arrived on the *Mayflower*. Few of them own their own homes. Few have a discernible family support system. Few have known anything other than rejection. There are few who believe that anyone really cares about their plight. Few churches would find them financially attractive, and yet God has called us to reach them for Him. For many, the church is the only stable thing they have known.

It brings to mind the story of the Samaritan woman at the well in John 4:4. This woman came to draw water in the middle of the day for fear of running into the townspeople who came early or at night when it was cooler. She was a Samaritan, and people despised her because of her mixed race. She came for water but her real need was for Jesus. These are the people who are reaching out for help, which the community does not readily offer. They are part of our ministering community. We find them or they find us. On the front of our vision brochure, which tells of the church and its ministry, are these words,

> "For I was hungry, and you fed me. I was thirsty, and you gave me a drink. I was a stranger, and you invited me into your home. I was naked, and you gave me clothing. I was sick, and you cared for me. I was in prison, and you visited me. ... Lord, when did we ever see you hungry, thirsty, or a stranger, or naked, or sick or in prison?"
>
> "I assure you, when you did it to one of the least of these my brothers and sisters, you were doing it to me!" [Matthew 25:35-36, 40]

Caller ID

Not long ago I failed to remember Jesus' words about one of *"the least of these my brothers and sisters,"* and God promptly reminded me. Out of frustration and irritation, I had turned my back on one of His lost, despised and disenfranchised people. My aggravation with constant phone calls from a young, delusional woman lost on the streets of Westerly caused me to momentarily lose sight of His vision. The woman was institutionalized for brief periods of time, and almost invariably after her treatment she would make her way back to the church. Her presence was annoying and bothersome to many people, but most galling to me were the numerous telephone calls she made to the church or to my home at any hour of the day or night, when she was in the hospital. She would disguise her voice or use aliases to get someone to answer the phone. The aggravation of the calls prompted me to have caller ID installed on my phone so I could avoid talking to her in the future. My joy in not listening to her was short lived as God brought me to repentance by reminding me of His words, *"I assure you, when you were doing it to one of the least of these my brothers and sisters, you were doing it to me!"* He made me aware that I was one of the very few contacts this young woman had with reality. At the same time, He reopened the door of my memory to a woman named Jamie Saunders.

God took me back to Pond Street Baptist Church in Providence around the fall of 1974. That was when I first took notice of Jamie Saunders. I don't remember the occasion of our first meeting, but in retrospect the circumstances are not important, for I believe Jamie was there to teach me a valuable lesson which would be vital for the implementation of God's revelation yet to come. What made her stand out in my mind was her faithfulness. She was always the first one at Bible Study and prayer meeting on Wednesday evening. Many times she was waiting at the locked church door, having braved the elements—rain, snow, or bitter cold. Her usual covering was a gray and black salt-and-pepper tattered overcoat, and a muted gray scarf loosely wound around her head. Jamie at 60 was a slight woman about five feet tall with a slightly bent frame. She had inconspicuous features except for one distinguishing mark: her right eye was noticeably protruding and a size larger than her left eye, a deformity that caused some people to fear her. Jamie appeared to be unhealthy and hardened by years of living on the street. She carried most of her belongings in a large paper bag, and her demeanor suggested mental illness. During prayer service Jamie would sit quietly for a time, but often without warning she would interrupt the prayer meeting with outbursts of loud, provocative, often damning words directed at any person in her proximity. Her actions caused annoyance, frustration and resentment to many people.

One Wednesday evening as I was leading prayer meeting, Jamie Saunders began loudly inveighing in her usual voice and style. I was very irritated and on edge waiting for what was predictably transpiring. I had no idea how to handle the situation, so I took what I considered a sensible and safe approach to quiet her down by declaring to those assembled that we should pray for Jamie Saunders. Hardly had the words left my lips when I again heard that familiar, small voice speaking and querying me. "Why do you want to pray for Jamie Saunders? Is it because she annoys you, or is it because you believe I can help her and you want that for her?" The answer was obvious. I immediately felt conviction for my sin and I asked God for His forgiveness, as I was reminded that Jamie was *one of the least of these*.

God had indeed taught me a lesson which would be critical if indeed I was to bear His heart of love and compassion to His people. I was convicted by my wrong motives and I vowed never to do that again. I kept my promise until recently, when my sin and selfishness led me to install caller ID on my telephone.

The ministry at Pleasant Street is a less than comfortable ministry. It is not for folk who are wishing for a quiet non-challenging Sunday worship. Our worship services are incredibly alive, meaningful, loving and hopeful. They are inviting, not condemning. However, our members come knowing it is the path to ministry. If one takes the time to note the many times Jesus retreated to the mountain or went to the other side of the lake to be refreshed with the Father, in almost every instance He came back to encounter the blind, the lame, the crippled, the infirmed calling out for help. He went from the top of the mountain to the valley of need. After Jesus was transfigured on the mountain Matthew records: *"When they arrived at the foot of the mountain, a huge crowd was waiting for them."* [Matthew 17:14] A man brought his son to be healed of his seizures. Mark says:

> "A vast crowd was there as he stepped from the boat, and he had compassion on them because they were like sheep without a shepherd. So he taught them many things." [Mark 6:34]

As a church, our members have come to understand what the vision in Westerly means to the larger community. More than half of our membership lives many miles from the church. Yet they have committed a great deal of time and money to support a ministry which they personally derive little support from other than on Sunday. They are willing to follow the Holy Spirit's direction for the church, and because of it they have seen many lives changed, witnessed miracles, and watched the fruit borne out of their obedience and faithfulness to God's promise that he will make a difference.

Our ministry's outreach has touched people in many places far beyond our local area. It has met needs of lay people as well as clergy. It has reached youth and families in crisis here and beyond our ministry area, and when people leave the locale they carry the vision of ministry of Pleasant Street wherever they go. On Tuesdays and Wednesdays I average six to eight hours of counseling. Eighty percent of these persons or families are not members of the church. Many come simply on the testimonies of others of what God has wrought in their lives. Some come great from distances. All come because they seek help, sometime as a last resort. I have watched God answer prayer. I experienced a literal transformation of people right before my very eyes. Many of these people have not come to join a church, they have come for help. When they leave, many of them feel they have experienced God. Several years ago I had a call at ten at night from a young minister in Providence who felt he was being attacked by demons. I invited him down and while he was on the way I called my prayer team together and began to pray for his safe arrival. After spending much time in prayer that night, he was set free and is now conducting an outreach ministry to homeless people in Oakland, California. Just two years ago, I spent many hours counseling a young minister recently graduated from seminary in Massachusetts. The young man lived in Boston and drove the two hours to Westerly every Tuesday for counseling. He is presently assisting the pastor in a church near Boston. Another young man from New London, has come to me seeking help in trying to sort out God's call for his life. Many people have come to the church for help and then went out and ministered the love of Christ to others. At Pleasant Street, we presently have on staff three licensed lay ministers who assist other churches in the area by filling their pulpits at least twice a month. I have counseled pastors, conducted training sessions for deacons in other churches and have taught in educational programs. As previously mentioned, we have been asked by middle school and high school youth to conduct lessons in their Bible study clubs. Many of those to whom we minister are associated with other churches or groups, so our time with them or ability to nurture them is limited. And yet when they move on they carry the Pleasant Street vision of ministry wherever they go.

What is remarkable is that we often hear from people or see them in other places and they usually have pleasant memories and testimonies of lessons learned at Pleasant Street. Further, I have invited pastors from most of the other churches in Westerly to preach and experience our ministry. Pastors of two of the major Roman Catholic churches have come, the rector of the large Episcopal church has preached here, the Seventh Day Baptist pastor and the pastor and ministers from Central Baptist Church, the largest Baptist church in the area, have likewise accepted our invitation. So, no longer do I bemoan the fact our church rolls are not expanding like others. I now celebrate the difference our small church is making in Westerly and surrounding communities.

Deborah Ervin previously lived in a town around 50 minutes from the church. She was so committed to Bible study that she would leave her job and then drive directly to the church in Westerly, often foregoing dinner. Her husband was a practicing Jehovah's Witness, so for her,

Bible study became her food for life, health and strength. She wrote to me from her new home in Florida of the effect it has on her life today.

"Good day, Pastor, Joshua, Friend. All month I have been thinking about contacting you since it was Pastors Appreciation Month. Here it is the last day of the month and I wanted to let you know how much I appreciate you. The years I spent with you [church and especially Bible study] have been very beneficial, and I am so much a better person for the knowledge and understanding I would not have acquired without your patience and guidance, she wrote, "Thank you for giving me a solid foundation which has enabled me to continue to grow and understand and teach others some of the real truths of the Old Testament, such as tithing. Erv is doing well, he is very serious about his deaconship and he teaches our Sunday school class. He is always studying and praying. Who would have believed it? He reminds me of Paul, from a Pharisee to Apostle. I believe that Erv was called by the Lord as Paul was. I've witnessed the transformation he has gone through and I'm still in awe of the change. I think you had more confidence than I did that he would turn around. My only solace was the fact that I knew once the Lord has you in the palm of His hands He will never leave you. I wasn't sure Erv would ever acknowledge the Lord whispering to him. Just goes to show you how patient He can be. Much love to you. Thank you for being who you are and entering my life when you did. Had you not been there I would probably be a Jehovah's Witness today, not knowing that I would be so far from the Truth and Eternal Life. I wish I could turn them all to Christ. But you know how blind they are."

Another person synonymous with our ministry is the Rev. Lydia Velez. Lydia remains one of the most wonderful and memorable persons of all. She came to visit Pleasant Street many years ago on the recommendation of a friend. Here her life was changed. She was nurtured and ministered to and grew up in the church possessing a great love for the Lord. Subsequently, Lydia felt called to professional ministry. She enrolled in Andover Newton Theological School in Newton Centre, Massachusetts and was later called to pastor a church of Spanish speaking immigrants from Central America. Her members came from Nicaragua, San Salvador, Guatemala, Ecuador, Dominican Republic and other neighboring countries. Iglesia Bautista De El Valle Church is located in Brentwood, New York, in the Central Islip area of Long

Island. Lydia Velez is a fine pastor, a wonderful Spirit-filled person and remains close to the church and the people who first cared for her and fostered her knowledge and growth in the Lord. Her church in New York is not large. In fact it would be considered very small by some standards. And yet this small group of people has a vision that the building they presently worship in will one day be their own. What is important to note about this small church is that it is made up of people like those at Pleasant Street who have no previous base in the community and are also in danger of slipping through the cracks. Lydia has said, "My foundation for ministry I learned at Pleasant Street."

"I didn't know my particular need at the beginning, but my pastor helped me to prioritize. He helped me focus on what is important. He counseled me to first get filled with Jesus. Allow the Word to get deep in you; know and grow in the Lord, the pastor would say. Pastor kept me on the right track, and to focus on my desire for ministry. God knew my need. Through this church, God began healing my life deeply. This was the beginning of God's redeeming work in my life," she wrote, "I was totally delivered from using alcohol and drugs. I went through a process of cleansing, emotionally and spiritually. My life drastically changed. The vision of Rev. McClure to reach the unloved reached out to me, and now I know I am loved."

What I have been attempting to point out is our ministry here in Westerly continues to impact lives far away from the pews. Each church's ministry is different. Each person called by God to pastor His people has been prepared from birth to be God's visible gift to the church. Indeed, it carries an awesome responsibility to be charged with the task of making God manifest and also knowing that the effectiveness of the task can only be measured by God himself. Since God calls us to the work and God Himself oversees the work, the results must come under His scrutiny alone.

But how often do we seize the place of God in the church and insert our own standard for success in ministry by using measures established by the world? Can the size of the church be the determining factor in the church's effectiveness in ministry? Is the number of pews occupied on Sunday morning the statistic for successful ministry? Does the number of choirs, boards or committees indicate fulfillment of God's desires for His church? Is it the number of deacons in the church or the credence of the pastor's degrees that prove God is resident in the ministry of the church?

I ask these questions because over the years I have heard each of these counts, along with others, cited as the way to measure the effectiveness of a church's ministry in people's lives. However, I now know that none of these alone can be a credible witness for Christ. None can be the solitary measure of whether we are, indeed, the living organism of God assembled under its head the Lord Jesus Christ, or if we are merely a great worldly organization—only constituted in the name of the Lord. I do not wish to be controversial or confrontational. However, I do not believe any of the elements above meet God's standard for the church. The only acceptable standard for the church is a changed or "transformed" heart, and the resulting fruit it produces. Jesus affirms this in [Matthew 7:20] saying, *"Yes, the way to identify a tree or a person is by the kind of fruit that is produced."*

The apostle Paul writes

> "But when the Holy Spirit controls our lives, he will produce this kind of fruit in us: love, joy, peace, patience, kindness, goodness, faithfulness, gentleness, and self-control. Here there is no conflict with the law." [Galatians 5:22, 23]

What I am suggesting is that we often use the wrong measure to determine whether we are successful in what God calls us to do. I thank God that He has allowed me to look beyond the trees and behold the forest. He has allowed me to discover the true worth of the vision of ministry He has for His church at Pleasant Street. May I never look at it any other way than through His eyes. And may I ever prove faithful to His trust in me to carry out His wishes.

CHAPTER TWENTY ONE

Christ Our Life

"Instead, there must be a spiritual renewal of your thoughts and attitudes. You must display a new nature because you are a new person, created in God's likeness—righteous, holy, and true."
Ephesians 4:23, 24

There are many people who wear the name Christian; however, my observations lead me to believe there are far fewer who have undergone real life change and live life daily in the Kingdom of God. Those who have experienced the Kingdom are living testimonies of the incredible transformation God has wrought in their lives. They are people created again, but in a new and different way. The apostle Paul explains, *"What this means is that those who become Christians become new persons. They are not the same anymore, for the old life is gone. A new life has begun!"* [2 Corinthians 5:17] It is then clear to all the difference Christ can make in people who are willing to open their lives to Him.

The Holy Spirit is the agent of change: The divine transformer, the construction manager, the building foreman, the interior outfitter and the finisher. He is the guarantee that the transformation will be completed from the old house to God's new home.

> "The Spirit is God's guarantee that he will give us everything he promised and that he has purchased us to be his own people. This is just one more reason for us to praise our glorious God." [Ephesians 1:14]

A new relationship with God is personal, intimate and real. A person no longer wonders what life can be like. They no longer have concerns about receiving the promise. They now live the life God prepared for them in Christ, freely and joyfully knowing it is already theirs. In essence they are becoming-being-changed into His likeness.

This means the Holy Spirit is at work, and God is in the center of the church's ministry. The manifestation of a changed life more than anything else proves, without question, that God is real. Here the invisible God becomes sight, and Christ is now seen living His life out in us. Transformation is well underway and becoming like Jesus is factual as we share in His divine nature. The remainder of this chapter will be given over to those whose lives witness real change. Like the apostle Paul they testify, "*I myself no longer live, but Christ lives in me. So I live my life in this earthly body by trusting in the Son of God, who loved me and gave himself for me.*" [Galatians 2:20]

Testimonials
Priscilla Lee: East Providence, Rhode Island

Priscilla was the oldest of five children. She was a non-practicing Catholic. Her marriage at age 16 had produced six children. I met Priscilla in the spring of 1978 while I was associate minister at Second Freewill Baptist Church later named Pond Street Baptist Church in Providence. She had come on the behest of her sister-in-law to dedicate her youngest child. God was prepared to give her much more than she sought. She describes what came after in her own words.

"The ceremony was wonderful. But the smiles and laughter camouflaged the feelings of worthlessness that plagued my soul. The dream would not go away. In my dream, Christ descended from the heavens. The skies literally opened, and all eyes could see Him. Jesus spoke to me and said that although I wasn't a "bad" person, I couldn't ascend to heaven. I was in Purgatory. I had to "earn" my way into heaven, I had to repent. As I discussed possible interpretations with the pastor, a gentleman stood near and listened attentively. After the discussion ended, the gentleman apologized for eavesdropping, and introduced himself. He was then Minister McClure.

"Although I didn't realize it, I was angry with God. My oldest child died at age 3 in 1964. She was hit by a car. I loved her so much. She was my first born. She belonged to me and no one could take her away. I wanted to die. I was also sexually molested. Feelings of shame, worthlessness, abandonment, and fear consumed my thoughts, and painful memories remained etched in my mind. Although I then had two other children, my despair made me feel that they were better off without me. Thoughts of suicide were my only escape. After a period of time, I left my husband. I now had four children. We moved into an apartment. Suicidal thoughts continued to lurk in my mind. I enjoyed smoking, drinking, and going to clubs. I didn't want to give it up. But another part of me wanted and desperately needed God to be with me and my family. Unfortunately the tug of war I fought within could not shake my demons. I attempted suicide.

"My sister-in-law sought out Rev. McClure to speak with me. He visited me at the hospital. Since I was receiving shock therapy, I cannot vividly recall six months of that time. However, I do remember the kind images of Rev. McClure speaking to me while I remained in my dreamy state. I always remembered Rev. McClure. I tried to put my life back together. The children and I moved back home with my husband. Rev. McClure continued to visit, and Rev. McClure began to also counsel my marriage. Rev. McClure was sympathetic, kind, gentle, and understanding. But most importantly, he never condemned. We shared many conversations and he always led me to the Scriptures. He never showed the frustration that he must have surely felt.

"I attempted suicide again. I failed again. Desperate to save my life, my mother knew that the only person I trusted was Rev. McClure. She contacted him, and again he found the words to give me strength. However, I would always say: Rev. McClure, intellectually I understand what you are saying, BUT … It was the BUT that always got me into trouble. I could not feel worthy of God. I had to clean myself up. I had to earn my way into heaven.

"The third and final suicide attempt was in 1988. It changed my life. I was in a coma and on life support for three days. I remember waking up and sensing I was in a strange place. I couldn't move. Where was I? Why wasn't I at work? Suddenly I heard someone whispering my name very softly. Then the voice said, 'That was a close one.' I replied, 'Not close enough.' It was Rev. McClure. We prayed.

"I began to attend Pleasant Street Baptist Church. I always sat in the back of the church. One particular Sunday morning, I was feeling extremely depressed and hopeless. After service completed, I walked to my car and cried. I said, 'Lord, I can't bear this burden any longer. I surrender it all to you. I cannot do it on my own, and I don't want to try anymore. I give it all to you.' Immediately, I felt lifted. I felt relief and peaceful. I knew at that moment that I was saved. Shortly thereafter, God also took away my desire for cigarettes and alcohol. I had tried many times to quit on my own, only to start over again. But this was different. I had no withdrawal symptoms. The desire was completely gone. Without my effort, those desires were taken from me. Divine intervention put Christ in my life. Oh Happy Day!"

Marie Thompson, Westerly, Rhode Island

Marie Thompson is a mother of three children and grandmother of eight. She is a lifelong resident of Westerly and lives just a few blocks from Pleasant Street Baptist Church. Marie had been raised as a Catholic, but one day she visited Pleasant Street Church upon invitation of a friend and has now become an integral part of our church family. She is a testimony that Pleasant Street Church has now become an established part of the ministering community in Westerly and surrounding areas. Marie is a spirit-filled woman who exudes the love of God. Her most outstanding characteristic is best described by the songwriter as a "sweet, sweet spirit." She recalls:

"My first meeting with Pastor McClure was a Wednesday night Bible study. My first impression of that meeting was how deeply spiritual a man was the pastor. He truly was blessed with his faith and understanding of God's will. Pastor reinforced some of my personal spiritual beliefs through study and interpretation of the Word of God. I was seeking comfort through faith in Jesus Christ. I believe I was brought to Pleasant Street Baptist Church. The people of the church are wonderful and share it in love and faith with all. The ministry of Pastor Joshua McClure has helped my life to change. I feel closer in my walk with my Savior Jesus Christ."

Stanley P. L. Fitzhugh Jr, Mattapoisett, Massachusetts

Stanley is my sister Arline's oldest son. He is a married, in his mid forties, a tall, fine-looking, physically imposing, man who is faced with the harsh reality of a career change because of a recently discovered blood disorder. Stanley, a Massachusetts State trooper, is facing retirement because of his condition. A Christian for many years, Stanley has rediscovered the joy of Christ in the Scriptures. His testimony bears witness to his confidence in placing his future in the Lord's hands.

> "Don't worry about anything; instead, pray about everything. Tell God what you need, and thank him for all he has done. If you do this, you will experience God's peace, which is far more wonderful than the human mind can understand. His peace will guard your hearts and minds as you live in Christ Jesus." [Philippians 4:6, 7]

"I was a Massachusetts State Trooper, six feet 2 inches, 240 pounds and could bench press 400 pounds. I was literally a poster child for the State Police: I was on brochures and billboards all across the state and everyone knew my name. Invincible, right? Wrong! I knew about Jesus, I grew up in a Christian family, had been baptized and gave my life to Christ years ago. But living in the world, I had all but forgotten who Christ was and my promise I made to Him years ago. That would all change on January 19, 2004 at 1:13 in the afternoon. I had been involved in a bad motor vehicle accident while on duty that day and it changed my life forever.

"As a result of the accident, I sustained a serious back and shoulder injury. I was placed on injured leave and started rehab. Everyone said how lucky I was to get out of that accident with only those injuries. While rehabbing, my activities were greatly diminished. I could not work out like I used to and my mobility was limited. Most of my time was spent on the couch, or some days I couldn't even get out of bed. Then on March 20, 2004, I woke up around 9:30 A. M. to horrible chest pain and my right calf was swollen and felt cramped up. I sat on the end of the bed hoping the pain would go away. It didn't.

"I decided to drive myself to the emergency room (by this time the pain had gotten worse). I made it to the hospital and sat down in a wheelchair. Next thing I knew I was hooked up to all kinds of machines, oxygen mask, etc. I've seen it many times on the job when people are in distress and death may or may not be near. They cry out to "Oh God please don't let me die.' Those very words came to my mind and out my mouth. After several tests the doctor came in and told me I had severe blood clots in both my lungs and that they were taking me to ICU. I stayed there for five days. He also said, 'You're a very lucky young man to have come in when you did, if you had waited any longer this would have been fatal.' I ended up in the hospital for three weeks. I have permanent lung damage and will be on medication for the rest of my life.

"However, the realization that I was no longer a trooper, the job I had loved and was committed to for years was really sinking in. I became very despondent, and I didn't know what I was going to do next. A week or two later my Uncle Josh called and told me he would be in the area and wanted to stop by and say Hi. I wasn't feeling very well and was in no mood for guests, but it was my Uncle so I said OK [Holy Spirit]. He stopped by, and we talked for a while. I told him what was happening, that I wasn't feeling too good about the situation with the job. After talking for a little while he said I should get some rest and that he would be leaving. But before he left, he said he wanted to pray, so we sat at the kitchen table and prayed. I will never forget that day. We prayed and prayed and as we did I could feel the stress, the anger and disappointment starting to lift from my body. Even the pain was starting to subside. I felt a happiness starting to take hold of my being. Then I realized what was happening to me: I knew that feeling, I've had it BEFORE. It was the Holy Spirit entering my soul. That was a very emotional time for me. I had missed that feeling; it felt so good for it to be back. After my Uncle left I started reading the scriptures again and studying the Word. A few weeks after that I went down and spent the weekend with him. We read the scriptures and talked for hours rejoicing in the Word well into the night. Since then I've been reading the Word daily, and the Word is changing my life DAILY. I now know everything's going to be fine. The Lord will find a way, another door will open. Praise God!"

Joe and Barbara Siner, North Stonington, Connecticut

Joe and Barbara are two people whose lives bear the imprint of Christ. They live in a country setting in North Stonington, Connecticut, approximately twenty minutes from Pleasant Street Baptist Church. They came to Pleasant Street with negative experiences, a trove of questions and skepticism about any involvement in the church. Their reason for coming at all was through the faith of a little child, their daughter Karalyn. God was then able to minister to their pain, overcome their fears and reservations and bring healing and wholeness to their lives. Joe and Barbara Siner today are visible fruit of God's vision of ministry for Pleasant Street Baptist Church. Barbara recalls the events that led to their life change:

"In 1992, my 11 year old daughter Karalyn was invited to attend a Friend's Day worship service at Pleasant Street Baptist Church in Westerly. She enjoyed herself so much that she asked if she could go back with her friend the next Sunday, and the next, and the next … soon she asked if she could join the church and be baptized. I told her that if she went to church for six months without excuse or complaint, she could indeed be baptized and join. Nearing the six months she reminded me of my promise and I thought it would be wise to attend a worship service and meet with the pastor. I did both and found a friendly church and a wonderful, intelligent, down-to-earth man as its head. I next week prodded my husband Joe to check out the church our daughter would be joining."

"The church and pastor resonated with Joe, and it took only a 'are we going to church this week?' to make it an unshakable habit. Joe was soon participating in the choir, cleanup, yard maintenance and eventually became a full active member. After a few years, he was asked to be a deacon. I am proud of Joe's work and the wonderful gentleness that has overtaken his spirit. On the other hand, my walk with the church was not such a straight line. While my husband was a fallen away son of a Baptist minister, I was a religiously stone-cold niece of a Catholic priest and a Catholic nun. The fire of the spirit that I felt and saw in the pastor and the men and women in the church was something I wanted. However, I struggled to find a way to get it without giving up my critical analysis and my family heritage. I edged closer over the years due to pastor's logical, spirit-filled and inspiring sermons and the day-to-day witnessing of the church members. One day my name was put forward for a deacon and many were shocked since I had not even become a member nor had I been baptized except as a baby.

"This time my loving pastor nailed my feet to the floor, so to speak. I told him what was holding me back in my spiritual walk. One afternoon we sat one on one. Pastor led me through the Scriptures and I literally saw the light. I am now baptized, a walking deacon, and the happiest I have ever been. Thanks to a loving God and my blessed Pastor Joshua McClure."

Thus, before us is the evidence that the God-given vision of ministry for Pleasant Street Baptist Church is being fulfilled. Its fruit can be observed daily in the many changed lives. And it can be seen in the diverseness of personal testimonies that the vision has visibly touched people in all walks of life, and in surrounding communities near and far from Westerly. The vision has reached out to embrace time, cultures, communities and continents. So many more people wanted to share their personal testimony of the change Christ has wrought in them but neither time nor the pages of this book could contain them all, so I offer you just a sampling of the difference Christ can make living His life out in us.

The people of Pleasant Street, along with this great cloud of witnesses, are also evidence of what God can accomplish through a small group of believers who are obedient to Him as He confirms once again the promise of His presence, *"For there are more on our side than on theirs."* [2 Kings 6:16] This once dying church has led people out of the darkness of sin and brought them into God's marvelous light of life, all because they ceased to tell God about their mountains. Instead they faithfully began to tell the mountains about their God. The church previously mentioned as moribund, on its way to extinction, whose guttering candle flame was all but snuffed out is now a divine luminescence that radiates light of Christ for miles around. Jesus' words commend, *"You are the light of the world—like a city on a mountain, glowing in the night for all to see."* [Matthew 5:14]

Pleasant Street Baptist Church, Westerly, now reflects the light of Christ because it heeded King Solomon's ominous warning, *"Where there is no vision the people perish."*

CHAPTER TWENTY TWO

Vision Unveiled

"Slowly, steadily, surely, the time approaches
when the vision will be fulfilled."
Habakkuk 2:3a

The writing of this book sets forth the footsteps of the vision of ministry for the people here in Westerly and its surrounding communities. For the past twenty-five years this has been my home and my appointed task before God. Much has been done, much is now underway, and much is yet to be done; all this at the hand of God.

The vision of many years ago has led to my initial attempt to transfer my thoughts from my heart to paper. This book is not about me. This is a love story of the God who I encountered in my life, the God who is my life, my everything, my all.

Since I have begun to write about what God has done, I feel even more compelled to make Him known. He has awakened my memory and has been pouring words from His heart into my understanding for a greater vision of Him; and in the process he took me into the place where His deep secrets reside.

Pleasant Street at one time had simply claimed squatter's rights on the top of a lone hill in the North End of Westerly. This was a community that had known a former glory; however, Pleasant Street Baptist Church was not counted among the names listed on their glory roster. Today much has changed. Transformation is beginning in the North End largely due to the visibility and intentional ministry of the church to its residents. New hope has spawned in the community. A past president of the Westerly Town Council, Barry Cole, proudly pointed out six years ago that Pleasant Street Baptist Church was now the hub of the North End. The same little white building on the hillside, once a quiet, unremarkable, old church on a side street, has now emerged as a busy, remarkable ministering community. No longer unnoticed, this church in the far southern extremity of Rhode Island is now sought out by people far and wide as a place where people care. Small, powerful, but far reaching, the church has undergone transformation energized by a vision from God.

On February 3, 2005, at 10 A.M. there was a reception held in the church fellowship hall to announce the commencement of work to renovate homes to aid the revitalization of the North End neighborhood. The reception was attended by the executive director and representatives from the Rhode Island Housing Authority, the Westerly Town Manager, members of the Westerly Town Council, the Westerly Police Chief and officers, state Representatives, the Washington Trust Bank, and the developer of the project, the North End Crime Watch and Community Development, Inc., along with newspapers from Rhode Island and Connecticut.

When I became pastor of Pleasant Street I had a dream of building affordable housing for low income families and elderly on a three and one quarter acre lot behind the church. This did not materialize because the targeted land was eventually sold. One day then Capt. Pete Plenninger of the Westerly Police Department contacted me and told me of a man living in the North End who had a similar dream for the area. Adrian Pelchat and I met, and we immediately bonded. We shared our vision for the North End and found we had much in common. Adrian was a man raised in the North End of Westerly, moving here 55 years ago. The last 25 years of his life had been spent watching his once proud neighborhood with its pristine houses, manicured lawns, distinctive porches and colorful flower boxes brought to its knees by blight, propelled by the greed of absentee landlords, abandoned houses and drugs. In 1992, the North End Crime Watch and Community Development was formed to address some of these problems. Pleasant Street Baptist Church has been its meeting place since. Today the drug problem in the North End has abated, partially due to a police sub-station in its midst. The absentee landlords are being pressured to improve or sell their properties, and along with this, home ownership / landlord tenant classes are available to prepare low income persons and families to purchase the renovated properties. Largely due to the resurrection of the church there is now a renaissance in the North End of Westerly.

These highly visible alterations now underway are bringing renewed hope to the minds and hearts of the people of the neighborhood. Along with this, Pleasant Street Church is about to undergo a physical transformation of its own which will make the present church building a multi-purpose worship center to complement the educational ministry. Earlier, I noted that the church stood alone for many years as a Sunday worship place. However, with the addition of the purchased properties, it has been slowly converting to a ministry center. Now plans have progressed, and financing is nearly in place to renovate the main church building, sanctuary, and fellowship hall on the street level to complete the conversion to an all encompassing ministry complex.

Movable chairs are planned for use in the sanctuary to allow for maximum use when the present space is expanded into a larger worship area that can be converted to other uses. Currently our pews seat 85 people. The new sanctuary will comfortably seat 120; however, when necessary additional chairs may be added. The choir seating will increase from fifteen to twenty-five. Dual use of the seating space will accommodate an expanded banquet area or space for larger programming when needed. The lower level of the church building will be redesigned for classrooms for Sunday school. This will allow for carefully planned growth until much larger quarters are needed for future expansion of the ministry. The entrance into the church will be relocated from its familiar surroundings near the west end of the building. The new church entry will be on the eastern end of the church adjoining the handicapped ramp. Immediately upon entering the church building, stairs on the right side will lead to the lower level. This will be a more centralized entryway affording more direct contact to the church office and ongoing ministry areas. These changes will bring the vision nearer to reality both spiritually and physically.

When the vision first arrived with me in 1986, it was summarily rejected by the church leaders. Little credit had been given to its Divine author, and it was easy for people to justify their actions by branding the vision as a personal desire of mine. This caused a chain reaction by many people in the congregation who echoed the words of the leaders and were resistant to a word from God. However, as it has been proven time and time again, God always has the last word.

There was a minority of people in the church who believed in the vision without seeing.

Love and Ophelia Freeman had moved to Westerly several years before from Staten Island, NY, and were well respected members of the church. Love Freeman was my choice for chairman of the Deacon Board, and he proved to be the most loyal friend and supporter a pastor could ever have. He and Ophelia immediately embraced the vision as God's will for the church and community and for their lives. From the very beginning they helped others to see God, and they supported the vision until Love died on December 28, 1996. The church property at 33½ Pleasant Street, "The Love Freeman House" in honor of his service to the church and ministry, is slated to be a retreat place for ministers and missionaries.

Following his death, Ophelia Freeman was elected chair of the diaconate and her humble loving dedication to the Lord has earned her the respect from persons both inside and outside the church. She is the only person I know who is always addressed as "Mrs. Freeman", never by her first name.

One of the most memorable persons of all was a woman named Rose Virginia Smith. Virginia was a woman infused with the presence of God. She had been a member of Pleasant Street for 45 years and lived a few doors down the street from the church during that time. After being in the home of Virginia and Charles Smith, you had a feeling of being in a place where God dwelled. I believe to this day I met the Lord many times there. On the third Sunday in February of 1997, I had the distinct privilege and pleasure of renewing the marriage vows of Virginia and Charles Smith on their 64th wedding anniversary. Three years later on September 9, 2000, her beloved Charles died. Virginia continued to attend church until her health began to fail and prohibited her going out. All the while, Virginia faithfully supported the vision God had allowed her to see. From the moment I presented the vision to her she carried that far away look in her eyes. On January 13, 2004, Virginia slipped quietly away into the presence of her God who had been waiting to greet her.

There was among us a woman whose family ties reach back almost to the founding of the church by Native Americans in the 1800's. Mary Sebastian, after hearing me expound on the vision for the church, came to me a few days later and declared, "Pastor, I see us going all the way down to the end of the block." I must admit I did not see what Mary saw. After much reflection, I realized God had given Mary eyes to see beyond what I had even dared. Mary Sebastian taught me a valuable lesson. My God was too small. Her God knew no bounds.

Another person not to be forgotten in the initial stages of the vision was Margueritta Tucker.

Margueritta has been in the church since arriving from Lynchburg, Virginia as a young girl in 1958. She liked the Westerly area and decided to make it her home, settling in with her grandmother Signora Glover, and her grandmother's sister, Janie Purnell. Margueritta is a quiet, determined, somewhat private individual who had, over the years, known many pastors and witnessed several changes in the church. However, it was not until she heard me share the vision of ministry with people that she became truly excited. She was able to peer into the nothingness with her eyes of faith to see what the church would one day become. Because of her deep love and devotion to Christ and her spiritual eyes to envision the deep things of God, Margueritta was chosen as chairperson of the vision council. She recently stated:

"When you came as the pastor, there was a greater sense of stability in the leadership. One thing had to be established. We had to be one body of believers with a leader reporting to God and following God's promptings. You provided the leadership that was desperately needed. As full-time pastor you gave continuity to worship. The church has grown with your teaching. With your new leadership came the opportunity for all to participate in the ministry of the church. Reaching out for others was very new to many in the church. We have now become a church that is known for helping people and accepting people whether they are old or young.

Our membership embraces African Americans, Caucasians, Asians, Native Americans and Latin Americans. Pleasant Street is a church for everyone and any one. It is now an integral part of the North End plus community and towns beyond. My hope is that everywhere we go, we will be simply known as people of the Kingdom."

Initially there were others reached by the ministry. All had their staunch faith rewarded by the miracle of vision. God had proved to be faithful to and through them as people who believed without seeing.

Transitions

In the hearts of these people the vision began to take shape, and with God opening up other's hearts it has grown to become the all encompassing vision of ministry that it is today. At this point I feel I am encroaching on the time when my part in implementing the vision is nearing its close, and my role must, of necessity, change to a more supportive mentoring function to make room for the Joshua God has been preparing to lead these people to the next level. I say this with some sense of sadness and mixed emotions. However, I am excited about the future for Pleasant Street, because I greatly anticipate that Pleasant Street is poised on the threshold of some extraordinary times. I have set some goals for myself and for the church along, with a plan of transition for moving forward into the next decade of ministry with new, younger, exciting, more physically able vital leadership. My goal for the future is to ensure that when I relinquish the reigns of pastoral leadership all that we had set out to do back in 1986 will be accomplished or fully underway, with one exception: a decision will have to be made whether to move forward with construction of a K-8 Christian Academy.

Meanwhile, my personal plans for the future are set. God has filled me with a new excitement and enthusiasm unparalled since the day I first met Him. He has blessed me to carry the vision forward with the pen and to put on paper the thoughts and words stored in the archives of my mind for such a time as this. For as long as He will allow, I will make known through writing and teaching the love and faithfulness and majesty of my incomparable Savior and Lord Jesus Christ.

Fulfillment

What I have come to learn is that the vision was not for Pleasant Street alone but for all of God's people everywhere. It did not begin in the heart of a man in Providence, in December of 1976, but it began in eternity, long before Joshua A. McClure was conceived. The vessel that bore the imagination of God is temporal but the vision is eternal. Finite as I am, I will one day be at rest in the bosom of the Lord. However, the vision from the heart of the infinite God will return in fulfillment of Him who spawned it.

But what of the vision's future course? What's next for the future of the ministry here at Pleasant Street? Will the vision for Pleasant Street continue? Yes. Will it achieve God's end? Yes. Of the vision itself, I am assured of its arrival. Through all of these years I have gained divine insights into the workings of God. The Holy Spirit has taken me into the inner courts and revealed to me *"even God's deep secrets."* [1 Corinthians 2:10b]

One of the most important lessons I have learned is that vision is passed down from generation to generation. This has its inception in the Scriptures and has been practiced since the people of God came into existence. In researching the history of the nation of Israel, I came upon a most amazing fact to which I attribute to the success of the Jews to this very day: the patriarchs taught us the value of passing on a blessing to their children—not merely a pat on the head for doing something commendable, but the impartation of a blessing from God before their sojourn into the world. When the father blessed his child, words would be spoken which would mark their future success or failure to eternity. Once spoken, these words could not be rescinded for any reason. When Esau realized his brother Jacob had tricked his father Isaac into giving him the blessing reserved for the firstborn son, Esau cried out to his father to bless him too, but Isaac replied, *"I blessed him with an irrevocable blessing before you came."* [Genesis 27:33b]

Several times in the church, particularly on Father's Day, I have called for all of our children to come forward and stand around the altar. It is then I call for the men and fathers of the church to lay hands on each of our children and pray a blessing of God into their lives. Will the vision continue? Certainly. Because God is today moving it along in the hearts and lives of our younger generation. A few years ago it was manifested in my now five-year-old grandchild, Cinphany Janine McClure-Snead. On several occasions before she was four years old, Cinphany was dressing herself, trying to write her name, or fixing her cereal and pouring her own milk. Each time Dorothy, her mother, offered to help. She was rebuffed. Each time, it appeared that Cinphany was having difficulty accomplishing her task, and Dorothy, like a concerned parent, offered her services. But Cinphany refused. Finally Dorothy was exasperated enough with her daughter to sit her down and inquire, "What's going on here? Why will you not allow me to help?" She wanted to know why Cinphany was so determined to succeed on her own. Cinphany calmly raised her head, demurely flashed her little eyes, and with a determined look on her face said, "Mommie! Grampoppie said that I can do anything. I can be anything I want to be. Grampoppie said I can do it." Cinphany remembered the blessing spoken into her young life when hands were laid on her, and she was applying to herself the words of the apostle Paul *"For I can do everything with the help of Christ who gives me the strength I need."* [Philippians 4:13] To Cinphany there is no goal she cannot achieve. Nothing is impossible in her young, fertile mind. I am confident the vision is in good hands. I can rest in this assurance. I have no fear. The vision will duly arrive in the throne room of God having achieved its divine purpose.

Conclusion

Oswald Chambers once remarked, "Every God-given vision will become real if we will only have patience. The vision that God gives is not some unattainable castle in the sky, but a vision of what God wants you to be down here. Allow the potter to put you on His wheel and whirl you around as He desires. Then as surely as God is God, and you are you, you will turn out as an exact likeness of the vision. But don't lose heart in the process. If you have ever had a vision from God, you may try as you will to be satisfied on a lower level, but God will never allow it."

Epilogue

> "No eye has seen, no ear has heard, and no mind has imagined
> what God has prepared for those who love him."
> 1 Corinthians 2:9

The writing of this book exposits God's message for His church today. I pray that the message is clear. Its one main character is God. Its one main theme is the love of God for His people. Its principal source is the heart of God. Its sole conveyance is a vision birthed in the heart of God. Its foremost recipient is the church, the people of God. Its primary purpose is to manifest God's Son, Jesus Christ, to bring light and life to a people walking in darkness.

This book is not about churches or church buildings, large or small, nor is it about recognition of great programs large or small. This book is about transformation. It is about change. It is about resurrection. It is about life. It is about people, real people. God's people—people in ultimate danger of slipping through the cracks. It is about a God who cares so much for His created beings He would do anything and everything to save them, free them, and preserve them.

Can present day stagnating, expiring churches find new life? Can complacency and apathy in the church be reversed? Can doubting and dying folk be resurrected? Is there today a definitive answer for God's query, *"Can these bones become living persons again?"*

Admittedly, today's church is in decline. Many churches are closing their doors while countless others are heading toward a spiritual graveyard. Numerous congregations are being aptly defined as "a group of people void of the Spirit of God" or as others have noted, "a church without God's presence." All of this adds relevancy today to the question asked by God of the prophet Ezekiel concerning His nation's demise. The problem for the church today is not church growth, rather it is church survival. Thus the book addresses the burning question of life and death.

Previously, God had shown Ezekiel the idolatrous rites in the high places scattered about the countryside. Now the prophet is about to be exposed to the sins of his countrymen which have their lodging at the very center of national life, sin which strikes at the very heart of God, in Jerusalem and its temple. The nation has repudiated the God who made it a people and has replaced Him by the gods of the surrounding countries. I cannot help think the nation of Israel is much like the church today, for it too is idolatrous. Today's church is steeped in doctrines, creeds and liturgies. It is rich in structure with boards, committees and hierarchy and in some cases human figures who claim to stand in for God. We may not call it blatant idolatry, but it qualifies as willful rejection and leaves little place for God. It is, in essence, secularized religion. Worship without God's presence. Song without spirit. Prayer without power. Liturgy without life. Pulpits with an absentee King. Churches void of the spirit. Stagnating, declining, expiring.

The frightening narrative in Chapter Ten shows God's answer. He is departing the temple. He is withdrawing His presence from among the people. God gets up and says, "I've had enough religion, I'm leaving." The sad thing is not one person tries to stop Him. He rises up from His throne and moves to the threshold of the temple ...Waiting. Waiting. He goes down the hallway and no one notices. People are yet singing and worshipping. He now goes from the Holy of Holies to the doorway. He moves from the door of the temple to the Eastern Gate. No one takes notice of His movements. Not one person says, "God is leaving." If the Spirit of God is leaving the building somebody ought to say something. The Glory of God now hovers over Mt. Zion east of the city ... waiting for someone to stop Him, but the church is singing, worshipping, praising without the presence of God and no one expresses concern. The one who birthed the church has departed. The reason for their being a church has been withdrawn. Religion is king.

How often does the contemporary church find itself confronted by this narrative? How often is the church challenged by God's query to the prophet, "*Son of man, can these bones live?*" Many are at a loss how to answer. Many are operating too securely inside of their intellectual comfort zone. Too often the church doesn't encourage people to break out of their insular spirituality, because their leaders have received no clear word from God. This leaves people at a loss. The only way they know is holding onto established doctrines and creeds, never even thinking about slipping out of the mundane to risk what God desires of the church. Keep singing. Keep praying. Keep worshipping. Do your committee work, read your Sunday bulletin. Tithe. Attend choir rehearsal. It's sufficient for God's presence—but remember, if you seriously seek after the vision of God's heart for the church you may have to surrender your will for His.

The contemporary church gathered is often viewed not as a living organism with a vision powerful, awe inspiring, loving, and exalted, but as buildings, operating boards, staff, budgets, programs and lavish structures—where the facilities are nice and faith is mere conversation. Occasionally we run into the poor, homeless, the hopeless, or the disenfranchised and we know there are indeed those Jesus qualified as *"the least of these my brothers and sisters."* [Matthew 25:45b]But for the moment we keep singing, we keep praying, we keep praising.

The answer lies in whether pastors or church leaders have received God's vision for the church. But even more dreadful is the answer for the people when the leader has no vision to share with them. *"Where there is no vision the people perish."*

Leaders must come to the realization that it's not what cognitive knowledge purports the church to be, rather, it is what the Holy Spirit reveals the church to be. *"But we know these things because God has revealed them to us by his Spirit, and his Spirit searches out everything and shows us even God's deep secrets."* [1 Corinthians 2:10] God has not abandoned His church. God still reveals His heart to the church. God still speaks through visions but the church must be open to see and hear. It then stands that God's vision is the prerequisite to resurrecting dead or dying churches.

God's vision can change churches into vital, living organisms that reclaim broken lives, change hearts, heal hurts, and bring glory to Him. Confirmation is seen in the fact that a small, once expiring congregation in Westerly, Rhode Island, is very much alive. It is the story of God's vision for His church and what can happen when people faithfully follow after His heart. It shows that a church leader or pastor armed with a lone vision from God can make a great impact on a larger community. This account which shows how a God ordained vision captured a man's heart and ignited a small, nondescript church into become an explosive, growing, dynamic ministry can be experienced by all. Vision can indelibly change the leader, the church, the community, and the people it was called to serve.

"*Son of man, can these bones live?*"
"O *Sovereign Lord, you alone know.*" [Ezekiel 37:3, NIV]
Yes, these bones can live. These bones can become living persons again.

"Now glory be to God! By his mighty power at work within us, he is able to accomplish infinitely more than we would ever dare to ask or hope. May he be given glory in the church and in Christ Jesus forever and ever through endless ages. Amen." [Ephesians 3:20, 2]

Index

A

Abel family	38
Abyssinian Baptist Church [NYC]	39
Active non Members	206
Adams, John	57
Advent Christian Colored Church	29
Afflerbach, Ray	110, 111
AIKD	110, 111, 113
Alessio, Bob G. [Deacon]	152, 154
A Little Bit of Love choir	26, 27, 174, 181, 182
Allied Woodcrafters	83, 84
AME Zion Churches	121
American Baptist Churches of Rhode Island [ABCORI]	60, 66, 129, 130-132
American Baptist Churches, USA	129, 130, 132
American Baptist Convention	130
American Custom Kitchens, Inc.	107, 108
American Institute of Kitchen Dealers [AIKD]	108, 110
Ammons, Gideon	29
Andover Newton Theological School	135, 138, 211
Arlington Furniture Company	84, 102
Arnold family name	38
Astorbilts, those	72, 86
Aunt Gertie	45
Aunt Helen	44, 53

B

Babcock Middle School	172, 180
Bahamas, Freeport	155
Bailey, Lillian & Preston	117
Bannister House Nursing Home	114
Barna, George	34, 196, 197
Barrington College	61

Baxter, Bob 107
Beeson Divinity School 160
Bell, Andrew J., Jr. 104, 114
Bell Funeral Service 114
Bilezikian, Dr. Gilbert 57
Billy Graham School of Missions. 34
black shoes 48
Bloom, Abe & Julie 103
Bloom, Ben 102, 104, 105
Boot camp [US Navy] 77
Boston University 107
Bok, Joan 114
Boy Scouts 71
Bradley, Jan & Jerry 191
Branhagen, Sister Gladys 41
Brodsky, Naomi 112
Broscious, David & Joan 110, 111
Bryant College 105
Burdett School of Business 91
Business Development Corporation 112
Business Opportunities, Inc. 112

C

Calvary Episcopal Church 96
Cancer 52, 94, 107
Cardi Box Company 76
Carter, President Jimmy 113
Carter, Rev. Ronald 63
Central Baptist Church 131, 174, 210
Central-Classical School Redevelopment Project 116
Certified Lay Ministry Program [ABCORI] 60, 129
Chambers, Oswald 197, 230
Champlin, Henry 29
Charismatic Movement 153
checkers 49
Chelsea High School 75, 76
Chester, South Carolina 38, 39

Child's Memorial Baptist Church 78
Christmas [1976] 58
Church of the Holy Spirit [Episcopal]. 177
Civil Rights Movement 105, 112
Civil War [1861 - 1865]. 38
Clark, Rev. Jack 58
Communion table. 107, 108, 161
Community College of RI 123
Coney Island 44
Coney Island Gospel Assembly Church. 53
Cook, Franklyn. 163
Cooper Tire Company 47
Cromwell, Rev. Raymond A. 78
CUE House [Dixwell Avenue Community House] 70, 71

D

Damage Control School. 77, 78
Davis, Minister Mallory. 121
Deacon's Alliance of Providence and Vicinity 63
DeFelice, Lorri & Joe. 175
Depression, the. 48
Diabetes 91
Dixwell Avenue Community House [CUE] 69, 74
Dixwell Avenue Congregational Church 39
Dorn, Deirdre. 181
Dortch, Isabel Smith 29
Dunn, Josephine Queen Esther 39
Dwight Grammar School. 50

E

Ebenezer Baptist Church. 120
elders 41
encyclopedias 50
Engler, Gary & Linda 174
Ervin, Deborah 210
Ewart, Bill & Joan 162, 164, 166

Executive Order #9981 [July 26, 1948] 85
Ezekiel, Prophet 13, 16, 65, 199, 201, 231, 234

F

Father Devine... 41
F.B. Hicks Company 102
fire, [PSBC]... 30, 107
First Church of God [Peacedale, RI].................... 63, 135
First Missionary Baptist Church [MS] 159
Fisherman, the 169, 170
Fitzhugh, Stanley P.L., Jr.................................. 218
Fontainebleau Hotel.................................... 110, 111
Ford, Henry 57
Ford Motor Co... 47
Fortes, Eddie 77
Freeman, Deacon Love..................................... 226
Freeman, Love & Ophelia 226
Fund Consultants.. 163
Furnwood Corporation................................. 80, 82

G

Glover, Signora.. 227
Gordon School.. 112
Graham, Billy.. 57, 157
Green Lake Baptist Assembly 129
Greenbrier Resort... 111
Greene, Steven 176
Greenville Baptist Church 129

H

Harper, Tom.. 34
Helligar, Clinton 203, 204
Heroo, Dr. Leonard 93
Hester, Chief Petty Officer William 79
Hillhouse High School 74
Holiday, Rev. Bernard 116

Honor, Della 38
Honor, Jerry 38
Honor Street 39
Horn, Bishop Rosa A. [Mother Horn] 41-44, 90
Hurricane Katrina [2005] 159
Hybels, Bill 57

I

Iglesia Bautista De El Valle Church 211
Indian Meetinghouse [Charlestown, RI] 30
Industrial National Bank 106
Interaction 132

J

James Robison Bible Conference 154
Jeffrey, Russell & Carey 173, 174
Jenkins, Pastor Alan 159
Johnson, Billy 70, 105
Johnson & Wales University 105
Journal of the Southern Baptist Convention SBC Life 15

K

Kilpatrick, Dr. David 129
King, Jr., Dr. Martin Luther 27, 57
Korean Conflict 77
Kowal, Connie & Henry 176, 177
Kuhn, Paul 176

L

Lambe, Rev. Harold J. 66, 67, 122, 125-, 127, 135, 137, 139, 140
Lawrence, T.E. 101, 159
Lawrence & Memorial Hospital 159
Lawson, Rev. Earl W. 131
Lee, Priscilla 216
letter of resignation 141
"Life Outreach International" 149

Lincoln School... 112
Living Waters Christian Academy........................ 28
Love Freeman House, the 166
Lydia Fellowship International Ministries 162

M

Mars, Rev. Kenneth 63, 64
Marshall, Joseph & Mary.................... 83, 84, 101, 102
Martin, Alice & George..................................... 116
Massachusetts Mental Hospital 90
McClure, Albert Theodore [Allen] 42, 94
McClure, Allison Ruth...................... 7, 124, 125, 181,
McClure, Arline Dorothy. 44, 45, 48, 49, 51-53, 72-75, 76, 91, 95, 218
McClure, Beverly Ruth 40, 53
McClure, Clara.. 93
McClure, Deborah Mae Debbie... 43, 44, 50, 51, 69, 70, 94, 95, 107
McClure, Doris Helen 5, 40, 44, 52, 53, 94
McClure, Dorothy Janine..................... 7, 122, 123, 229
McClure, Dorothy Josephine E.
 [Stedman]... 39-41, 45, 47-51, 53, 70-75, 79-82, 86, 90-92, 109
McClure, Edward Daniel Eddie....................... 40, 50, 51
McClure, Esther Frances 5, 53, 91, 92, 94
McCl;ure, Ida Ruth
 [May] [Mrs. Joshua A.] 58, 78, 86, 110, 111, 122, 126
McClure, Joel Arnold..................................... 40, 53
McClure, Leslie Dianne.................................... 7, 123
McClure, Vanessa [Mrs. Wesley A.] 158
McClure, Warren Joseph 40, 51, 52
McClure, Wesley Allan 7, 115, 125, 158,
McClure, William 38
McClure-Snead, Cinphany Janine................... 37, 229, 230
McGhee, Rev. Hugh 66, 67, 124
McKay, Clarence [Bubby]............................. 116, 117
McKay, Larry.. 117
McKay, Louise 116
Merritt Parkway... 47
Meyer. F.B. 38

Miller, Calvin 37, 119, 120, 160
Miller, G. William 113
Moses Brown School 112
motto [PSBC] 28
muffins [pumpkin raisin] 96
Mulligan, Edward. 114
My Utmost For His Highest 197

N

Nardone, William. 175
Narragansett Electric Company. 27, 114, 115
Native Americans. 27, 30, 158, 227
New England Electric System 114
New London Day. 182
NICA. 125
Nichols, Guy 114
NIMBY 121
North End [Westerly] 25, 31, 223-225, 227
Northbrook United Methodist Church 95
Northeastern University. 124
Norwood Baptist Church. 131
Nouwen, Henri. 89, 189, 190

O

"Oatmeal Flat". 47, 48
Olney Street Baptist Church 64, 122, 125
ordination. 129-132
Outreach ministry 28, 151, 161, 174, 210

P

Packard Roadster 74
Pallin, Ralph & Hyman 75, 76
Pallin's Storage Garage. 75
Paradies, Klaus 108, 109
Paton, John. 157

Patterson, Ralph.................................... 130
Pentecostal Holiness Church of Prayer and Deliverance 25, 41
Phelps, Jerry....................................... 175
Pilgrim Way Baptist Church 131
Pinelawn Memorial Cemetery........................... 53
Pleasant Street Baptist Church 25-33, 66, 67, 122, 123, 126,
                          129, 131, 132, 135, 136, 141, 142, 151,
                          161-163, 166, 174, 175, 182-184, 217, 218, 220-224
Plenninger, Capt. Pete [WPD] 224
Pond Street Baptist Church 58, 60, 61, 58, 60, 63,
                        65-67, 92, 116, 117, 120, 125, 207
Powell, Jr., Rev. Adam Clayton......................... 39
Powell, Reverend Adam Clayton 39
Progressive Black Businessmen's Association................ 112
Providence County Day School 112
P.S. 129 [Brooklyn] 45

Q

Queenie 78

R

Ramseur, Carolyn................................... 151
Randall, R. C. Father Jake 153
Rangers, the 70
Ranier, Thom S..................................... 34
Registry of Ministerial Leaders 132
Rhode Island Department of Education 174
Rhode Island Hospital Trust National Bank 106, 107
Rhode Island Housing Authority....................... 224
Rhode Island Urban Project........................... 113
Robison, James........................... 149, 150, 154, 171
Robinson, Yvonne................................... 181
Rocky Hill School 112
Roger Williams College............................... 105
Roman Catholic Church 152, 206
Roosevelt, President Franklin Delano 48

Roosevelt, Theodore 147
Rutgers University 124

S

Sackett Street Elementary School 27
San Filippo, Pastor Jack 52
Saunders, Jamie 207, 208
Schoonmaker, Dr. Paul. 132
Scott, Rev. Frank 118
Sebastian, Mary 227
Second Freewill Baptist Church. 216
Seven Bassinets. 179, 181, 182, 185
Seventh Day Baptist Church 210
Sewell, Lucille [Walker]. 50
shoeshine business 51
Shrello Associates. 105
Siner, Joe & Barbara. 220
Siner, Karalyn. 220, 221
Smith, Charles & Virginia 226
Smith, Malcolm 154, 155
South Providence Neighborhood Ministries 27
Southern Baptist Theological Seminary. 34
St. Clare's Roman Catholic Church 152
St. Jame's Baptist Church. 66, 125
St. John's Episcopal Church 125
St. Patrick's Roman Catholic Church. 153
Standing Committee on the Ministry [SCOM] 129-132
Stedman, Charles Benjamin. 39
Stedman, Dorothy Josephine E. [Mrs. Albert T. McClure] 39
Stedman, Frances, sister 49
Stenhouse, Jean. 174, 175
Stetzer, Ed, Ph.D 16, 33
Suffolk University. 125
Sunbury Bible Church 110

T

Tabernacle Baptist Church. 122

Textron Inc. 112, 113
Thompson, George 70, 71
Thompson, Marie. 218
TIME-2 Project. 113
Toscano, Joseph 171, 172
Tower Street Elementary School 123
Trinity College & Seminary. 138
Troup Junior High School 71
Truman, President Harry S. 79, 84
Tucker, Minister Margueritta. 92, 94, 95, 227

U

UMass Medical Center 92
Union Baptist Churches
    [Cambridge, MA] 92
    [Pawtucket, RI] 63
University of Rhode Island. 105, 123
Urban League of RI 113
U.S. Navy Photographic Center 77, 78
Uzanas, Ray & Loretta. 96

V

Velez, Rev. Lydia 211, 212
Vision of ministry. 19, 28, 58, 132, 142, 149, 151, 153, 161-164,
               166, 167, 174, 175, 180, 209, 210, 221-223, 227, 228
Vision, the 59-60, 135-140, 142, 143, 148-156, 161-167,
               171-177, 179, 180, 190, 191, 195-202, 222-231, 233
Vitale, Frank. 172

W

Wal-Mart Supercenter. 174
Washington Trust Bank 123, 124
Watkins, Rev. Dr. Readus. 107
Watson, Josiah 29
Westerly Planning Board 172
Westerly Police Chief. 224

Westerly Town Council 223, 224
Westerly Zoning Board 166, 172, 175
Wheaton College 57
Wheeler School, Mary C.. . . . . 112, 125
Wilberforce, William 57
William Bloom & Son 84, 102-104, 115-116, 126
Williams, James N.. 113
Williams, Rev. Cornelius 64
Willow Creek Community Church 57
Wilson, Dolores 70
Woodlawn Cemetery 91, 92, 94
Wounded Healer, the 89, 190
Wright, Wilbur & Orville 57

Y

YMCA [Westerly-Pawcatuck] 96, 151, 181, 188
Youth Alive Ministries 26, 181

Z

Zion Gospel Temple. 92, 93

Bibliograpy

Books

Barna, George. *Revolution*. Carol Stream, IL: Tyndale House Publishers, Inc, 2005

Bell, Andrew J. Jr. *An Assessment of Life in Rhode Island as an African American in the Era from 1918 To 1993*. New York, Vantage Press, 1997.

Chambers, Oswald. *My Utmost for His Highest*. Grand Rapids, MI: Discovery House Publishers, 1935.

Graham, Billy. Angels, God's Secret Agents. Garden City, NY: Doubleday, 1975.

Hybels, Bill. *Courageous Leadership*. Grand Rapids, MI: Zondervan, 2002.

Meyer, F. B. *Changed by the Master's Touch*. Springdale, PA: Whitaker House, 1985.

Miller, Calvin. *The Unchained Soul*. Minneapolis, MN: Bethany House Publishers, 1975.

Miller, Calvin. *Into The Depths of God*. Minneapolis MN: Bethany House Publishers, 2000.

Miller, Calvin. *Miracles and Wonders*. Lebanon, IN: Warner Faith, 2003.

Monroe, Myles. *The Principles and Power of Vision*. New Kensington PA: Whitaker House, 2003.

Nouwen, Henri. *The Wounded Healer*. NY: Image, 1979. Written in response to the often asked question: "What does it mean to be a minister in contemporary society?"

The Life In The Spirit Seminars. Developed By The Word Of God. ANN ARBOR, MI: Servant Books, 1979.

Periodicals

Dortch, Isabelle Smith. Pleasant Street *[Westerly, RI]* Baptist Church. {Mrs. Dortch was the church's clerk from 1927 to 1971. She completed this history on June 6, 1971.]

Miller, G. William. "A Look at the 100 Most Influential People in the History of the Amarillo Area." Amarillo *Globe*. May 19, 2000.

Lawrence, T. E. "Papers of T. E. Lawrence" {c. 1894-1970} University of Oxford, Bodelian Library.

Stetzer, Ed. "Finding New Life For Struggling Churches." SBC LIFE. Southern Baptist Convention. February 2004.

Schoonmaker, Paul. "*Where there is no vision the people perish*" American Baptist Churches of Rhode Island. interACTion. Volume X, Issue 1, Winter 02 – 03

SONGS

Dorsey, Thomas A. "Highway to Heaven," *Precious Lord, The Great Gospel Songs of Thomas A Dorsey*, 1974

Dixon, Jessy. "I Am Redeemed" Words and Music by Rev. Jessy Dixon, Chicago Community Choir.

INTERVIEWS

With Robison, James and Betty. LIFE Outreach International, P. O. Box 982000 Fort Worth, TX.

With Smith, Malcolm. Unconditional Love Ministries, P. O. Box 1599, Bandera, TX, 2004.

TATE PUBLISHING & *Enterprises*

Tate Publishing is commited to excellence in the publishing industry. Our staff of highly trained professionals, including editors, graphic designers, and marketing personnel, work together to produce the very finest books available. The company reflects the philosophy established by the founders, based on Psalms 68:11,

"THE LORD GAVE THE WORD AND GREAT WAS THE COMPANY OF THOSE WHO PUBLISHED IT."

If you would like further information, please call
1.888.361.9473
or visit our website
www.tatepublishing.com

TATE PUBLISHING & *Enterprises*, LLC
127 E. Trade Center Terrace
Mustang, Oklahoma 73064 USA